The New Brand Spirit

*To Maria, my wife, and to my children Simon, Philipp and Ayla
who together represent my hope for the future.*

– Christian Conrad

*To the memory and inspiration of Paolo Ettorre, Chairman of Saatchi & Saatchi
Europe, who always believed in doing well by doing good and embodied that in his
love for his family, friends and employees; and in loving memory of my father,
Bill Thompson, whose sense of duty, responsibility and loyalty will accompany
me all of my life.*

– Marjorie Ellis Thompson

*In memory of my grandmother, Cheung, for all her love, trust and support
throughout my life, whose positive spirit will never fade.*

– Phyllis Kong

The New Brand Spirit

How Communicating Sustainability
Builds Brands, Reputations and Profits

CHRISTIAN CONRAD and
MARJORIE ELLIS THOMPSON

Routledge
Taylor & Francis Group

LONDON AND NEW YORK

First published in paperback 2024

First published 2013 by Gower Publishing

Published 2016 by Routledge
4 Park Square, Milton Park, Abingdon, Oxon OX14 4RN

and by Routledge
605 Third Avenue, New York, NY 10158

Routledge is an imprint of the Taylor & Francis Group, an informa business

Publisher's Note
The publisher has gone to great lengths to ensure the quality of this reprint but points out that some imperfections in the original copies may be apparent.

British Library Cataloguing in Publication Data
A catalogue record for this book is available from the British Library.

The Library of Congress has cataloged the printed edition as follows:
Conrad, Christian A., 1966–
    The new brand spirit : how communicating sustainability builds brands, reputations and profits / by Christian Conrad and Marjorie Thompson.
        pages cm
    Includes bibliographical references and index.
    ISBN 978-0-566-09244-2 (hardback : alk. paper) – ISBN 978-1-4094-6577-5 (ebook) – ISBN 978-1-4094-6578-2 (epub)
    1. Social marketing. 2. Sustainable development–Social aspects. 3. Social responsibility of business. I. Thompson, Marjorie, 1957– II. Title.

    HF5414.C667 2013
    658.8'27–dc23
                                                                        2013020293

ISBN: 978-0-566-09244-2 (hbk)
ISBN: 978-1-03-283842-7 (pbk)
ISBN: 978-1-315-55524-9 (ebk)

DOI: 10.4324/9781315555249

Contents

PART III SUMMARY AND OUTLOOK

List of Figures

List of Tables

About the Authors

Christian Conrad

Christian Conrad is Managing Partner of sustainability consultancy brands & values, which he co-founded in 2004 and supports clients in developing sustainability strategies, implementing them into the business and communicating them to stakeholders. In a consumer marketing career of more than 10 years, he worked for blue chip brands such as Kellogg's, where he was Marketing Director, and Unilever. He holds a degree in economics from the University of Mannheim, Germany.

Marjorie Ellis Thompson

Marjorie E. Thompson is Managing Director of C-3i, a communications consultancy she founded in 2002. She has previously worked for some of Britain's most famous brands including Saatchi and Saatchi, the Commission for Racial Equality, The Royal College of Nursing and The Campaign for Nuclear Disarmament. With Hamish Pringle she is the author of *Brand Spirit*, a bestselling Amazon Business Book of the Year.

Foreword

HAMISH PRINGLE

Edward de Bono wrote this in his foreword to *Brand Spirit* in 1999:

> *Cause Related Marketing is all about synergies and alliances. All three parties involved benefit and that is why CRM is very much of the moment and has so much potential.*
>
> *The charitable cause benefits because it gets so much publicity far beyond what it could otherwise afford to buy. In most cases there is also a direct financial benefit as a proportion of profits or price resulting from the trading aspects of the partnership arrangement.*
>
> *The vendor benefits because the commercial company involved is seen as making a social contribution through giving prominence and money to the cause. The vendor also benefits if the association leads to positive image attributes and increased sales of the brand.*
>
> *The consumer benefits because of the double reward of obtaining the product and also benefiting the charity or cause. The customer feels better because, at no extra cost, he or she is doing good.*

As de Bono forecast, the potential has been realized and CRM has widened out into the much bigger world of corporate social responsibility, or CSR. In 1999 there were but a handful of pioneers, with Marjorie Thompson in the vanguard, but now she and co-author Christian Conrad have found no less than 95 people to interview from eight different stakeholder perspectives. Their work has shown the diversity in expectations and paradigms that all communicators in this field need to take into account, but the core principles remain.

When people move up Maslow's Hierarchy of Needs, many of them need 'higher-order' reasons to get out of bed in the morning. And businesses have to reflect these needs in order to continue to sustain their continuing 'permission to trade' economically, socially and environmentally. Just consider the implications as more and more products acquire a service dimension and the service sector itself becomes ever larger. In this context, the commitment and motivation of the employees involved in delivering the brand promise is crucial. It's much more likely that a brand ambassador will go the extra mile if they truly believe in it, and the brand's promise to its public will have increased credibility if its internal values are aligned with its external ones.

This goes to the heart of the war for talent, because this new generation is the first to see corporate responsibility as a 'hygiene factor' when considering a job. Yes, pay and conditions are important to these young people, but so too is their prospective employer's 'reason to be'. We've known for a long time of the power of a single organizing principle to marshal the combined strength of a workforce, and a core purpose which speaks to self-realization is even more motivating to them.

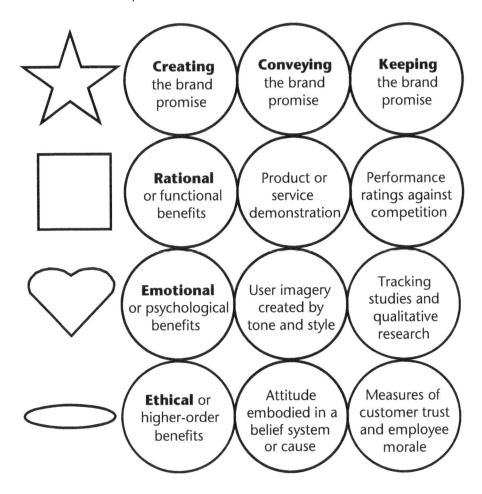

Figure F.1   The Brand Promise System
Source: Reproduced by kind permission by Hamish Pringle, Brand Beliefs Ltd.

To achieve this sense of purpose, companies nowadays need to subscribe sincerely to the idea of delivering on the triple bottom line. It is not enough just to return profits to shareholders. In addition, companies have to account for their impact on the environment, and on society at large. In *Brand Spirit*, we showed how people's expectations of brands have evolved so they need to have a mix of rational-functional, emotional-psychological and ethical-spiritual values when attempting to deliver a compelling brand promise. Today, we associate CSR communications with the wider issue of how a corporate, service or product brand is constructed and how it presents itself to stakeholders. This is summarized in the Brand Promise System set out in Figure F.1, but beware: there is no one-size-fits-all solution.

To arrive at the right balance, it's important to look at the business from multiple points of view. Managers need to take into account the market sector, competitive positionings and target audience in order to discern the best centre of gravity for their brand's promise. There are many successful examples where rational-functional benefits are to the fore, and similarly, there are others where emotional-psychological benefits are more compelling. But increasing numbers of brands are realizing that in order to be great, it's essential to be 'good'.

Having said that, it's helpful for those companies and brands seeking competitive advantage based on being 'good' that by no means everyone agrees with this proposition. For example, in the context of the environmental component within a brand's ethical or higher-order benefits, the authors cite Marks & Spencer (M&S) research which indicates that 10 per cent of consumers are really enthusiastic (so-called 'Green Crusaders'), 35 per cent are willing to be green if it does not cost anything, while 35 per cent are 'Defeatist' with a 'What can I do – it doesn't make any difference?' attitude, and the remaining 20 per cent are hostile, and absolutely not interested.

So it's perfectly possible to segment the market along these lines, and there may well be a place for 'refusenik' businesses for a long time to come. However, I believe that these companies and brands are fighting against an inexorable tide. This is being caused by the gravitational pull of massively influential retailers like Walmart, M&S and IKEA which have CSR front and centre of their supply chain policies. It's also being driven by leading brand marketing companies like Unilever, Procter & Gamble, Cadbury and Bacardi, which are changing the competitive landscape in their respective sectors.

While declaring itself not to be a 'how to' book, this comprehensive work nevertheless provides practitioners with plenty of valuable guidance. And with its combination of interviews and current case studies, this book makes an important contribution to the debate on how society, the economy and the environment should inter-relate – the New Brand Spirit, indeed.

Acknowledgements

This book kicked off with a workshop in Bremen in September 2009. The idea of the concept of 'letting stakeholders talk' came from Martin Blumberg, partner at brands & values[1] sustainability consultants, at whose offices the workshop was held. Without a lot of help from a number of people, this venture would never have been concluded. In fact, even despite that help, chances were that it – as with many similar schemes – could have become a victim of the financial crisis that hit the consulting industry leading to a delay of 12 to 18 months. We are happy we finally made it, though, and want to thank all those who helped us realize it as well as the ceaseless patience of Gower Publishing Director Jonathan Norman.

The backbone of the enterprise was our tireless team of editorial assistants: Ann-Kathrin Bracht, who set up the first workshop together with Caroline Zamor; Kristin Stengel, Hanna Stahl, Anna Backmann and Agata Bonn, who scheduled interviews, transcribed them and organized a sometimes chaotic author team, and last but certainly not least, the amazing Phyllis Kong, who did a fantastic job in preparing the cases and chasing visual materials and without whom we would not have been able to complete the project. There were many who helped us to obtain interviews or case materials, and among them we would specifically like to mention Dominic Burch, Gloria Abramoff, Maria Kalligeros Alan Leaman and Lucy Richardson, Jon Thompson, Robin McQuay, Katie King, Veronica Scheubel, Peter Gündling and Anne Reifenberg. Marjorie's father Dr Bill Thompson became seriously ill in the summer of 2012, and though ill, provided many of the synonyms for words we had overused in the initial drafts as she worked on copies sent by Phyllis and Christian in Switzerland and kindly printed out by John Mastrocola and his team at the Newport Beach Nursing and Rehabilitation Home where she was staying with her father.

We'd like to say a big thank you to all those who generously took the time to speak with us, most of whom are therefore mentioned or quoted in the book; it was an honour that so many were willing to share their perspectives and views with us. Having said that, willingness varied between stakeholder groups – non-governmental organizations and companies in the consumer goods category were particularly responsive, while shareholders and the media were not exactly forthcoming and therefore not represented as broadly as we would have liked.

Finally, a big thank you to our families, friends and colleagues who had to make sacrifices because we were using our spare time to research and write or were not always available for business opportunities, weekends or holidays.

---

1   Christian Conrad, co-author of this book, is co-founder of brands & values management consultants.

Reviews of The New Brand Spirit

Marjorie Ellis Thompson pioneered Corporate Social Responsibility twenty years ago when she established a specialist unit within Saatchi & Saatchi. At that time Marketing Directors shied away, disbelieving they could find mutual benefit between their brands and not-for-profit causes. Well those same Marketing Directors can now read the error of their ways in this definitive compendium of success stories. Choose to ignore Conrad and Thompson at your peril.
Marcus Brown, Executive Vice President, Young & Rubicam, EMEA

A new approach to CSR is necessary in the light of the changing global economy and the current perception of sustainability. The New Brand Spirit *gives an unprecedented 360° view of CSR, providing clear guiding principles for the implementation of CSR policies and initiatives, offering invaluable advice based on first-hand experience of some of the foremost players in this field.*
Annette Ettorre, President, 'Paolo Ettorre – Socially Correct' Association
(www.sociallycorrect.it)

Introduction

'Corporate social responsibility communication' is a controversial term. Many people don't like the notion of corporate social responsibility (CSR) itself, and communication is seen by many as the prime motive to engage in CSR in the first place. There are critics who shout 'Greenwashing!' or 'Cover-up!' at every opportunity, while consumers, on the other hand, state they don't feel sufficiently well-informed. Often, CSR experts use their very specific professional language in a way that outsiders, those who are not 'in the know' simply cannot follow. There are many different perspectives on the subject, accompanied by a lot of debate and discussion, but there is also a substantial amount of confusion. While there are companies which excel at communicating their socially responsible activities, many others simply lack the knowledge and experience, and occasionally the resources, to find the 'right' way to do it.

Originally, this book was meant to be a successor to *Brand Spirit*, published in 1999 and authored by Hamish Pringle and Marjorie Thompson. *Brand Spirit* focused on Cause Related Marketing, and generated considerable interest because it showcased many good examples and explained exactly what worked and what didn't in this specific marketing discipline. The world has since moved on; while Cause Related Marketing still exists, the communication of social and environmental topics and issues by companies has become so much broader that we decided to take a different approach. Surveying the current landscape, we realized that what makes communicating CSR or sustainability so complex and sometimes confusing is that there are myriad and varied perspectives on it, and accompanying those perspectives there are heterogenous expectations. Each stakeholder defines the subject matter – CSR, CR or sustainability – in their own way and has a specific view on what companies should both do and communicate. We attempt to portray these differing perspectives here. We will show that it is key for each stakeholder group to seek to understand the other party, and to want to engage in dialogue rather than to see communication as a one-way street. At the same time there are tradeoffs between the various stakeholder agendas, and those tradeoffs need to be addressed.

Our approach in this book is to 'let stakeholders talk'. We have spoken to 95 experts from eight different stakeholder perspectives who were generous enough to share their view on CSR communication – what it is, when it works and when it does not work, how it can add value and where the challenges lie. The eight stakeholder perspectives we have chosen, without claiming to be all-encompassing, are:

- civil society and non-governmental organizations (NGOs);
- the public sector (government, government organizations, intergovernmental organizations);
- suppliers;
- employees;
- customers (consumers and business-to-business customers);

- shareholders;
- (social) media
- academia and experts.

The Stakeholder Map in Figure I.1 illustrates the relationships between the company and its stakeholder groups and shows the relative distance of each group from the organization's core business and value chain.

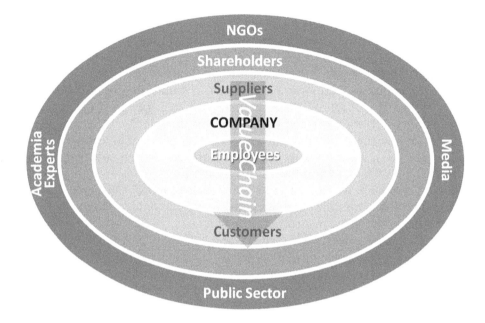

Figure I.1   The Stakeholder Map

The focus of our interviews was always how businesses communicate – not so much how the stakeholders themselves do so. However, as real communication is dialogue and many experts prefer the term 'engagement', the way in which specific stakeholders communicate in the context of CSR will be an additional focus. One-way communication will not build trust in the same the way as open and honest two-way communication will.

The book is divided into two parts: Part I is based on the interviews we conducted, and Part II features best practice cases from each stakeholder perspective. Most of the cases are also based on at least one or two interviews.

Every chapter in Part I features one of the most insightful interviews. Most of the other interviews find their way into the text in the form of quotations. Just as in the original *Brand Spirit*, the best practice cases in Part II are a key feature of the book. More than pointing out shortcomings in existing CSR communication, our motivation is to showcase examples that have inspired us and that others may be able to learn from. Also, they really bring to life what otherwise may seem academic. Good examples do exist!

This book is primarily for practitioners, for sustainability managers who are trying to grapple with whether and how to communicate what their company does in sustainability, for marketers thinking of how to integrate social and environmental messages into their brand communication, for corporate communications professionals and public relations (PR) people who seek ways to manage the balance between risk and opportunity and for human resources (HR) managers looking for ways to build strong employer brands. We are not academics, even though we have very much benefited from the dialogue with academics who are experts in this field. While being practical and for practitioners, *The New Brand Spirit* is not a 'how to' book, not a manual. It aims to inspire and to provide insights, as well as some principles and guidelines.

The Interviews

The Questionnaire

What do I associate with CSR communication? Dressing on a rotten salad!
Robert Rubinstein, CEO of TBLI Group

The answer came without hesitation from the Triple Bottom Line (TBLI) pioneer, a Brooklyn, New York City native, now residing in Amsterdam, the Netherlands, whose TBLI conferences bring together international corporate business and finance companies and aim to 're-educate the financial world'. I could sense the anger in his voice when he spat out the words 'rotten salad'. The rotten salad, he explained is his characterization of what companies actually do in the area of sustainability and corporate responsibility which they then cover with smooth communication – with dressing. Robert Rubinstein, like many others we spoke to, perceives a great discrepancy between the walk and the talk of companies when it comes to CSR. There needs to be a fine and artful balance between the two – if there is too much talk relative to the walk, then the outcome tends be at least a little superficial. If on the other hand there is hardly any or no communication of substantial commitment, there is a real missed opportunity to create positive brand value and to build reputation by adding credible, open and honest communication.

What becomes very clear when talking to different stakeholders is that the perceptions of what CSR is and what CSR communication is tend to vary significantly. We found that some views and perspectives can be constructively aligned, while others are so divergent that it is hard to reconcile them. One reason for this may be fundamentally different paradigms, values and beliefs or 'dogmas'. This is particularly true for the view of certain parts of civil society. Our aim is to show where the convergence is, but also where there may be a need for companies to agree to disagree with some of their stakeholders.

What do you associate with CSR?

Overall, there is scepticism and even dislike of the term 'CSR' or 'corporate social responsibility' among many of our interviewees. We chose it because internationally, we felt it was the term with the broadest understanding – which may, in hindsight, be a mistaken assumption, judging from the response we received. For some, 'corporate responsibility' without the 'social' is a better term, as it seems more inclusive of environmental issues. For others 'corporate sustainability' is the more all-encompassing and suitable term because sustainability covers the three dimensions 'economic', 'environmental' and 'social' and has a time dimension to it ('future generations') that stresses the long-term view companies ought to take more than 'corporate social responsibility' does. For some, 'corporate social responsibility' is dated. As Hugh Burkitt of The Marketing Society (UK) and Business in the Community (UK) puts it:

> CSR is an old-fashioned notion of how companies should behave – but it is stuck somewhere in the Corporate Affairs department. We in the BitC team looking at this feel we have moved on, we think CSR has been discredited because it was seen as a kind of side show, because it was not handled by those in charge. Companies today need to move towards sustainability.

Peter Kruse, a German communications expert, is concerned that CSR is a blunt instrument used to create a shiny surface on a society that is increasingly blind to anything but monetary value.

There is also the pragmatic view that the terminology does not matter that much. Uwe Kleinert of Coca-Cola Germany says:

> Our concern is that businesses act and produce and move in their market in a way that is responsible toward all stakeholders including future generations. Coming back to the term, we left out 'social' and included 'sustainability' to make it clear that we care for both.

This view states that it is about how companies *behave*, how they go about their business. Or as Nancy Baxter, formerly of Wells Fargo (US) puts it: 'CSR is a business practice and a discipline within an organization to address and focus on the issues of being a good corporate citizen.' British CSR expert Mallen Baker agrees, and maintains that CSR is about how companies manage the business process to produce an overall positive impact on society. Even more pragmatic is the definition of SustainAbility's Jean-Philippe Renaut, for whom CSR encompasses 'all corporate initiatives that improve the sustainability performance of an organization'.

The other, more philosophical, perspective takes the position that CSR is about the role of business in society. The Natural Step founder Karl-Henrik Robèrt states:

> It is about the overall need to integrate business into the objectives of society at large, to consider the larger impacts of business on society, not just on shareholders. In that respect, CSR is so wide that it is difficult to pinpoint exactly what it means. Actually, while being a good starting point when talking about the role of business in society, it has become a bit flaky. In the mid to longer term we must get rid of CSR as it has the tendency to create a permanent and unhealthy dichotomy between business and society. We need to integrate the two but then we don't need to shout so much about it anymore. If CSR creates this dichotomy it leads businesses astray and may be more dangerous than not having an agenda at all. In the full business case for sustainability businesses understand that taking into consideration all social and environmental concerns is good for business and then CSR is not needed any more.

What do you associate with CSR communication?

From our interviews we can identify two camps: those who perceive CSR communication as necessary or even positive, and those who see it as a 'cover-up', as a new area of public relations, and point out that a lot of it is either boring or mere window-dressing. It is strongly associated with reporting, and there has been significant change in this field over the past decade.

The negative associations are twofold: the majority of the critics feel there is too much CSR communication, while there is a group that is concerned that so far, many key stakeholders do not have sufficient understanding of the subject. 'There is a real gap of understanding and knowledge in this area and a real need to clarify the term(s) that people who are not in the profession would use', says one Fortune 500 corporate spokesperson who does not want to be named.

For many, the first thought is CSR or sustainability reporting. While that is important, it is not the focus of this book. There are many books, many research reports, which focus on reporting. We include reporting where it is mentioned by our interviewees, and include one case on integrated reporting (Case 14: Novo Nordisk, Chapter 16). However, many of the key lessons we learned from many of the interviews and case studies can be applied to reporting. Reporting is one format, one medium, that can be used in communicating CSR and sustainability. Our aim is to show the diversity and complexity that have developed within the subject matter. If there is one message that we want to get across, then it is this: that there is no one-size-fits-all. Marketing and PR professionals will be surprised that we even mention this point, as to them it seems so evident. But it needs to be said. The principles of marketing and corporate communication apply to CSR and sustainability communication!

Each chapter follows the structure of the questionnaire.

We start by looking at CSR communication from the stakeholders' side. What do they expect of companies' CSR or sustainability communication (Question 1)? And how do they see their role in the context of this communication (Question 2)? Question 3 looks into the issues and challenges that companies face when talking to the particular stakeholder group. Questions 4 and 5 reflect on what works (best practice examples) and what does not work (greenwashing examples). The final question gives some hint as to why some communication works and others do not – key success factors of CSR communication to their stakeholder group.

Interview with Robert Rubinstein, TBLI

WHAT DO YOU ASSOCIATE WITH CSR COMMUNICATION?

A salad dressing on rotten salad. A lot of companies don't integrate sustainability into their organization. A lot of it is basically bullshit – you know the level of bullshit depending on where it is parked in the organization. Unless it is embedded in the organization, core business, it is only an add-on, an external thing, not part of business activity. I have never understood corporate volunteering if it has not got anything to do with core business. CSR has been damaging to the whole sustainability movement – not created an economy. It is investing in toxic waste and planting flowers around it. They want to feel good about the garbage they are doing. I have never been a fan of CSR – it is Oprah Winfrey ribbon-cutting nonsense. An example is Porter and his 'effective philanthropy'. CSR is basically communication without a strict definition. Our definition of 'sustainable investment' is much stricter – you don't get a membership to the fitness club. It would be different if I changed it to 'sustainability communication', defined as 'While you are making money are your products or services worsening or damaging the sustainability and environmental balance?' Social balance is more profitable, environmental balance is, in the end, more profitable through lesser use of resources! Many companies say 'We are actively engaged in stakeholder dialogue'– but that does not mean you are making progress – see Obama and health care.[1]

WHAT ARE YOUR EXPECTATIONS REGARDING CSR COMMUNICATION OF COMPANIES?

Have your company audited whether or not it is actually maintaining or improving the sustainability balance, for example according to The Natural Step. The key issue is: do companies really want to do this? Ninety-nine per cent only want to do 'CSR-lite', and it is very difficult to get from the dark to the light side. Take the Dow Jones Sustainability Index (DJSI): the ones who score the highest are the biggest CO_2 polluters, because they report. SRI fund managers do not look at taxes in terms of determining the sustainability of a business, it is not an issue for them, even though that means: no social contribution. Audit results need to be communicated properly. The audit companies are whores, would do it if you paid them. That is why they are supporting the present system. Yoda said: 'Do or do not, there is no try.' I am just tired of listening to companies chatting about this. TBLI[2] has the focus: show self-interest, show the opportunities, show the money flows and the progress that has already been achieved. We see the money flows that we directly or indirectly create, and that is why we focus on the financial sector – it is much easier to convince than other sectors. If they see the money, opportunities, self-interest, they will do it. They are very predictable and easier to manipulate than other industries. And I mean asset managers and asset owners, not regulators!

WHAT IS THE ROLE OF SHAREHOLDERS IN THE CONTEXT OF CSR COMMUNICATION OF COMPANIES?

They are not doing what they are supposed to do. They could be more challenging, should integrate sustainability into their portfolio rather than giving 5 per cent to charity! But the whole process is in a state of flux, it is changing, just needs to be moved faster! Their understanding is not very good, they are not very good at what they do. In general, there is a significant movement in the right direction, though, and I have confidence in the greed of people. The EU should do the same thing for pension systems as they do to telecoms and energy and offer a choice – either adhere to ESG[3] to manage money or otherwise ....

---

1   The interview was conducted in 2010, when US health care reforms were being introduced.

2   Triple Bottom Line Investing Group, Robert Rubinstein's company which organizes the largest international conference in sustainable finance and investing, as well as providing advisory services on ESG (environmental, social and governance) and impact investing.

3   'ESG (environmental, social and governance) – is a generic term used in capital markets and used by investors to evaluate corporate behaviour and to determine the future financial performance of companies. ESG factors are a subset of non financial performance indicators that includes sustainable, ethical and corporate governance issues such as managing the company's carbon footprint and ensuring there are systems in place to ensure accountability'; *Financial Times* Lexicon, http://lexicon.ft.com/Term?term=ESG (accessed 20 October 2011).

CAN YOU SHARE ANY BEST PRACTICE EXAMPLES OF CSR COMMUNICATION?

Look at the Corporate Register awards for the best reports, GRI is just copying that. I am only interested in the actual sustainability effect, not the communication.

HOW DO YOU DEFINE 'GREENWASHING' AND COULD YOU NAME EXAMPLES?

All CSR communication is greenwashing. Maybe not the right term, certainly people who are doing it think they are doing well, there is not enough awareness. But take banks – the main impact they are having is about where they put the money.

WHAT DO YOU CONSIDER TO BE KEY SUCCESS FACTORS OF EFFECTIVE CSR COMMUNICATION FROM AN INVESTOR OR SHAREHOLDER PERSPECTIVE?

Authenticity. Show that it is really integrated into your core business activity – not an add-on. And don't rely on reporting – fund managers don't read the CSR reports. Take MTR, the Hong Kong transport company, as an example of authenticity: the boss of MTR is a big fan of sustainability. He went to Copenhagen,[4] really trying to push the equation, authentic, passionate, trying to push the concept also within his organization.

---

4   Referring to the 2009 Copenhagen Climate Change Conference.

1 Communicating Sustainability – the Civil Society Perspective

CSR communication should be all about linking a company's core activities back to real corporate sustainability.
Dax Lovegrove, Head of Business & Industry Relations, WWF-UK

The world of NGOs and 'civil society' is a multifaceted tapestry of organizations and movements with varying perspectives and agendas. It can therefore be argued that it is particularly challenging to paint a coherent picture of what this stakeholder group's expectations of CSR communication are. Simply speaking, there are two kinds of NGOs – those which can be labelled 'campaigning NGOs' and those that we will call 'collaborating NGOs'. Campaigning NGOs see it as their mission to bring specific social and environmental issues to public attention and thus onto the societal agenda. In their relationship with business they often seek to expose corporate (mis-)behaviour in the context of those issues. They are less interested in dialogue with companies, but see it as their objective to encourage public awareness as well as regulatory pressure on businesses, and in that way influence their behaviour. Collaborating NGOs take the approach of seeking solutions to social and environmental issues through dialogue with businesses (and other stakeholders). They actively engage and even partner with companies, seeking win–win solutions between social and environmental objectives on the one hand and the economic objectives of business on the other. Obviously there are overlaps between collaborating and campaigning NGOs: few are 'purebreds'. Oxfam and Greenpeace can be seen as prominent examples of campaigning NGOs, yet they are also in dialogue with businesses. On the other hand, the WWF and the Rainforest Alliance are organizations that could be labelled 'collaborating NGOs', yet they also campaign for their respective causes. Good examples of organizations that increasingly do both in relative balance are the Fairtrade Foundation and the Fair Labor Association.

Both groups of civil society organizations are relevant to CSR communication for different reasons, and companies seeking to move towards corporate sustainability and aiming for effective communication of their activities need to take these different roles into account.

What do you associate with CSR and CSR communication?

CSR AND CSR COMMUNICATION ARE SUSPICIOUS

In most cases, NGOs have a paradigm that fundamentally differs from that of businesses. NGOs take a social or environmental perspective. While companies focus on generating (economic) profit and creating value for their shareholders, their aim is to improve social or environmental conditions. They therefore view corporate behaviour primarily through the lens of its social and environmental rather than its economic impact, while many of them assume that businesses are solely driven by economic motives. Consequently, they are at least latently suspicious of companies that engage in CSR and CSR communication because they question their motives. Are the efforts for real, or are they 'just marketing' – jumping on the green bandwagon, merely the latest trick to sell more (green) products?

Apart from 'CSR = marketing', other popular NGO associations with CSR are that it is just a smokescreen to cover up the fact that social and environmental responsibility is not really part of how a business is run. 'At best CSR is about companies choosing the way they do business – putting social concerns at the core of how they do business, make their money, deal with their suppliers. But that does not happen,' says Harriet Lamb, Executive Director of the Fairtrade Foundation UK and a leading campaigner for fair trade. She adds: 'CSR communication at its best is (when) companies communicate what they have done and achieved. Often though it consists of wishy-washy wishlists of how they would like to change the world, constructing a lovely picture which does not always ring true.'

'CSR communication is about company programmes to meet growing consumer, stakeholder and shareholder expectations around environmental and social responsibility,' maintains Chris Wille of the Rainforest Alliance. WWF's Anthony Kleanthous, co-author of *Let Them Eat Cake*,[1] a report focusing on the social responsibility of communications professionals for sustainable consumption, agrees: 'CSR should focus on how to make life better for customers and consumers, in sustainable ways. It's about helping them to change the way they live, and to extract more value from less material.' Comic Relief pioneer and Pilotlight founder Jane Tewson (now with Igniting Change in Australia) associates 'misguided and flawed attempts to add a second dimension to a single dimension structure – that is, social benevolence to capitalistic principles and practices' with CSR communication, rather than what it could be doing, namely bringing together maverick groups of people – for example, business leaders and marginalized, vulnerable people from the fringes of society – and inspiring individuals to change their behaviour. She herself did this, bringing top media and business people together with refugees and homeless people.

---

1   Anthony Kleanthous and Jules Peck, *Let Them Eat Cake: Satisfying the New Consumer Appetite for Responsible Brands* (London: WWF-UK, 2006), http://assets.wwfcmsuat.rroom.net/assets/downloads/let_them_eat_cake_full.pdf (accessed 10 July 2013).

What are the expectations of NGOS regarding CSR communication of companies?

SUBSTANCE FIRST – AND COMMUNICATE IT WITH INTEGRITY AND HUMILITY

If we had to sum up the NGO expectations of CSR communications in two words, it would be 'substance first'. Substance implies positive social and environmental outcomes, tangible results of the activities companies undertake when aiming to balance their economic objectives with social and environmental impacts. But what does that mean? What do NGOs see as substance? On one level it is about 'demonstrating how business is really changing and what it is genuinely doing', according to Dax Lovegrove of WWF. Stephen Howard of Business in the Community thinks there is a lack of trust because too many companies make statements of intent like 'We want to be green' or 'We will do this and that' without really following up on those claims. Howard emphasizes:

> The secret is to keep it simple, not to have a lot of lists of community organizations that you give money to, but rather how responsible thinking helps you to grow your business, how you link CSR to the engine room of the business. You have to be transparent and honest.

He points out that large segments of society do not believe that responsible business is good business, but feel that 'all this talk about the environment and so on is just baloney'. Since the banking crisis, more and more people are more convinced than ever that businesses, particularly the financial sector, are only in it for the short term. This common-sense observation feeds cynicism about 'marketing stuff' and looks for substance and proof of the verbal claims companies make about CSR. Jane Tewson of Igniting Change feels that companies would have the potential to create significant positive social outcomes and benefits for the community if they 'started in their own backyards, with their own staff and working conditions and if it then includes genuine two- way dialogue with the people and issues they are trying to engage with and genuine change in individual behaviour and corporate structure'.

Substance is about both what companies do and how they communicate it. The following seven points summarize the key expectations that NGOs have of companies' CSR communication:

1. **Start in your own backyard** – Change begins in the organization, in the business itself.
2. **Link CSR to core business** – CSR and sustainability need to be linked to the 'engine room' of the business, to the products and services that a company offers and to the way these products and services are produced.
3. **Be transparent and honest** – This implies stating objectives and reporting on them. NGOs expect businesses to make themselves accountable to society.
4. **Focus on results** – What are the positive social or environmental outcomes? Reporting on results is still far less popular amongst corporates than communicating intent.
5. **Maintain constant dialogue** – with key stakeholders, particularly NGOs and civil society. This will make sure there is no greenwashing and will ensure change and progress.

6. **Advertise and communicate only in proportion to results** – NGOs often criticize companies for being too aggressive in communicating their 'good deeds'. What they expect instead is that businesses will partner with NGOs and promote them and their causes.
7. **Take responsibility for sustainable consumption** – Companies ought to inspire and empower consumers to move towards sustainable lifestyles with the products and services they offer.

The first six points all relate to building trust with NGOs and civil society. Assuming that this trust is not already there helps to understand why 'starting in one's own backyard' is important: it implies integrity, 'walking the talk', and thus results in trustworthiness – trust from the inside out. Seen from the NGOs' view, perhaps more than from some of the other stakeholder perspectives, social responsibility has to start with the responsibility a company has for its own employees and for its own organization. The next and most important step is to link CSR to the core business – to what products and services a business offers and to how these products and services are sourced, produced and used. This does not primarily mean becoming a donor to NGOs and seeing CSR as a new term for supporting charities, which has been and still is widespread practice. In other words, in the CSR context, NGOs are interested more in how a business makes its money rather than how it spends it. Paul Brown of The Prince's Trust understands that companies are keen to communicate the success of their CSR programmes but feels that it would be good to know what their business objectives are. Nigel Stanley, Head of Campaigns and Communications for the UK's Trades Union Congress (TUC), adds: 'Where a company chooses to promote its product by not talking about the product but by talking about itself, what does that say about the product?'

It is not surprising that NGOs are particularly looking for communication of societal impacts, and the actual social or environmental results of businesses' CSR activities. They want to know what the positive effect is, the benefits society gains from a company's efforts to link CSR to its core business. And even if what the company does is not as closely linked to core business as expected, at least there should be clear records of the positive impact. An example could be Danone brand Volvic's Cause Related Marketing '1 litre for 10 litres' programme. The programme is closely linked to the product (bottled water), yet it still is an initiative that could be criticized by some NGOs as 'charity' or 'just marketing', because it has no direct link to how the business makes its money or how and where the water is sourced and the product is manufactured. It is acknowledged as one of the more successful and credible international Cause Related Marketing programmes which may be due to the fact that it really communicates the results of its collaboration with UNICEF or World Vision in a number of African countries, on the packaging, instore, online and in its advertising.[2]

Monitoring and reporting on results is, however, closely linked to transparency. From an NGO's perspective, credible and trustworthy reporting on impact and results implies two things: (1) not just reporting what works, but also what does not work, and (2) having impartial and third-party verification of the impact. Reporting just on the successes and leaving out potential negative impacts or at least challenges to creating a positive impact does not help to support credibility and build trust. And when – as in the case of the

---

2   The programme was first launched in Germany in 2005, where it ran until 2010. It was first adopted in France in 2006, and since then in Japan, the US, Canada, the UK, and in 2010 in the Middle East. Together with an NGO partner, in the majority of cases UNICEF, wells are built in a number of African countries (Ethiopia, Mali, Malawi, Ghana, Zambia, Sudan and Niger), providing clean drinking water to more than a quarter of a million people.

relationship between civil society and big business – trust is at a relatively low level, self-reporting will in many cases not be sufficient to raise the level of trust. Also, it may be wise to have others speak for you. As Stephen Howard of Business in the Community puts it: 'It starts with having something substantive to say. Maybe communicating is not something that you should do – rather, let others talk for you, with higher credibility.'

Third-party verification sounds like control and assumes an environment of low trust. If there is a serious stakeholder relationship between the business and civil society, it will be based on mutual respect, honesty and dialogue. Open disclosure of targets and results makes common sense, and ensures there is no greenwashing. Sally Uren of Forum for the Future expresses it in a nutshell: 'When you communicate openly, it is much harder to greenwash. Some rules: set absolute targets for key impact areas; transparently disclose those targets; be honest and: keep a constant dialogue. This will reduce your chances of being accused of greenwash.' Over and above not greenwashing, dialogue, engagement and partnership between companies and NGOs will help bring about change for good. WWF-UK's Anthony Kleanthous[3] says:

> Greenpeace is looking for 'no greenwash', looking for companies first to do no harm. Overall the concern of campaigning NGOs with an anti-business ethos is that companies do make a commitment not to sell unsustainable products any more. NGOs like the WWF, on the other hand, are looking for corporate partnerships. These partnerships typically involve a combination of: funding (for WWF and its various programmes); communication by both parties of a client-sponsored WWF programme; and change within the corporation itself (such as production efficiencies and new product development). WWF vets its potential corporate partners as part of a pre-contract due diligence process; if WWF feels that its reputation may be compromised by association with the prospective partner, then it will either not engage, or it will engage behind closed doors, in a partnership for change.

Another aspect of 'substance first' is that NGOs believe that communication needs to be proportionate to the results. Greenwashing is often seen as just that: little or no substance, and big communication or hype. Many Cause Related Marketing campaigns are criticized because the amount of advertising spending behind them is seen as out of sync with the investment in the social causes. The advertising by power companies for their renewable energy subsidiaries is over-proportionate relative to the minute share of the overall business of these large companies. In the view of campaigning NGOs like Greenpeace, this is a sign that they are more interested in the image effect of building some wind power turbines than really transforming their businesses away from an emphasis on fossil fuels to one focused on renewables. There has been a lot of criticism of PRODUCT RED, an innovative Cause Related brand initiative co-founded and heavily promoted by rock star Bono of the band U2 where select high-profile brands launch 'red' products.[4] With every sale of each of those specific products a donation is given to the Global Fund, a grant-giving organization focusing on fighting AIDS, malaria and tuberculosis. While the Global Fund is one of the single largest contributors to all global HIV/AIDS, malaria and tuberculosis programmes and PRODUCT RED is the largest private donor to the fund (to date it has generated over $150 million for HIV/AIDS programmes in Africa), PRODUCT RED has been accused of spending significantly more on advertising the products than on

---

3   Now with Here Tomorrow, with WWF-UK at the time of the interview.

4   Brands include Nike, American Express, Apple, Starbucks, Converse and Armani.

donations, and therefore of profiting from using disease and suffering as a marketing vehicle. As this line of criticism holds true for many Cause Related Marketing campaigns that are large-scale and involve advertising, it needs to be taken into consideration by any company aiming to link its CSR activities directly to the sales of its products. Marketers will defend their activities by arguing that the advertising would be conducted anyway as a means of positioning the product or brand successfully in a competitive environment and to generate awareness and thus sales. The only difference in the Cause Related context is that not only does the campaign create brand awareness, but it also creates awareness for the cause and potentially the partner NGO, and could be seen as a significant contribution in kind to the cause or NGO. This argument is more likely to be accepted by collaborating NGOs than by campaigning NGOs.

Moving away from a quantitative view balancing substance and communication is the expectation that business should show humility. This is a point Harriet Lamb of Fairtrade Foundation UK makes:

Approach [CSR communication] with humility! Showing off angers the public. Humility means showing respect to NGOs and civil society who are ready to criticize businesses that are over-claiming. It can also mean being ready to run blogs and take public questions and concerns seriously and enter into a real dialogue.

NGOs which see the potential of working hand-in-hand with business to transform society by making it more sustainable have an expectation that business should inspire and empower consumers in order to drive sustainable consumption.

Thus far, even in 'developed' countries, when it comes to consumer awareness of sustainability in the context of consumption, sustainable consumption is still stuck in a niche. The challenge seen by NGOs and increasingly by major retailers is to move into the mainstream. As Anthony Kleanthous of WWF puts it:

In the UK, which is fairly typical of Europe, 10–20 per cent of consumers care a lot about environmental and social issues, and shop accordingly. The real impact, however, lies in the mainstream, which remains largely untapped. Some early and high-profile product failures undermined the confidence of many FMCG [fast-moving consumer goods] brands in the commercial potential of sustainable mainstream products, but the potential is huge. Mainstream consumers want to be responsible, but, unlike the deep greens, they are not willing to compromise on performance. If you can reassure them on that front, then a metaphorical green tick on pack or above your door is worth real market share. It's the holy grail of sustainable consumption: guilt-free shopping! That is why innovation is so important.

Put differently, companies that communicate through their products, through advertising and via PR have clout when it comes to empowering and inspiring consumers – so they are at least partly responsible for sustainable consumption. Advertisers and marketers are actually aware of this responsibility. This is one of the findings of research in Germany and Austria conducted by marketing weeklies w&v [Werben und Verkaufen, Germany] and HORIZONT [Austria] in collaboration with sustainability consultancy brands & values.[5]

---

5   Respondents were readers of the online portals of *Werben & Verkaufen* and *HORIZONT*. The research was conducted online in November and December 2010 with over 900 respondents across both countries. Results were published in

What is the role of NGOs in the context of CSR communication of companies?

BETWEEN WATCHDOG AND PARTNER

The role of NGOs can be to keep organizations honest. Most companies don't intend to mislead people, they may do it unwittingly because they have not scrutinized their data. NGOs and civil society can be third-party scrutinizers, not evaluating and not verifying data but pronouncing on the validity and significance of data and keeping companies and brands honest.

Sally Uren, Forum for the Future

NGOs take on one or more of three roles in the context of CSR communication: (1) watchdogs, (2) partners and (3) lobbyists for civil society.

Watchdogs

In line with the key expectation 'substance first', NGOs that act as watchdogs see their main responsibility as making sure that what companies communicate is actually based on substance. As Dax Lovegrove of WWF says, substance means it is based on a solid foundation of sustainability. NGOs should be scrutinizers, according to Sally Uren – and taking that role seriously can mean that they expose communication they don't see as honest or as being a half-truth. For example, Greenpeace publishes greenwashing lists, German NGO FoodWatch exposes what it considers mislabelling and unhealthy foods produced by food manufacturers, Oxfam draws attention to the situation in the coffee supply chain, and the Clean Clothes Campaign creates awareness of the living and working conditions in fashion and apparel production. A more recent example of an NGO acting as a watchdog is the case of BP – even before the oil spill in the Gulf of Mexico in April 2010. According to trade union spokesperson Nigel Stanley:

Carbon offsetting is a good example of how sustainability-related activities by companies can become meaningless. In this instance, BP was investing a bit in solar energy and changed its vision [to 'Beyond Petroleum'], but as soon as the market wavered and top personnel changed, they ditched these efforts – on the one hand they were progressive, but the cost cutting and outsourcing went on and their record deteriorated on health and safety.

Stanley refers to the significant criticism of BP's focus on the bottom line rather than creating substance behind its claim of becoming a 'new' petroleum company that went beyond oil and fossil fuels. These campaigns were catalysed when disaster struck on the oil rig 'Deepwater Horizon'. In the aftermath of the largest oil spill in history, NGOs as well as the media dissected BP's CSR and sustainability-related communication and showed the discrepancies between what the multinational aspired to verbally and its actions.

However, if scrutiny only means exposing negative performance, that is only half the story, in the view of Harriet Lamb of the Fairtrade Foundation:

January 2011, and a second phase was run in December 2012. For more detailed results and charts, see Chapter 6.

In some cases NGOs can hold companies to account – 'you claimed xyz and you haven't delivered. This is what you say, this is what you do and they don't line up'. And very often companies do react to pressure so there is a role for this 'naming and shaming'. But we offer carrots and sticks, not just sticks. NGOs are also good at celebrating the good for example by putting together rankings like in fish and seafood. That way they reward the achievements of those that do well and create an effect of encouragement and raising standards alike.

Partners

NGOs often act as partners, especially if they are of the collaborating kind. Jane Tewson neatly summarizes what NGOs can do as partners of business:

When it comes to the role of NGOs and civil society, they might consider: alerting companies who are interested to the potential flaws (that I perceive) in the current process of CSR communication, inspiring businesses to think anew about being part of positive social change, encourage them to start with their own people to see if their practices and guidelines are fair and based on sound ethical grounds and expose them to scrutiny, if they fail to take sufficient account of the human and environmental costs of their operations, influencing the legislative context within which companies operate in favour of social justice, human rights and ecological sustainability, inspiring authentic two-way dialogue between companies and stakeholders (especially marginalized stakeholders) where companies demonstrate clear commitment and – last but not least – working in partnership with them to develop ethical, entrepreneurial products and services which meet pressing social and environmental needs.

As partners, they may even challenge companies to be bolder in what they communicate. It is true that one of the expectations of NGOs is that businesses should be humble when communicating their social and environmental activities and impacts. But at the same time, as Dax Lovegrove of the WWF sees it, if they aren't bold in how they communicate, they will not inspire and empower their customers and consumers to actually purchase greener products and lead greener lifestyles.

Another role as partners of companies is for NGOs to act as vehicles for businesses to channel their community support – and also to help them communicate the results of that support. Paul Brown of The Prince's Trust says:

Charities and NGOs tend to be the organizations that are actually delivering community benefit. They are the vehicles through which businesses can channel their community support and achieve their social objectives. Businesses, rightly, demand evidence of what their investment has achieved and so the charity partners have a duty to report back and demonstrate the benefits. This in turn, gives the business partner the opportunity to communicate the good work they are doing.

Best Practice Case: Lifebuoy's Global Handwashing Behaviour Change Programme

Figure 1.1   Colourful cartoon characters prompt children to remember to wash with soap before eating

Source: Reproduced courtesy of Unilever plc.

This is a classic example of a brand and a company in partnership with NGOS creating awareness and encouraging successful behavioural change on an unprecedented scale. Recognized as one the early brands that were truly global, Lifebuoy's initial mission, 'protection from infection through personal hygiene', evolved into 'clean hands help guard your health', and from that it was not a big step to 'health insurance for millions of children'.

Lifebuoy re-launched in the Indian market in 2002, supporting the largest hygiene education campaign ever, with the World Bank and UNICEF, and by the end of 2009 had reached 130 million people in 50,000 villages, along with double-digit growth. With 13 partners in the Public Private Partnership for Handwashing with Soap (PPPHW), Unilever through Lifebuoy was able to extend its campaign in 2008 to 23 countries in Asia and Africa.

In the words of one of its NGO partners, what was significant was their 'incredible market knowledge and reach'. The key here was obviously Lifebuoy's assessment from the beginning of a tremendous untapped consumer base and the realization that through partnership, the aim of making a difference to children's health was a perfect fit with the same NGO goal of saving children's lives, in particular from diseases manifesting themselves through diarrhoea and other symptoms linked to poor or absent hygiene. So the partnership element was crucial, as well as being able to monitor not only commercial growth but actual lives saved country by country. In addition, the NGO aim dovetailed perfectly with Unilever's realization that it could improve its performance in these emerging markets.

For the full Best Practice Case 1, see Chapter 10, page 151.

Lobbyists

From a societal point of view, NGOs additionally play the role of lobbyists for marginalized groups or social and environmental issues that don't have sufficient advocacy. Raising awareness of serious societal challenges, sometimes in collaboration with the media, is perhaps the most important role that NGOs have. They create the projection screen for sustainability in the public domain, on which companies and other stakeholder groups can act and communicate. Why this is important can be studied in those markets where there are few such NGOs, and where public awareness of social and environmental issues is usually significantly lower than in countries where NGOs actively campaign as lobbyists. Eastern European countries are an example, as there was very little 'civil society' to speak of following the overthrow of Communism. And the lack of awareness makes it more difficult for companies to create understanding and positive acknowledgement by consumers for what they may be doing in the CSR or sustainability realm. As an example, climate change is much less of an issue in Eastern than in Western European countries, partly because environmental NGOs do not have the same support base and clout there as they have in the West. For companies trying to explain the benefits of engaging in reducing their carbon footprints to consumers, this poses the challenge of doing the NGOs' 'job' of raising awareness of the issue as well as communicating their response to it. Businesses lobby for their (market-oriented, often vested) interests, and NGOs are trying to balance these activities by lobbying for what they perceive as the interests of either the common good or for causes that otherwise have little or no voice, such as underprivileged or socially excluded groups or 'free' goods, like water, natural resources, biodiversity or the climate, for which, so far, market mechanisms do not function. Harriet Lamb of the Fairtrade Foundation adds:

Agenda-setting is important. If things are not on the agenda, there is no business case. If civil society has said it loud and clear there is a business case. Just caring means: it is tricky to be competitive. The goodwill is beaten by the bad case. There has to be a business case otherwise it will not last and will not be sustainable.

Understanding the different roles

Businesses need to understand, respect and even appreciate the different roles of NGOs in order to develop effective CSR communication that really creates value for the business and productively engages with this key stakeholder group. Creating win–win situations between business and civil society may mean that companies support their civil society partners in their agenda-setting efforts by lending them a hand in the communications department and supporting them in driving awareness about specific social and environmental issues among the public at large or their targeted consumer group. And when the roles of watchdogs, partners and lobbyists come together, NGOs can become standard-setters, which define in a multi-stakeholder process what 'good' looks like and create a framework for sustainable behaviour, aiming to link sellers and buyers, producers and customers, brands and consumers behind a common social and/or environmental interest. Good examples of organizations that fuse these roles are Fairtrade, The Rainforest Alliance and the Forest Stewardship Council (FSC) in the business-to-consumer field, but partly also in the business-to-business context. These NGOs create standards on one hand and brands and labels on the other as vehicles of communication. Chris Wille of the Rainforest Alliance explains:

> Some NGOs have standards and certification programs and can go much further in demanding, guiding, verifying and rewarding positive company actions. The Rainforest Alliance pioneered this concept. We developed the first standards for responsible forest management and the first comprehensive standards for sustainable agriculture. The forestry standard is now managed by FSC and the agriculture standard by the Sustainable Agriculture Network. These standards and the supporting certification programs allow companies to make significant changes in the way they do business, incorporating sustainability into their supply chains and (especially important in the context of this interview) what the companies can claim in their CSR reports, advertising and other public-facing messaging. A certification program gives companies an independent, third-party endorsement of their claims that they can use even at the retail level. In agriculture, we have used standards and certification to help companies make dramatic changes. Sector leaders such as Chiquita, Kraft, Unilever, Tchibo, Tetley, Mars, Nespresso and others have overhauled their business models, starting with sustainable sourcing.

Partners pay for the use of the Rainforest Alliance or Fairtrade label or seal separately from the remuneration for using and helping to implement the standards. As most NGOs do not have large advertising, promotion and PR budgets they rely heavily on the usage of their labels and communications support from their corporate partners to drive awareness and build their brand. That may very well make sense for companies if they in return are given the space by NGOs that 'gives them the permission to care', as Harriet Lamb puts it:

> There is a role for NGOs to create that space, the political space to make big bold moves that are about creating societal change. Companies need to be part of that space and NGOs have the critical role of helping to change the environment in which businesses operate. As an example: if a company is going to invest millions to change fridges to higher environmental standards that is a big investment and they need to be able to present it as an attractive business case to their shareholders. If NGOs continue to create pressure by campaigning, the issue will be taken seriously, legal frameworks may change or be modified and the business case becomes convincing

for the company and its shareholders. Another example is Sainsbury's [a UK grocery chain] and their Fairtrade bananas. Switching to 100 per cent Fairtrade bananas costs them millions and they can only do it because they are sure that more people will come to their shops as a result; it benefits their brand and contributes to their financial success. As Justin King, CEO of J. Sainsbury plc, would say: 'I know it works because I know the public has requested Fairtrade.'

What are the key issues from a business perspective in communicating CSR to NGOs?

ALIGNING TWO VERY DIFFERENT PARADIGMS

Between humility and boldness

There are, no doubt, both opportunities and issues for companies when communicating CSR and sustainability-related messages to NGOs. Due to the difference in viewpoints there are seeming or even apparent inconsistencies and contradictions. On one hand NGOs ask for humility when it comes to communicating CSR – 'communicate less and not as loudly' – on the other they challenge companies to be bold, to inspire customers and consumers to change their lifestyles to bring about social change. On the one hand they ask companies to build substance before communicating, on the other they are quick to bash companies that have taken great care not to communicate prematurely once they have their 'coming out' and start leveraging their substance in marketing and advertising. A good example of this is Chiquita, as Chris Wille of the Rainforest Alliance remembers:

> *They worked for 10 years with the Rainforest Alliance to clean up their farms, and then started talking about it and using the RFA [Rainforest Alliance] seal. They did get some credit, some media and activists were impressed, but by sticking their necks out, Chiquita got a lot of negative press and got more attention than they had before. We have seen that in other areas, too, that companies that are doing well and talking about it get more criticism than if they were not doing anything.*

Beware of inconsistencies

Inconsistencies always challenge NGOs, which often take a strong stand on specific social and environmental topics like climate change or obesity. Sally Uren of Forum for the Future provides an example:

> *Social issues such as obesity and nutrition can be very complex. When big multinationals pledge their commitment to improve nutrition at the bottom of the pyramid but at the same time have a large number of high calorie and low nutritional value products in their portfolio they draw criticism for inconsistency. This criticism has been levelled at many brands, from PepsiCo to Unilever, the answer is for these businesses to be honest and commit to continuous improvement.*

Another example is consumption versus resource efficiency: 'Consumption is another issue – companies make money selling stuff (if they are profitable), so how do you align the objective of expanding market share while at the same time reducing your carbon footprint? Decoupling carbon emissions from business growth is essential in these instances.'

Understanding the NGO agenda

As a result of being criticized for inconsistency, companies may feel that their serious efforts to improve their social and environmental performance are not acknowledged, nor is the complexity of the task they are taking on – of aligning social and environmental performance with economic performance. One reason why NGOs have to be intolerant of inconsistency is that they are as accountable to their key stakeholders as companies are to their shareholders. While shareholders want a return, the constituents of NGOs – often their donors or activists volunteering for them – want progress on the cause they are supporting, and that includes media headlines and exposing 'baddies', like well-known brands or companies. If NGOs appear to compromise on their central tenets, they risk losing the trust of their followers and supporters, which in turn may put their 'business case' at risk. Despite this dilemma, Chris Wille of the Rainforest Alliance asks for a more differentiated approach:

> As NGOs we have to allow companies to change and to stop blacklisting them, like Nestlé. Nestlé is still blacklisted for issues that date back 10–15 years, despite a lot of substantial change. If the blacklisting persists even if a company takes action, why should it bother to change?

He adds that the tide is turning towards more balanced feedback by NGOs about businesses' CSR activities and towards growing acceptance of them, and cites seven points:

> (1) Success stories like Chiquita; (2) more NGOs working with companies like WWF and more recently even Greenpeace (McDonald's, Nestlé); (3) social media; (4) the media are getting more mature, journalists are beginning to understand the issue better and recognize that the old 'us versus them' dynamic is no longer as valid as it used to be; (5) the corporate world now has much more credibility (recent studies show that when the general public is surveyed about 'Who do you trust?', companies have improved rankings compared to those of politicians); (6) there is little regard for government regulation, so business has an increased role, and (7) growth in (the) certification movement – even though there still is a lot of conflict, competition and confusion, its success speaks for itself: it has gone mainstream and has brought the good efforts of companies to millions of consumers, and consumers trust independent seals.

Consumer interest versus NGO interest

In our conversation, the TUC's Nigel Stanley pointed out another dilemma – we could call it the 'Can they afford to care?' dilemma. He uses Walmart, the world's largest and much-campaigned-against retailer, as an example:

The left hates Walmart and the poor love it. They are the kind of people who cannot afford to go to farmers' markets. Walmart provides an awful lot of jobs and their customers don't really care about having an ethical stance or not. They can't afford to care!

So Walmart is in a dilemma, at least theoretically. On the one hand it wants to improve its reputation and work on the dialogue with key stakeholders, including NGOs. On the other hand, improving its overall reputation will not (have an) impact on the image it has and wants to retain with its key customers: that of the retailer they can afford and that gives them the things they need for a fair price.

Walmart's Personal Sustainability Plan may be a move in the right direction.[6] The programme follows the rationale Stephen Howard of BitC outlines:

You need to have more than a communications campaign – just communication gets you only that far. The question is: How do you build a brand and a reputation as a consequence of your responsible actions? You need to ask how you retain and recruit employees Do you consider community engagement and involvement? That is important for staff!

The best communications campaigns, directed towards customers as well as towards NGOs, are the employees who act as ambassadors for your business and brand. Seen from an NGO perspective, having members of staff speak for you voluntarily and with conviction, will build credibility and authenticity. If the community involvement results in positive social action, it will ultimately help in building the brand.

Will they ever trust us?

'The most effective way to get input from NGOs is through partnership,' says Dax Lovegrove of the WWF. 'Businesses are far more likely to listen and be open behind closed doors, based on a relationship of trust.' And building this relationship of trust with NGOs and civil society is probably the number one challenge for companies, which may have to dare to take the first step if there is a long-term history of conflicting opinions and antagonism. However, if this trust is developed and grows, a partnership with an NGO or with several NGOs can help businesses to improve overall societal trust and reputation.

Partnership works best if the NGO is involved both in creating the substance with the company and subsequently in any communication. That is reflected in the above-mentioned growth in certification, like that of the Rainforest Alliance, Fairtrade or the FSC, just to mention three of the many schemes and labels. This co-creation works, whether the label is used actively by the company or brand or whether it chooses to create its own mark, authorized by the NGO or in collaboration with the NGO. That is the path premium coffee brand Nespresso has chosen. Nespresso's sustainability initiatives are bundled under its own label, ecolaboration. Its sourcing initiative is the AAA Sustainable Quality Program in partnership with the Rainforest Alliance, which provides the certification and third-party endorsement. The reason this endorsement is important is trust. Despite the observation made by Chris Wille above that trust in companies has grown, at least relatively, the public has a lot more confidence in NGOs.

---

6   This is briefly described in Chapter 4; see the interview with Erica Jones, International Corporate Affairs Manager, Walmart, pp. 67–9.

Partnering with NGOs therefore has the potential to transfer trust to corporate or product brands. According to Harriet Lamb, the Fairtrade Foundation conducted research in 18 countries on the public perception of companies and found that 70 per cent of respondents were looking for a third-party verifier. She further quoted another piece of research conducted by the think-tank AccountAbility that found that trust in companies was declining, while that in NGOs was increasing.

Best Practice Case: Fairtrade Comes of Age

Figure 1.2   African farmers picking fairly traded cotton, meeting consumer demand for sustainably sourced materials

Source: Reproduced courtesy of Fairtrade International.

Fairtrade's experience demonstrates the evolution of a brand from 'worthiness' and niche positioning to a mass-market, strong consumer brand. Furthermore, this has been done without resorting to huge spending on advertising.

Its heritage goes back to the 1950s, when it was essentially a collaboration between enlightened European and American importers of commodities from developing countries. In the late 1980s and early 1990s a number of organizations, notably the Dutch development agency Max Havelaar, among others, campaigned to alter international trade practices and developed certification marks.

In 2004 the Fairtrade Labelling Organization (FLO) was divided in two: FLO itself dealt with standards and labelling and was responsible for strategy, and FLO-CERT dealt with auditing producers and traders.

Nowadays, 1.2 million workers and farmers, covering 905 producer organizations in 63 countries across Africa, Asia and Latin America, as well as their families, benefit directly from Fairtrade. The brand has built public awareness, and through this, increased consumer demand, moving it from something that represented products that were not necessarily high-quality but were ethical to something desirable in quality and price.

The main point here is that the ethical dimension of a brand cannot compensate for any deficits.

The International Social and Environmental Accreditation and Labelling Alliance is one of seven such bodies acknowledged as having the highest ethical standards, and it is arguably the best-known.

Fairtrade continues to promote changes in conventional trade, and all its producers are able to have a voice through various committees which feed into its board. Not only has profit grown exponentially, but premiums are distributed to communities.

In conclusion, the example of the UK grocery chain Sainsbury's in selling Fairtrade bananas has truly transformed it into a genuine brand, and not merely a label.

For the full Best Practice Case 2, see Chapter 10, page 161.

Can you share any best practice examples of CSR communication?

Table 1.1 shows the brands and programmes which were mentioned in the interviews.

Table 1.1   Brands and programmes referenced in the interviews

Brand, company, programme	No. of mentions
Top 4	
Marks & Spencer 'Look behind the label' and Plan A	4
Unilever Corporate Sustainability	3
Cadbury Fair Trade chocolate and sustainability reporting/stakeholder dialogue	3
P&G Ariel 'Turn to 30°' and Excel Gel	2

Brand, company, programme	No. of mentions
Single Mentions Grouped by Industry:	
(Fast-moving) Consumer Goods (Including Top 4):	16
Chiquita partnership with Rainforest Alliance; Diageo talking about drinking less; SAB Miller 10-point plan; Nespresso Ecolaboration; Nestlé Creating Shared Value/Corporate Sustainability; Tate & Lyle sugar; innocent; Lavazza	8
Retail (Including Top 4):	7
Marks & Spencer, Walmart, Tchibo	3
Food Service:	
Starbucks collaboration with The Prince's Trust; Caribou	2
Media:	
Sky–Carbon Trust partnership	1

Harriet Lamb of the Fairtrade Foundation says: 'Marks & Spencer's Plan A is completely brilliant. It covers everything under the umbrella of sustainability communication, first the stakeholders, then the press. People still talk about it, because of the vision that holds it all together.' Anthony Kleanthous of the WWF agrees, and goes a step further:

> *The most successful campaign if you take the consumer perspective is 'Look behind the label' by Marks & Spencer. That really took CSR messages to the consumer and was their most successful campaign ever run – completely 360° marketing! It really improved the image of the M&S brand and encouraged sustainable consumption with consumers. They evolved it into Plan A, which is more than a communications campaign, very substantial with goals and indicators, where everyone is involved. Plan A shows that it is about changing the way the company works and then resulting in communication.*

Stephen Howard of BitC commends the iconic British retail brand for 'being very careful in the way they word it' and for:

> *having the courage in a difficult environment to launch this [Plan A] as 'the right thing to do',[7] convincing the staff first, then the customers. What Plan A is basically saying is that 'You are telling us that you want performance, value and sustainability. We will give you that and that will make us a better company and we will have a lot of good results.' It is a very strategic decision to run a business, not just marketing.*

Unilever is commended for 'weaving sustainability into the corporate brand', according to Dax Lovegrove of WWF. Sally Uren of Forum for the Future agrees: 'Unilever and big multinationals do it well. At a corporate level they have a co-ordinated and logical approach.'

Cadbury is mentioned as a best practice example for both its sustainability reporting and its partnership with Fair Trade and the move to 100 per cent Fair Trade cocoa in its biggest brand, Dairy Milk. 'Cadbury's initiative is big and well phased,' says Harriet Lamb

---

7   Since the re-launch of Plan A in 2010, Marks & Spencer now actually calls its approach 'The right thing to do'.

of the Fairtrade Foundation. 'They talked to NGOs early, went to Parliament and then to the press, then to the public, making sure that as many people as possible heard it directly from them.' Sally Uren calls Cadbury (now part of the Mondelez group of brands) a sector leader, referring to its corporate sustainability communication.

Procter & Gamble is mentioned because it delivers on taking the consumer perspective and links its sustainability message directly to product performance 'P&G's Ariel "Turn to 30" is a good example of creating a virtuous circle of delivering performance and environmental value,' says BitC's Stephen Howard. 'The product is bought because it is good and has a clear benefit.' Anthony Kleanthous agrees: 'It is not really different from selling any other washing powder – now the benefit is lower impact on the environment and cost-saving.'

Chris Wille of the Rainforest Alliance says:

Chiquita is the best story to tell, because it is just one product, bananas. They have a vertically integrated single product supply chain and it is a very well known, much researched business. And: there are whole leagues of NGOs and political commissions focused on pointing out issues in bananas.

An entire industry is highlighted by Paul Brown of The Prince's Trust, and not surprisingly it is the (British) retail trade:

Some of the best examples can be seen on the high street. In the UK, the major supermarkets each support a leading charity. The partnerships are brought to life in-store, engaging and motivating customers and colleagues alike. I am sure, behind the scenes, there are sophisticated communications exercises aimed at stakeholders and opinion-formers. But, for immediate, wide-scale impact, the activation in-store is quite impressive.

Brown points out that The Prince's Trust currently works with Starbucks, which, as well as raising vital funds to support the Trust's programmes, is helping it 'to tell our story through a series of communications with their customers in store. They are, in effect, a media channel which is really valuable to us,' proving that CSR communication can play an important role for NGOs.

Another case that was acknowledged is Virgin Unite. Jane Tewson of Igniting Change explains:

I truly believe that healthy businesses need healthy communities around them and vice versa. I am privileged to sit on the board of Virgin Unite, which is committed to using business as a force for good. Unite has a developing relationship with Kids Company in London and very vibrant and inspiring conversations always take place when we visit there. Virgin Care had some of the wonderful young people from Kids Company work with them to better understand what young people needed from healthcare services and have now taken on board many of their suggestions. Listening to the people who really understand the issues must be a part of any company's work to partner with their communities. It must be a partnership filled with dignity and respect for everyone involved ....

Going through the examples the NGO interviewees alluded to, three points stand out:

1. **Involvement** – NGOs become passionate when stakeholders are truly involved – interestingly enough, consumers in particular.
2. **Professionalism** – A logical, co-ordinated, strategic approach is appreciated.
3. **Courage** – NGOs may be very critical but they recognize when a company and its management is convinced of what they are doing and move ahead boldly.

The example that fulfils all three criteria is Marks & Spencer.

How do you define 'greenwashing'? Examples?

WORDS WITHOUT SUBSTANCE

If it's words and nothing behind it, no examples, no clear link to business strategy.
Stephen Howard, Business in the Community

The most basic form of greenwashing is when companies tout an environmental product or service – even though their core business is polluting or unsustainable. There can be a lot of exaggeration and spin behind environmental claims, and companies which tout their green credentials have been known to simultaneously lobby against environmental regulation.
Nigel Stanley, Trades Union Congress

Paul Brown of The Prince's Trust alludes to the basic 'substance first' credo stating: 'When companies spend more time talking about their CSR projects, community investment, environment and sustainability programmes than actually doing them they are often accused of greenwashing. The communications campaign needs to be proportionate to the investment.' And Nigel Stanley adds that greenwashing implies 'style but not substance, random claims about sustainability credentials about product, service or brand'.

The examples given include whole industries, areas of activity and specific companies: 'One of the more fashionable activities of the recent past has been that carbon offsetting has emerged as one of the biggest areas of potential greenwashing: shouldn't we be focusing on reducing our carbon footprint, rather than paying a tax to continue polluting, sometimes to rather dodgy schemes?' Many interviewees thought that Shell's advertisement showing flowers coming out of power station chimneys deserved the negative attention that it received.

It is another oil company that Sally Uren mentions, however, for a different reason: 'Exxon has no targets, no integrity behind its communications, one-dimensional advertising, single-issue, no substance.'

Anthony Kleanthous tries to provide advice on how to avoid greenwashing:

CSR messages need to be both true and credible. Past transgressions may undermine present credibility, even when the necessary lessons have been learned, and change implemented. Nestlé has learned this the hard way. This is why good CSR communications usually focus on specific claims of superior process efficiency or product performance. Bad ones can fall into a variety of traps, such as immateriality. For example, if I were Volvic, I would shout less about building wells in African villages and more about how I'm reducing the (enormous) environmental impacts of transporting a heavy product like water all over the world in plastic bottles.

I might do what Coca-Cola (sort of) did, and launch a branded range of bottled local tap water. Granted, Coke's Dasani brand tanked spectacularly in the UK, but that's because the brand was ill-conceived and an early batch was found to contain harmful chemicals.

What do you consider to be the key success factors of effective CSR communication?

RELEVANCE – SUBSTANCE – INTEGRITY – BOLDNESS – PROFESSIONALISM – HUMILITY

The feedback can be summarized into six key success factors from the NGO perspective:

1. **Relevance** – 'People are resistant to changing their habits,' says Anthony Kleanthous, 'including the way they choose, buy and consume products and services. If you want them to change, then you have to be relevant; you have to deliver tangible benefits, you have to communicate those benefits at just the right moments, and you have to choose the most credible vehicles for your messages. This might involve direct communications with consumers, or it might involve seeding messages amongst a core group of influential and connected consumers and other opinion formers.' Tangible benefits are key for Jane Tewson, too: 'both for people in the company and people in the community. Don't just pay lip-service to social and environmental change!'

2. **Substance** – 'Somehow you've got to be seen as not just sincere, but verifiable and clearly stating that this is important to your long-term success. That is the really powerful message!', emphasizes Stephen Howard. 'Take chocolate as an example: you want to be sure that you have a sustainable source of quality chocolate, that is where the virtuous circle comes in. People will believe it – and if it is bullshit, you will get caught!'.

3. **Integrity** – Effective communication works from the inside out, and it has a lot to do with how the company that communicates walks the talk in its own organization. Jane Tewson points out that there is a connection between healthy companies and healthy communities. And a healthy company is recognized by a 'happy, motivated and inspired workforce'.

4. **Boldness** – Dax Lovegrove cites the 2010 Renault advertisement (see the full interview below), and comments: 'It is a clear articulation of the dilemma of climate change and the freedom dichotomy – yet it creates a simple aspiration to be climate friendly. It is simple, yet bold and challenging, an articulation of what it means to embrace sustainability from a consumer perspective.'

5. **Professionalism** – 'And then [once a company has embedded sustainability in its core values, processes and business model] it is just [good, professional] marketing – the same stuff as in all other messages i.e. memorability, credibility and relevance' stresses Anthony Kleanthous and points out that it is very much about choosing the right media channel for what you want to achieve: 'Be single minded and ask yourself: what is most likely to influence change in behaviour? Very rarely it is direct sustainability communication and above the line messaging that reaches consumers in a way that affects their behaviour. You need to be more clever. An example is offsetting: if you want people to do that, you make it very easy for them! That brings about change in

behaviour – and the internet is the most important and appropriate channel for CSR messages!'

6. **Humility** – Whenever there is considerable CSR or sustainability substance, there are also partners and there will always be imperfection. Humility and recognition of partners will always strengthen credibility and trust. Paul Brown concurs: 'If the communication shows both the charity and the business partner in a positive light, then it has been a success. If it demonstrates real, tangible, quantifiable results, then it is likely to have a positive effect.'

Interview with Dax Lovegrove, WWF-UK

WHAT DO YOU ASSOCIATE WITH CSR COMMUNICATION?

CSR communication should be all about linking a company's core activities back to real corporate sustainability.

WHAT ARE YOUR EXPECTATIONS REGARDING CSR COMMUNICATION OF COMPANIES?

CSR communications should be demonstrating how business is really changing and what it is genuinely doing.

WHAT IS THE ROLE OF NGOS IN THE CONTEXT OF CSR COMMUNICATION OF COMPANIES?

NGOs' role is to check that CSR communications are based on a solid foundation of sustainability. Also to challenge companies to make their communications bold enough. Do they inspire and empower their customers to buy greener products and lead greener lifestyles? Do they drive reform? How do they manage the issues of creating competitive advantage for the company yet striving for the common good? In this context, some NGOs take a more aggressive stance than others towards policing companies.

WHAT ARE THE ISSUES FROM A BUSINESS PERSPECTIVE IN COMMUNICATING CSR TO NGOS?

The most effective way to get input from NGOs is through partnerships. Businesses are far more likely to listen 'behind closed doors' based on a relationship of trust.

CAN YOU SHARE ANY BEST PRACTICE EXAMPLES OF CSR COMMUNICATION?

Marks & Spencer's Plan A is always cited as best practice, and rightly so as it does genuinely keep pushing the boundaries. Another one is SAB Miller's 'Ten point plan', covering a wide range of aspects, both social and environmental – for example, HIV, water footprinting, carbon footprinting and responsible drinking. I like the way Unilever is weaving sustainability into its corporate brand. Last but not least, I would mention

Sky's Carbon Trust partnership, which, for example, covered the Copenhagen Climate Summit well in December 2009.

HOW DO YOU DEFINE 'GREENWASHING' AND COULD YOU NAME EXAMPLES?

Power companies are good examples of greenwashing. All their CSR communication is about their involvement in wind farms, but it is a very minor part of their business. The oil sector is another one – they are busy recarbonizing rather than decarbonizing. WWF is leading a toxic fuels campaign to persuade oil companies to be more transparent around the environmental risk of some of their recent and planned oil explorations. You could also mention airlines that talk about improvements in aircraft efficiency but don't address the fact that the overall volumes of air traffic are increasing, thus increasing the carbon footprint of the industry.

WHAT DO YOU CONSIDER TO BE KEY SUCCESS FACTORS OF EFFECTIVE CSR COMMUNICATION FROM AN NGO PERSPECTIVE?

Boldness, honesty and communicating from a consumer perspective. Take the recent Renault advert as an example.[8] It's a clear articulation of the dilemma of climate change and the freedom dichotomy – our freedom as car drivers directly impinges on the freedom of others. It creates a simple aspiration to be climate-friendly, and it is a simple yet bold and challenging articulation of what it means to embrace sustainability from a consumer perspective.

Key Messages in a Nutshell

Table 1.2   Chapter 1 key messages in a nutshell

Expectations of NGOs towards CSR communication	Start in your own backyard Link CSR to core business Be transparent and honest Focus on results Maintain constant dialogue Advertise and communicate only in proportion to results Take responsibility for sustainable consumption
Roles of NGOs in the context of CSR communication	Watchdogs Partners Lobbyists

8   Referring to the 'Drive the Change' campaign started in January 2010 across Europe. The advert positioned Renault as a responsible auto maker that claims to drive both social issues (equality, mass mobility) and environmental issues (climate change, resource-efficiency) with its product offerings (for example, electric vehicles). The advert was taken off air after the British Advertising Standards Authority (ASA) banned it in March 2010 following consumer complaints, saying it was misleading because it gave the impression that the entire production, use and disposal of the vehicles shown would be free of emissions and other detrimental effects on the environment. The ASA stated: 'Because Renault was unable to substantiate that, when including the emissions from production to disposal the vehicle would not result in any emissions, we concluded the claim was likely to mislead.'

Issues of CSR communication to NGOs	Between humility and boldness Beware of inconsistencies Understanding the NGO agenda Consumer interest versus NGO interest Will they ever trust us?
Key success factors for communicating CSR to NGOs	Relevance Substance Integrity Boldness Professionalism Humility

2 *Communicating Sustainability – the Public Sector Perspective*

> *Good CSR communication implies that you see what the issues are and ... involve government as early as possible in the process.*
> Toni Symonds, California State Assembly

'Public sector' is defined in relatively broad terms – we have spoken to representatives of state and local governments as well as national government and international inter-governmental organizations. What they all have in common is that they are primarily publicly funded and have a direct or indirect influence on the conditions companies operate under, either by shaping laws and regulations or by being involved in creating international agreements and guidelines.

The framework for CSR and CSR communication differs between countries due to the variations in their legal or economic systems and thus the public perception of the companies and their role in society. In the context of CSR communication, this is reflected, for instance, in whether CSR reporting is voluntary or required by law, as in France and Denmark. Another example is the area of labour relations. In Germany all companies with more than 20 employees are required to have a labour council. Labour councils are one element of 'employee participation' or 'co-determination' in the management of business, something that does not exist to such an extent as a legal requirement in most other countries.

What do you associate with CSR and CSR communication?

ANYTHING YOU DO ACTUALLY COMMUNICATES

'CSR is about how money is made not how money is spent,' says Matthias Stausberg, Head of Media Relations & Public Affairs at the UN Global Compact. To him, 'corporate social responsibility' is a controversial term; he prefers 'corporate sustainability'. Blaine Collison of the US government's Environmental Protection Agency (EPA) tends to agree: 'CSR is not a favourite term.' He would understand CSR to 'capture a broad array of voluntary corporate activity in the areas of the social and environmental framework'. For Toni Symonds of the California State Assembly, 'CSR is not something that is extra – it is about the integrity and the conscious management of the company over the long term.' That means managing with integrity, being truly risk-conscious and working towards long-term value-creation. Being risk-conscious means being aware of the fact that externalized costs[1] can be internalized by changes in laws and regulations very quickly. Actively engaging in CSR can therefore be a way to deal proactively with such risk areas.

It should, however, be seen holistically, according to Dr Rolf Bösinger of the German Federal Ministry of Labour and Social Affairs, CSR needs to cover fair treatment of employees as well as sparing and efficient use of natural resources and socially and environmentally responsible production along the value chain. A key point he makes is that CSR is never a substitute for public framework-setting, but can be the springboard for win–win agreements and projects between political institutions and business.

CSR communication is mostly associated with annual CSR reports, and is perceived as 'a crowded landscape', according to Blaine Collison. While he sees a lot of positive developments, he worries about the information overload generated by newsletters and countless CSR reports. In particular, he feels it is very hard to select the leaders from the laggards, as a lot of the information is more anecdotal than quantifiable and benchmarked.

Matthias Stausberg takes a wider view – 'Doing the right thing and talking about it' – which is similar to the definition Dr Rolf Bösinger uses: 'CSR communication is about companies that wish to portray corporate social responsibility as their company philosophy to the outside world and manage their core business applying better rules.' Having said that, portraying CSR to the outside world is not a simple and straightforward task: in the age of social media, it is much more than reporting because 'anything you do actually communicates', according to Toni Symonds. Global Compact's Matthias Stausberg[2] maintains that this is why the 'classical corporate communications' function may not be ideally equipped to handle the challenges of CSR communication: from developing and disseminating CSR or sustainability reports to internal communication about 'what we are doing, how we are doing, what is our sustainability strategy to what does it mean for you as an employee'. Therefore, whoever is responsible for the communication of CSR needs to be closely involved with the development of the sustainability or CSR strategy, and thus has to be placed very close to the leadership of the company.

What are the expectations of the public sector regarding CSR communication of companies?

THE FIVE CS – FROM CORRECT TO CREDIBLE

The public sector expectations can be summarized as the 'Five Cs': Correct, Clear, Complete, Comparable and Credible:

1. **Correct** – This means that the information communicated needs to be fact-based and accurate, which these days is fairly easy to check. Correct, however, also means that communication is always backed by action. Matthias Stausberg cites BP as an

---

1   Costs that are incurred by a company through its activity, but are not allocated to it, but to the general public – like effects on air or water quality, a lot of CO_2 emissions, effects on biodiversity or impacts on human living conditions or quality of life.

2   Matthias Stausberg was Head of Public Affairs & Media Relations and Spokesperson for the United Nations Global Compact between September 2002 and October 2012, since November 2012 he has been Community Director at Virgin Unite (UK).

example where there was a major schism between the image that was created by a 'sort of brand narrative' and the actual sustainability-related behaviour: 'They spent years building a mirage of sustainability that they did not live up to.'

2. **Clear** – The public sector expects transparency and disclosure from companies in the area of CSR and sustainability. Companies need to show what they actually do to minimize specific social and environmental risks in an easy to understand way. Information about companies' performance, programmes and policies in these areas need to be readily accessible to the public, not just to policy makers. This may include information on where they are not doing well thus far.

3. **Complete** – CSR communication needs to be more than merely self-congratulatory. It needs to cover all relevant social and environmental issues, including those where performance could be improved. A widely accepted definition of what is 'complete' is the Global Reporting Initiative (GRI) set of guidelines. However, this may only serve as a general guideline as 'expectations [of stakeholders] will increase over time', says Matthias Stausberg, and they may be industry- or even company-specific.

4. **Comparable** – Public sector stakeholders expect that the CSR performance of companies can be benchmarked against that of other companies. A prerequisite to benchmarking is quite obviously that communication is based on quantitative metrics, not only on narrative. If, in an ideal world, those metrics are standardized, they will allow 'apple to apple' comparison, otherwise known as benchmarking.

5. **Credible** – From a public sector point of view, credibility primarily relies on consistency between a company's actions in the area of CSR and its communication. However, CSR communication also needs to be consistent with other corporate communications. If that kind of consistency is absent, it is an indicator that CSR is not integrated into the core business.

What is the role of the public sector in the context of CSR communication or companies?

STOP THE PLAYING FIELD FROM SPINNING

Regulation should stop the playing field from spinning.

Toni Symonds, California State Assembly

'Part of the role [of government] is to provide some of the market context, set benchmarks and performance targets that constitute minimum and exemplary levels,' states Blaine Collison of the US EPA. This applies to CSR in general as well as specifically to CSR communication. Setting the framework implies providing guidance, direction and a playing field that is reasonably constant and predictable. However, 'that role is not generally fulfilled', according to Toni Symonds, because 'long-term vision and consistency is very tricky due to short-term public expectations and the short-term rewards of political actors'. A changing regulatory environment potentially creates huge risks for companies, and is therefore an obstacle to CSR communication that meets the expectations of the public sector. If, on the other hand, governments provide direction and leadership, as the French government has recently with its national experiment on carbon labelling, it can create fertile ground for innovation and progress. The same goes for mandatory sustainability reporting for businesses, as in France, the Netherlands and Denmark: the respective guidelines provide a framework and facilitate transparency and comparability between reports, and according to recent research by Harvard Business School, leads to increased social responsibility among business leaders.[3] Strategic policy documents on specific topics are more of a recommendation than a regulation, but nevertheless provide guidance to companies, and in addition can clarify stakeholder expectations.[4]

Leadership also means leading by example. Just as governments can be good examples in terms of sustainable (business) practices, for example by setting and following green public procurement rules, they can be good examples in terms of their CSR or sustainability communication. The German Federal Government as well as selected federal government agencies report on progress made in terms of the national sustainability strategy as well as annual key performance indicator reports. Under the Greening Government Commitment, the UK government encourages public bodies and businesses alike to disclose their sustainability performance via annual reports and accounts. The Sustainability Reporting Guidance published by HM Treasury provides the framework for public sector sustainability reporting and ensures that 'apples are compared to apples' – that the information is accurate and comparable between reports.[5] Similarly, the Australian government requires all government organizations to report on their environmental performance in their annual reports.[6]

Governments can also act as facilitators for effective CSR communication. They can create and promote labels, like the German Bio-Siegel (or Bio-label, indicating that goods are organic) or the above-mentioned French CO_2 labelling initiative, or develop information portals that provide an easy-to-use digest of corporate sustainability information to consumers. As Dr Rolf Bösinger of the German Federal Ministry of Labour and Social Affairs explains:

Consumers need quick and easy guidance on the CSR behaviour of companies. CSR reports offer some initial guidance, but comparing them can be cumbersome. That is why the ministry responsible for CSR, the Federal Ministry of Labour and Social Issues wants to offer a practical guide where relevant information is collated and presented in a targeted manner, for example via an Internet portal. The objective would be that consumers use this CSR information in making their purchasing decisions.

3   Ioannis Ioannou and George Serafeim, *The Consequences of Mandatory Corporate Sustainability Reporting*, Harvard Business School Working Paper 11-100, 26 October 2012, www.hbs.edu/faculty/Publication%20Files/11-100_35684ae7-fcdc-4aae-9626-de4b2acb1748.pdf (accessed 10 June 2013).

4   An example is the policy strategy on food labelling published in September 2011 by the Council of Academic Advisors for Consumer and Nutrition and Agricultural Policy to the German Federal Ministry for Food, Agriculture and Consumer Protection.

5   'The purpose of this guidance is to facilitate the completion of sustainability reports in the public sector. It sets out the Minimum Requirements, some best practice guidance and the underlying principles to be adopted in preparing the information. It is aligned with the "Greening Government Commitments", applicable to Central Government bodies, to ensure consistency, with the ambition to strive for a single reporting mechanism in the future'; HM Treasury, *Public Sector Annual Reports: Sustainability Reporting – Guidance for 2011–12 Reporting*, 19 December 2011, www.hm-treasury.gov.uk/d/psar_sustainability_reporting_guidance20112.pdf (accessed 10 June 12013), p. 4.

6   Under Section 516A of the Environmental Protection and Biodiversity Conservation Act 1999.

Best Practice Case: German Bio-label

Figure 2.1   **'Now you can compare apples with pears' – Bio-labelling with a sense of humour**

Source: Reproduced courtesy of Bundesministerium für Ernährung, Landwirtschaft und Verbraucherschutz (Germany) and Wire Advertising.

A crisis can have very positive results. This is the story behind the development of the German Bio-label, which came about due to the European BSE ('mad cow disease') crisis in 2001–2002. In an unprecedented collaboration between various stakeholders and with the wholehearted support of the German government, it can be described as an unqualified success.

With a backdrop of two ministerial resignations and a confusing market of multiple organic products, the government decided that there needed to be a simplified label, which at the very least would meet European Union organic farm guidelines. It convened stakeholder consultations which included everyone: consumer groups, representatives from the food industry, and traditional farmers as well as organic farmers. It was decided that simplicity was paramount – an anxious public must be able to view the process in a way that made it both transparent and accessible. The government backed this up with a major advertising campaign which ensured that even now, the Bio-label is the best-known sustainability label in Germany.

The success of the initiative can be seen in that there are more and more farmers choosing to become organic, whereas before an organic farmer was viewed as a bit of an oddity in farming communities; organic has now moved from a niche to becoming a market segment of its own, and the emphasis throughout the consultation process was one of two-way communication and engagement, with voluntary participation.

Dr Ingo Braune of the German Ministry of Food, Agriculture and Consumer Protection sees the German approach has having been most effective, as measured in the market growth of the organic sector as well as the fact that all of the big discounter chains have developed their own 'Bio' lines. In contrast, the European Union's top-down and regulatory approach to developing an EU-wide label in 2011 is, he feels, not likely to be as successful for just these reasons.

For the full Best Practice Case 3, see Chapter 11, page 169.

As an alternative, governments can even run national sustainability awareness programmes, like the Swedish government in 1989.[7]

Matthias Stausberg of the UN Global Compact points out that governments and (inter-)governmental organizations have very distinct roles. Governments are, in his view, primarily regulators, and have both soft and hard power options to drive the CSR agenda. Hard options include regulations – for instance, by making sustainability reporting mandatory – and soft power options can include incentive schemes – like the German Deutscher Nachhaltigkeitspreis, an award scheme under the tutelage of the Federal Government that rewards best practice sustainability performance. Inter-governmental organizations like the United Nations Global Compact primarily offer a platform for dialogue, experimentation and information. They bring companies together to talk about sustainability strategies, practices, and how to best communicate them. 'I am not talking only about disclosure, but also about other forms of communicating, about good performance or responding to critical issues,' concludes Matthias Stausberg.

---

7   See The Natural Step case study in Chapter 9.

What are the key issues and opportunities from a business perspective in communicating CSR to the public sector?

ALIGNING LOBBYING AND CSR COMMUNICATION

The major challenge, particularly for large businesses, is to align lobbying (or, to be more 'politically correct', advocacy) efforts with CSR communication. That links back to the observation by public sector representatives that in many cases CSR or sustainability communications staff are not sufficiently linked to those in the business handling strategy development and implementation. Lobbyists, on the other hand, are (by default) linked very closely to the core business objectives, as their goal is to gain political favour for those objectives. As Matthias Stausberg of the UN Global Compact puts it: 'If you want to communicate sustainability effectively, you need to link the decision making process with communications and make sure it is reflected in all [communications] from marketing and advertising to human resource policies to supply chain management to PR and government relations.' Linked to this challenge is a warning to treat the government side with respect. California State Assembly representative Toni Symonds states that 'it doesn't help the process if you (the business) think they (government officials) don't know', and cites the positive example of a mobile homes manufacturer which communicated well.

Best Practice Case: The French Environmental Labelling Experiment

The French CO_2 labelling initiative, or 'national experimentation', goes one step further: it offers businesses a platform to experiment in a real-life market situation with labelling options, providing a framework with minimum requirements and a fixed period after which the results will be evaluated.

In a unique approach to make the public aware that domestic consumption, and that of food in particular, is responsible for the majority of CO_2 emissions, the French government developed a labelling pilot scheme with retailers such as Casino.

With the advent of 'Le Grenelle Environmental Multistakeholders Stage One', consumers were given the right to have environmental information on products. In Stage Two it would become a legal requirement to display carbon and environmental indicators on product packaging.

In 2006, Groupe Casino introduced lifecycle assessments on 26 branded products. By 2007, following the establishment of a think-tank bringing together governmental and business interests at EU level, Grenelle Stage One was introduced, and in 2008–2009 Casino had 100 of its own-brand products labelled.

Figure 2.2   Retailer Groupe Casino was one of the drivers behind the French Environmental Labelling Experiment

Source: Reproduced courtesy of Groupe Casino.

With the advent of 2010 and the development of Grenelle Stage Two, businesses were invited to participate. There were 230 applications from companies to take part, of which 168 were selected; these were broken down into 25 per cent being large companies, 45 per cent medium-sized and 30 per cent small companies. The pilot began in July 2011 with consultation with brands and companies prior to the implementation of mandatory labelling. This is expected to begin sometime in 2013 after the conclusion of a 12-month voluntary phase at the end of 2012. Once this is concluded, results will be presented to the French National Assembly.

In addition, efforts to gain 'broad stakeholder engagement' are planned, seeking the views of NGOs and consumers to be included in the report for parliamentary consideration. This will also involve manufacturers and retailers, so that they can have some input into the process.

A more in-depth look at Casino, which is very much seen as a French 'pioneer' in the field of sustainability, including the improved efficiency and cost savings it has made while improving its reputation and consumer trust, is also included in the Best Practice Case Study.

For the full Best Practice Case 4, see Chapter 11, page 175.

Can you share any best practice examples of CSR communication?

Table 2.1 shows the brands and programmes that were mentioned in the interviews.

Table 2.1   Brands and programmes referenced in the interviews

Brand, company, programme	No. of mentions
Carbon Disclosure Project reports	1
Ceres Reports	1
DuPont on water conservation	1
Patagonia Sustainability vision and transparency in the supply chain	1
Gap, first sustainability report, 2004	1
Pfizer internal communications programme on the Global Compact	1
Siemens's reaction to corruption scandal	1

The examples mentioned in Table 2.1 can be divided into two groups: company-specific communication, and structured third-party reports like Carbon Disclosure Project reports and the Ceres Reports.[8] For the EPA's Blaine Collison, the latter are valuable sources, as they have 'good metrics (and) good quantified data'. As multi-company or sector reports (they) help to assess 'who is leading, just getting started, (and) who is not participating' and provide a broader overview than individual corporate reports.

DuPont is cited by Toni Symonds as a best practice CSR communications example. She specifically refers to sustainability discussions 'where DuPont did some of the earliest work on how water conservation work saved them money'. DuPont's work in the CSR field helped the California state government ('they took the time to do research in such a way that government could pick it up, they felt it was their responsibility to develop this model') so that it selected DuPont as a good example in 2003 in the context of developing the state's CSR plan. Thus 'DuPont influenced the legislative process' and is an example of how 'CSR provides the opportunity for business to partner with the government to create a new alignment of the success of business and the success of society'.

Matthias Stausberg commends Patagonia for its strong vision of corporate responsibility and sustainability, and more specifically its communication for creating remarkable transparency in the supply chain: 'a very comprehensive supply chain website that illustrates for every product their product line, what material it's made of, where it comes from, where and by whom it is manufactured and what the challenges and issues are. They maximize the use of different available [communication] channels.' He further outlines how best practice can be defined in a number of ways: responding to criticism,

---

8   Ceres is a US-based not-for-profit organization that leads a national coalition of investors, environmental organizations and other public interest groups working with companies to address sustainability challenges such as global climate change and water scarcity. It publishes regular reports on specific sustainability issues plus an annual report outlining the progress made. Founded in 1989, Ceres launched the Global Reporting Initiative (GRI), has partnered with large corporations on specific sustainability engagements (for example, Ford committing to a 30 per cent carbon emissions reduction target by 2020) and is behind the Investor Network on Climate Risk (INCR), a group of leading investors managing almost $10 trillion in assets, and the Business for Innovative Climate and Energy Policy (BICEP), a coalition of 20 leading consumer brand companies.

documenting production and supply chain activities, responsible lobbying, and internal communications, specifically in-house training programmes to bring employees on board. On a very different note, he points out how well Siemens reacted in the context of the corruption scandals it was involved in – management were 'very outspoken and clear about it. Not only that they completely restructured the leadership of the company and their approach to [governance] but they also shared that information with others and are actively engaged in all [Global Compact's] anticorruption work in which they play a leading role.'

How do you define 'greenwashing'? Examples?

WORDS – NO OR DECEPTIVE ACTION

In its very simplest form, greenwashing is 'words not backed up by actions,' according to Matthias Stausberg. Dr Ralf Bösinger takes the view that greenwashing is just a new form of spin, related to sustainability issues:

> Spin in the environmental or social balance sheet of a company becomes very apparent when specific achievements that are irrelevant to the overall business are singled out and used to suggest to consumers or the general public that the company is following a socially responsible strategy. If this specific positive environmental or social performance achievement is out of sync with the overall behaviour of the company, we call it greenwashing.

In other words: if companies do not re-engineer their core business according to social and environmental criteria, greenwashing is very often lurking around the corner. It has to be more, much more than just individual PR-stunts or marketing gimmicks. As Matthias Stausberg puts it, he finds it:

> very aggravating how companies are trying to use sustainability for their advertising purposes. You see a Cadillac designed in suggestive green. You hear the term 'sustainability' being used, but once you dig into the details you find maybe one or two products that are Forest Stewardship Council- or Marine Stewardship Council-certified without sincere efforts to make a strategic difference for the company.

At the same time, he warns that due to the erosion of trust in multinational companies, it has become increasingly difficult to get away with greenwashing as more and more stakeholder groups look behind the rhetoric. Greenwashing therefore poses a very high risk of further undermining trust, or even exposing companies to yet more reputational crises.

What do you consider to be the key success factors of effective CSR communication?'

CREDIBILITY, TRUTHFULNESS, TRANSPARENCY, A HOLISTIC APPROACH AND A STRATEGIC COMMITMENT

There is agreement that *credibility*, *truthfulness* and *transparency* are the key success factors. When it comes to implementing or living up to those values, Matthias Stausberg points out that what is needed is a *holistic approach* to CSR communication – not just reporting, not just external communication. What is required is internal communication that motivates employees and makes them into ambassadors and multipliers. It includes a responsible approach to advertising and marketing as well as responsible lobbying and, according to Matthias Stausberg, 'touches all corporate functions that have a communicative role. Sustainability communications have to find a way to align these. The prerequisite is a *strategic commitment to sustainability* – policy development and implementation of these policies must come first, communication can never come first.' A holistic and strategic approach may, however, include something else in order to bring CSR communication to life, according to Willi Lemke, the United Nations Secretary General's Special Adviser on Sport for Development and Peace, and that is 'innovation and creativity'.

Interview with Toni Symonds, California State Assembly

WHAT DO YOU ASSOCIATE WITH CSR COMMUNICATION?

Sustainability reports, websites, but also annual reports and sponsoring. However, with new technologies like Twitter, it is changing. It is about how the community is learning about what the company is doing. It is important to bear in mind that you are constantly communicating, not just when you report or sponsor something. Anything you do actually communicates. (Do the wives of your senior staff run around in fur? – For some companies that may be very serious.) Consistency of the message with how the company acts is key.

WHAT ARE YOUR EXPECTATIONS REGARDING CSR COMMUNICATION OF COMPANIES?

When they are consciously communicating, they need to be correct and accurate, and to project a basic understanding of sustainability. Accuracy, by the way, is very easy to check these days! We want to see from all levels of organizations that they understand the company's business model and philosophy. If not, there can be great inconsistency between line managers and the CEO/board. It is important that all communications pull in the same direction; external communications are dependent on internal communications.

WHAT IS THE ROLE OF THE PUBLIC SECTOR IN THE CONTEXT OF CSR COMMUNICATION OF COMPANIES?

To set the frame. To make sure that apples are compared to apples and that information is accurate. Rewarding correct behaviour and recognizing poor behaviour. That role is not generally fulfilled, because due to short-term public expectations and short-term rewards for political actors, long-term vision and consistency in this area is hard to achieve. Also in the US, as a fairly young country, success has been built on the premise of boundless resources and success that is measured in growth – something that is challenged by the ideas of CSR and sustainability. In fact, sustainability runs counter to this underlying paradigm, so we need a massive paradigm shift in the public sector, too, and to be able to provide new answers to the question, 'What is success?' Despite this massive challenge of defining objectives, from a business point of view, specifically in the context of sustainability and CSR communication, regulation should stop the playing field from spinning. Companies have to be able to run their model without permanently taking a huge risk that too many variables in the regulatory environment change too quickly.

WHAT ARE THE ISSUES FROM A BUSINESS PERSPECTIVE IN COMMUNICATING CSR TO THE PUBLIC SECTOR?

There is a lot of lobbying and advocacy on all political levels. For instance, most companies are represented politically in some form or another in California, including many foreign companies. It is important first to ensure that the business model and corporate policies are aligned with the policy goals of the government. As an example for how not to do it, there is a Canadian tar sand company that is the second largest Canadian trading partner with California. The Speaker of the House of Representatives did not want that company represented in California as it violated the Californian Greenhouse Gas Policy. In this context, as with all areas of lobbying, companies should not assume that government is stupid or uneducated – we may just have a different opinion. Chevron is a positive example: they chose to have high-level lobbyists in Sacramento, both those that can hold scientific discussions and those that are excellent lobbying experts. IBM has very good representation, and were able to bring their expertise into the discussions on e-waste. It is about mutual respect! It is surprising that business underestimates the political side's ability to smell spin and thinks that the civil servants do not understand the issues – they make the laws, which is a difficult, complex process. Good CSR communication implies [the ability] to see where/what the issues are, and that means you need to involve government as early as possible in the process. Understanding the structures, understanding where they are coming from and engaging, and thus moving forward. As an example I can cite the case of mobile homes. They often have very high indoor air pollution. Manufactured housing producers in California proactively reduced indoor air pollution by half. Two years later, the Air Resources Board decided they wanted to do something about indoor air pollution. The company needed to make sure that policy makers understood what they had achieved on their own (including third-party verification) and talk about what further reduction could be implemented. Due to the good communication, the producers were rewarded, which gave them a competitive edge against other mobile home manufacturers from other states.

CAN YOU SHARE ANY BEST PRACTICE EXAMPLES OF CSR COMMUNICATION?

DuPont, in the early sustainability discussions. They did some of the earliest work on how water conservation work saved them money. As partners in the World Business Council on Sustainable Development they took the time to do research in such a way that government could pick it up. We then used DuPont as an example to develop our CSR policy. In November 2003 California had the first growth and economic development strategy in the nation with an integrated CSR policy. So DuPont influenced the legislative process. It shows that the private sector can be a partner to the public sector in achieving economic success. Our CSR policy document, called *The Governor's Environmental Goals and Policy Report*, reflects this new alignment of the success of business and the success of society. We see that the corporate model is changing and there is an alignment of interest between government, big investors and large multinational corporations in the area of sustainability.

Key Messages in a Nutshell

Table 2.2   Chapter 2 key messages in a nutshell

Expectations of the public sector of CSR communication	The 5 Cs: Correct Clear Complete Comparable Credible
Roles of the public sector in the context of CSR communication	Provide the framework Be an example Facilitate best practice
Issues of CSR communication to the public sector	Aligning lobbying with CSR communication
Key success factors for communicating CSR to the public sector	Credibility Truthfulness Transparency Holistic approach to CSR communication Strategic commitment to sustainability

3 *Communicating Sustainability – the Supplier Perspective*

The key success factor is full engagement with a clear incentive system.
Ying Sun, SusA Shanghai

Sustainability in the supply chain deals with working conditions and the social and environmental context of the various stages of value-creation up to a final product. Sweatshops, low wages and child labour are regularly exposed; many companies have experienced scandals and reputational damage as a result, including such well known and significant brands as Nike, IKEA, Mattel or Hennes & Mauritz. The issues are complex, and in many cases there are no simple answers. NGOs often adopt the position of advocates on behalf of poor and disadvantaged workers, and businesses focus on auditing to signal compliance. There is evidence that suggests that a lot of audit results are not consistent with the actual social or environmental situations in factories in China or Bangladesh, and sometimes the objectives for improvement of living conditions propagated by NGOs may not be the same as those that workers themselves would want to achieve, if consulted. Quite obviously, this area is a minefield for CSR communication because there are many different views, a general lack of transparency and no 100 per cent solutions. We have spoken to experts in the field, both from an environmental and a social perspective, two of whom actually work with factory employees and factory managers at a grassroots level to improve working conditions sustainably in a collaborative process, which is explained in more depth as a case study below. The other two case studies illustrate the environmental aspects of sustainability communication and the importance of traceability in creating transparency as a means of product-related CSR communication.

What do you associate with CSR and CSR communication?

ENGAGEMENT, DIALOGUE AND A LONG-TERM WIN–WIN PERSPECTIVE

'CSR is ultimately about corporations recognizing that they have a role in and responsibility towards society besides making money,' says Thomas Krick, CSR Consultant for PwC in Germany:[1]

---

1   At the time of the interview, Head of International Development at TwoTomorrows (Europe) Ltd, London.

Both role and responsibility derive from the potential negative and positive impacts of their value chains. It's obvious that companies should ensure that their operations and services have minimal negative impacts on people and the environment. However, it is also important to consider the positive impacts. For example, the world's largest telecommunication companies are very good at facilitating communication between people. Their unique capacity and position to do this means that people expect these companies not just to leverage it for the benefit of shareholders, but also for the benefit of society. In fact, many of the currently most interesting long-term shareholder propositions are where there is alignment between profitable opportunity and societal demand for sustainable solutions.

For sustainable packaging expert Barbara McCutchen, CSR is synonymous with sustainability, meaning taking responsibility for the social, environmental and economic impacts and opportunities related to the company's operations. Ying Sun of SusA Shanghai, who works to improve conditions at factory floor level in China, states that for her it implies sustainability in the whole supply chain, not just at one level of it, taking a holistic view of social, environmental and economic interdependencies. According to Sebastian Siegele of Berlin-based consultancy Sustainability Agents (SusA), CSR means that the social responsibility of organizations is mirrored in its core business. While charity is also a kind of responsibility, it is not possible to balance out destructive elements in the core business with charity.

'CSR communication means that organizations communicate about how they are increasing value added while reducing the environmental or social footprint,' says Dawn Rittenhouse of DuPont. At DuPont, it is therefore called 'sustainable growth communication', implying that the company's products and services can help, for instance, in reducing greenhouse gas emissions or water consumption, thus offering customers reasons to work with DuPont. Sustainability expert Brian Wagner of Packaging & Technology Integrated Solutions (PTIS) makes the point that while corporate communications used to be relatively simple and straightforward, the transparency requirements that sustainability communications pose raise the bar and require first and foremost that all lines of communication with all different stakeholders are consistent – a challenge which many companies are not set up to remedy.

Sebastian Siegele identifies another challenge when confronted with the term 'CSR communication': it is sometimes difficult to communicate success and progress effectively because achievements at the production or service level do not match stakeholders' expectations. One example is improvements in working conditions. If a reduction in weekly working hours in a Chinese factory from 80 hours to 70 hours is achieved, that is already a major success and good starting point. However, as Western stakeholders expect a maximum 60-hour working week, a company that has achieved this improvement by working collaboratively with its suppliers and its factories has a hard time communicating this, not least as there is no definition of what constitutes an improvement and there is a lack of criteria at the supplier level. He suggests that the paradigm of communication in the context of supplying factories needs to change even more towards a continuous dialogue than it perhaps does in other areas. The starting point should rather be that labour conditions today are not in fact where we would like them to be, and indeed the reality is that many audit reports are faked or manipulated; the communication of these reports is based on a mindset that reflects Western ideas, and auditing based on a top-down and control approach. It is important to turn this around: suppliers should communicate whatever progress they make, but at the same time they need to communicate in the other direction, with the workers on whose behalf consumers want to exert pressure to improve working conditions. These men and women on the factory floor are usually never asked what they want, what an improvement would look like for them, but really they are the key stakeholders who need to define the agenda. 'Jane Doe's moral outrage about labour conditions actually is a form of post-colonialism,' claims Siegele provocatively, 'which is why the Clean Clothes Campaign is named as it is and not "the Campaign for Improved Working Conditions in Textile Production" or similar.' He calls on the stakeholders involved, including trade unions, to 'stop the cold war' and move to a culture of open discussion. Doing so would entail a ceasefire on companies wanting to go down the route of dialogue and real improvement which want to communicate what they are doing without being attacked. This would also involve acknowledging that virtually all products are produced in violation of labour standards somewhere in the supply chain.

Thomas Krick picks up on the notion of dialogue: his interpretation of CSR communication is that it primarily has been one-way communication rather than engagement, which is, as Sebastian Siegele describes it, a two-way process: 'A good CSR report, for instance, is one that actually stimulates dialogue and perhaps asks questions rather than just providing all the answers.' Having said that, CSR communication also implies taking a stand and measuring itself against very diverse stakeholder expectations, not just being diplomatic.

What are the expectations of suppliers regarding the CSR communication of companies?

COMMUNICATING OPENLY, FAIRLY AND WITH A WIN–WIN MINDSET

Consistency

In many ways, suppliers' expectations are similar to those of other stakeholder groups: clarity, truthfulness and accuracy. More specifically, they find consistency between what is reported to the general public in CSR reports, the internal communication and the messages they receive down the supply chain very important. Brian Wagner argues that there is a need for a new model with a single person responsible for creating a unified message that goes out to all stakeholders, 'up' as well as 'down' the supply chain.

Transparency

Most important, however, is suppliers' expectation that they will be seen and accepted as partners, and that requires transparency, dialogue and a win–win mindset:

> The key expectation is to create real transparency and to focus on the objectives, getting things done. In our case that means: we want to improve the lives of workers and managers on the factory floor, and workers honestly do not have time for drawn-out stakeholder dialogues without tangible results. The problems, for instance in Bangladesh, are so pressing due to the skyrocketing prices of staple foods, especially rice, and that shapes the workers' perspective. They need small steps, as long as they happen quickly.

So suppliers want to be engaged with, but they also want their immediate needs to be respected and understood. And they want to understand the company's motives – hence transparency. Thomas Krick underlines this need for transparency. In his view, transparency is a cornerstone of responsible communication, and this implies transparency about the company's activities, about the way it uses renewable and finite resources, and about how it distributes and redistributes wealth. In the absence of transparency, it is impossible to engage stakeholders in a credible and progressive dialogue about corporate responsibility and sustainability, which Krick would consider as the kind of communication all companies and their stakeholders should strive towards.

Win–win mindset

DuPont is a supplier as well as a customer, so Dawn Rittenhouse is familiar with both perspectives. Often she is invited by customers to present what DuPont is doing in terms of sustainability. As quite a few of them are not as advanced in sustainability as the chemicals giant, they expect to learn about the tangible business benefits that sustainability-led innovations implemented by their more experienced supplier may offer them. As an example, she mentions TiO_2, titanium dioxide, used as a whitener. This product disperses more easily than conventional whiteners and uses less energy in the mixing process, and as a result the total cost is lower despite the higher cost per unit of whitener. Lower costs and better environmental performance make this product a compelling proposition for customers. So in this case the supplier is expected to communicate the sustainability-related benefits of the product to its customers effectively, and in the process enhance their knowledge about sustainability.

Best Practice Case: The Tchibo and GIZ Worldwide Enhancement of Social Quality (WE) Project

Figure 3.1   A WE Project workshop with workers in Bangladesh

Source: Reproduced courtesy of Tchibo GmbH.

Because of the Clean Clothes Campaign's highlighting of workplace health and safety conditions in factories in Bangladesh, German retailer Tchibo set up a Corporate Responsibility Department to make sustainability integral to its future activity.

Having decided that the social audit route was not for it due to its 'top-down' approach, Tchibo worked with the German Development agency GIZ (also known as the Society for International Cooperation) and the consultants SusA to develop an alternative. This put human rights – the relationships between managers and employees – at the heart of the project. It is these relationships which can affect production adversely.

Tchibo recognized early on that it would need trainers who were local to the factories and who were not only able to communicate in the local languages but had cultural knowledge as well, to be able to engage in dialogue going beyond merely meeting standards.

By 2007, there were 18 local trainers in 40 plants in China, Bangladesh and Thailand. A programme of workshops and stakeholder conferences took place. The training and consultation was ultimately not just about managers informing employees, but getting employee participation. The next step was to set up supplier workshops, so that following the pilot in 2010, the aim was to roll out the programme to 500 suppliers in Tchibo's textile and non-food business during 2011–13.

With a focus on transparency, integration, training and participation, the goal was to include workers, managers at all levels (senior as well as middle and junior), buyers, governments, trade unions, NGOs and international organizations in the improvement process.

For the full Best Practice Case 5, see Chapter 12, page 181.

What is the role of suppliers in the context of the CSR communication of companies?

CHANGE AGENTS FOR SUSTAINABILITY THROUGH INNOVATION AND PRODUCTIVITY IMPROVEMENT

Sustainable innovator

Linked to customer expectations, Dawn Rittenhouse explains that 'if a supplier can innovate sustainably he needs to communicate so that the customer can understand the benefits'. Conversely, if customers – or, down the line, consumers – do not perceive the sustainability performance, for example reducing the environmental footprint, as a tangible benefit on a similar level to a monetary benefit, 'it will drive the challenge back into the supply chain to further innovate so that the consumer sees the benefit'. In other words: one key role of suppliers in the context of CSR or sustainability communication is to innovate to create sustainable product features that are perceived by customers or consumers as tangible benefits, including economically (or monetarily).

Brian Wagner (PTIS) puts the ball back in the customers' court and claims that the responsibility does not just lie with the suppliers. If procurement officers take purchasing decisions based on price alone and do not factor in the sustainability benchmarks the company has set itself, it will be extremely challenging for the supplier to deliver those innovative sustainability benefits because there is simply no incentive. Nevertheless, he claims that suppliers need to be more proactive even in an arena or sector lacking customer standards, and cites the packaging element as being full of good examples of sustainability-led innovation – for instance, MedVestVaco and Sanoco are tied for second place in the Dow Jones Sustainability Index. A number of packaging companies have implemented ISO 14000/14001,[2] and consider this environmental management norm a helpful means for improving performance.

Setting sustainability standards

Setting sustainability standards is a key role for suppliers. This means collaborating with one another, setting industry standards and working on consistent messaging for customers. Chris Wille of the Rainforest Alliance underscores the importance of such standards and mentions the Forest Stewardship Council standard in forestry and the Sustainable Agriculture Network for agricultural products as good examples which the Rainforest Alliance was instrumental in shaping:

> *These standards and the supporting certification programs allow companies to make significant changes in the way they do business, incorporate sustainability into their supply chains and what they can claim in their CSR reports, advertising and other public-facing messaging. A certification program gives a company an independent, third-party endorsement of its claims that it can use even at the retail level.*

He claims that many sector leaders in the FMCG sector like Kraft, Chiquita, Unilever or Mars have overhauled their business models towards sustainability, starting with sustainable sourcing.

---

2   ISO 14000 is the International Standard Organisation's family of environmental management standards. ISO 14001 sets out the criteria for an environmental management system and can be certified by an independent certification organisation. Source: http://www.iso.org/iso/home/standards/management-standards/iso14000.htm (retrieved 14 August 2013).

Best Practice Case: ROMP – Fully Traceable Organic Fashion

ROMP

TRACEABILITY

What is traceability?

For all products in our shops, you can trace back to every process and material used in production of item.

How to use?

Every product has unique code. Enter code in the field below and press 'trace'. It is that simple. Traceability data will open in new browser window.

Traceability code:

[   ]

Trace

Our product code:

[   ]

Find product

home

Figure 3.2   ROMP uniquely combined high-end fashion with full online traceability for each product

Source: Reproduced courtesy of Janusz Krek, web design (www.kreksi.net).

A very ambitious project which was arguably before its time, the brainchild of Greg Sturmer, who had been a dealer in sheepskin and organic leather, in collaboration with acknowledged high fashion designer Nina Morgan-Jones, the ROMP case study illustrates the complexity of putting sustainability at the heart of a business. However, the legacy of the innovative software developed shows that many in the fashion industry could be a lot more proactive than they currently are.

ROMP brought together organic leather with state-of-the-art design, incorporating complete transparency in the supply chain. At its height, prominent chart-topping female rock stars wore ROMP products, including at the MTV Awards. This was truly eco-fashion, putting style first, with the added value of a 'point of sale value proposition'.

Customers at the ROMP store in Los Angeles could look at plasma screens and see where the item they'd purchased had travelled, from farm to the finished product in their hands. The traceability software, developed by a company called Historic Futures, was in a clothing tag made from tannery waste containing California poppy seeds – with the added bonus that the nitrogen fertilizer used on ROMP suppliers' farms actually made flowers grow better. The product's components contained none of the conventional chemicals used to treat animal disease, toxic dyes, metals or other traditionally-used substances.

Fashion industry observers admit that Greg Sturmer was ahead of his time, wanting to tell a great story rather than 'just resolving business issues in the supply chain'. This story encompassed the UK Soil Association's certification, the farms, the abattoirs, the tanneries, the factory in Slovenia and the design. As a result, having begun in 2002, by 2003 he was considered to be five years ahead of the big brands, which only started to show an interest in sustainability in 2010. However, by 2009, ROMP, hit by recession, was no more.

For the full Best Practice Case 6, see Chapter 12, page 192.

Enabling transparency

Ying Sun points out that stakeholders like factory workers and managers on the supplier side have a key role, even though in most instances they unable to play it because they do not have a voice at the moment: 'Their stories should be more significant in order to help the outside world understand what the conditions on the production floor are, to communicate their concerns to get more attention from the agent companies, importers, buyers, retailers and even the end consumers in the western world.' Through factory floor training, they learn that they themselves can set standards and influence brands on the other side of the globe. Brands that recognize this, like the German retailer Tchibo, empower suppliers and give them an opportunity to define their own benchmarks, thus providing them with motivation. Empowering factory workers and managers enables a dialogue between workers and managers, and both learn to value and respect each other. This creates a paradigm shift and a whole new dynamic. The suppliers' role then changes, from being one concerned with compliance through audits and benchmarks to that of making improvements and increasing productivity. This sets up a win–win situation: better working conditions for the workers, and the same or better business results (in terms of quality, price and quantity) for the managers and customers.

What are the key issues from a business perspective in communicating CSR to suppliers?

FROM SPOT MARKET TO LONG-TERM SUPPLIER ENGAGEMENT

'One key test is the purchasing behaviour of companies,' responds Ying Sun. It all depends on whether purchasing departments are aiming to build long-term relationships with their suppliers and whether they put sufficient resources into capacity-building to work jointly with their strategic sourcing partners to tackle the sustainability issues. She argues that while it is all very well to run pilot projects, the key goal from a communications standpoint is to scale up these projects into full-blown mainstream sourcing policies across the board, which implies a paradigm shift. The paradigm shift is away from spot-market buying that is purely price-driven to long-term relationships with suppliers where the criteria are price plus quality, price plus sustainability.

Brian Wagner agrees that if a company communicates sustainability well to its suppliers, it offers them a way to differentiate themselves so that they avoid commoditization: 'The CSR story should help [suppliers] strengthen benefit over price.' But obviously, it also means that customers need to set clear expectations for their suppliers. If customers are able to understand the status of their eco-footprint, they can establish high standards for improvement and communicate assertively how to bring them about, (or raise them.) Changing the paradigm, and with it modifying the key performance indicators for purchasers, suggests that sustainability has to be fully embedded into the business. This in turn implies that there are key performance indicators for sustainability that affect every decision-maker within the operation: 'with everyone from the CEO down to the part-time worker knowing what the key focus areas are for the organization. Recognizing that sustainability is a journey, organizations will present where they are on that journey and explain the targets they have,' says Barbara McCutchen. 'Then it becomes a business imperative – embedded.'

Can you share any best-practice examples of CSR communication?

Table 3.1 shows the brands and programmes shown that were mentioned in the interviews.

Table 3.1   Brands and programmes referenced in the interviews

Brand, company, programme	No. of mentions
Tchibo, WE project	3
(Fast-moving) Consumer Goods	
Nike; Chiquita Rainforest Alliance; Nespresso Ecolaboration; Unilever Lipton Rainforest Alliance; Nestlé, Creating Shared Value; innocent; Campbell's Soup; Kraft Rainforest Alliance	9
Retailers (Including Tchibo)	8
IKEA, sustainable sourcing system IWAY; Metro, supplier policy; Lidl	5
Industry	
GE, ecomagination; Sonoco S3, turned waste into profit centre for Kraft; Husky (blow-moulding machine manufacturer)	3
Food Service	
McDonald's; Caribou	2
IT	
HP; Intel	2
Chemicals	
DuPont	1
Office Equipment	
Herman Miller	1

German retailer Tchibo is mentioned three times for its pioneering supplier-oriented WE Project, which is presented as a case study in this chapter. In the context of this project, the company engages with workers and managers at grassroots level to improve working conditions in a tangible way and at the same time increase productivity, creating a true 'triple win' between workers, factory owners and Tchibo as the customer. The key is changing from one-way communication to two-way communication.

Chris Wille's favourite example is Chiquita: 'It is the best story to tell – just one product and a vertically integrated supply chain. It is a very well-known and much researched business and there are whole leagues of NGOs and political commissions focused on pointing out issues in the banana trade.' It is remarkable that the Rainforest Alliance is mentioned explicitly four times and implicitly once (Nespresso Ecolaboration).

Barbara McCutchen and Mike Richmond point out that it is best practice to provide clear goals and metrics and monitor how you are progressing, for example in terms of water, waste or energy reduction. In these categories, suppliers can focus on their own contribution to such measures, especially if they are third-party manufacturers of the customer's products. Nike is mentioned as being very respectful in dealing with suppliers in this sector, having been heavily criticized in the past for its treatment of them.

How do you define 'greenwashing'? Examples?

MISLEADING OR UNSUBSTANTIATED CLAIMS

'Making unsubstantiated or inflated claims with the intention of covering up a problem or making the company seem more progressive than it really is' – this is how Chris Wille defines greenwashing. He goes on to say that the media are full of examples of greenwashing, although today it is much less blatant than it was about a decade ago. Nowadays, he claims it is less deliberate and more the result of carelessness or of ignorance about what sustainability really requires: 'This is aided by the media and some NGOs that promote the notion that one can "save the world" simply by changing lightbulbs or taking a reusable carrier bag to the supermarket.'

Barbara McCutchen makes it a little more specific:

Greenwashing is stating that an environmental improvement or benefit exists when it does not. It is a misleading statement of benefit. This is anything from biodegradable plastics in packaging that goes into landfills because there are no other recycling processes available to having the environmental metrics of a company portrayed as covering the corporation but only including office facilities since manufacturing is fully third-party outsourced.

Brian Wagner cites the packaging industry as an example:

Every year there are large packaging exhibitions like the PackExpo. Most exhibitors at PackExpo are machinery companies, and in 2008 sustainability was the main issue. Unfortunately, most of these companies went wrong in their communication – misleading claims, exaggerating what they were doing – and that is true greenwashing. Many companies in the US are driven by the Walmart packaging scorecard but doing nothing else in their business that is right socially or environmentally, so they think that sustainability is all about reducing packaging materials, overlooking the fact that sometimes packaging can save food waste and the net-net effect is positive. Tesco, the British retailer, backed off their aggressive pack reduction goals as waste would go up and perceived quality would go down.

Thus, greenwashing can be the result of businesses not understanding what CSR means holistically to the business or industry across the value chain.

What do you consider to be the key success factors of effective CSR communication?

ACCOUNTABILITY – HONESTY – ENGAGEMENT – PARTNERSHIP – MEASURABLE – RESULTS

Accountability

This involves establishing clear expectations about the role of suppliers in meeting their CSR goals and clearly articulating these expectations in a supplier code of conduct, acknowledging the cost impact of sustainability standards.

Honesty

There needs to be transparency and honesty, both with suppliers (managing expectations) and consumers. As many workers still do not understand sustainability on the factory floor, it may be necessary to educate them about it. Companies need to 'tell true stories to end customers,' adds Ying Sun.

Engagement

There must be true dialogue, two-way communication including at the grassroots level.

Partnership

The paradigm shift from purely price-driven procurement behaviour to long-term partnerships implies very different supplier communication. It means solving sustainability issues together with suppliers, seeing the workers, managers and farmers as the key stakeholders who need to be involved as integral to the process of developing more sustainable solutions.

Measurable

'Develop metrics based on international standards (for example, the ISO 14000 family) or DJSI (Dow Jones Sustainability Index) expectations, using lifecycle inventory measurements as the basis for communication to suppliers,' says Brian Wagner. Add to that traceability data where available, or create them, suggests Mike Richmond.

Results

There is a need to present results: 'Stories about constructive steps forward haven't been told ... while problem- oriented stories exist. What we need are solution-oriented stories to tell customers so that they understand what their role is, what they can do,' says Ying Sun. 'Solve problems and talk about it – managers and workers expect small continuous steps, that is what they like,' adds Sebastian Siegele.

Interview with Ying Sun, SusA Shanghai

WHAT DO YOU ASSOCIATE WITH CSR COMMUNICATION?

To be honest, I never put CSR communication together as a term before this questionnaire. To me, it is a key foundation of effective and healthy supply chain management. Without communication, it would not work in a productive way. For me, it has to be based on mutual respect between all stakeholders and on transparency. It cannot be ad hoc, one-off, but has to be frequent, ongoing and long-term. I would think that communication should be solution- not conflict-oriented. It needs to be dialogue-oriented, seeking solutions together, with the aim of reaching win–win situations. Therefore, you have to be patient, you cannot expect overnight changes, but aim for continuous improvement.

WHAT ARE YOUR EXPECTATIONS REGARDING THE CSR COMMUNICATION OF COMPANIES?

Companies have to be patient and realistic because of all the constraints and local conditions. It has so much to do with company culture and with that of their brands. They need to focus on achieving small steps and a continuous improvement process that achieves sustainable change rather than aiming for quick fixes. While there are differences between communication to the external world and communication within the supply chain, the principles are the same: the key messages need to be consistent, transparency is essential, and they need to take into account the challenging realities of the supply chain, those which have an influence on all stakeholders.

WHAT IS THE ROLE OF SUPPLIERS IN THE CONTEXT OF THE CSR COMMUNICATION OF COMPANIES?

They really have a key role, even though they are not playing it fully yet. There are many lower tiers of suppliers that live in a very difficult environment for basic survival and do not have a voice at the moment. Their stories should play a larger role to help the outside world understand about the conditions on the production floor, to communicate their situations, to gain more attention from the agent companies, the importers, the buyers, retailers and even end- consumers in the Western world. The suppliers – the workers and managers on the factory floor – are starting to realize that they need to communicate. They have no structured ideas about how to do this more than on an ad hoc basis, though. But through training and other efforts, we have raised their awareness; however, it will take time before they can do it in a more strategic and structured way. Some of them tell us: 'From what I have learned from you through training and workshops, I can pass on my knowledge to lower-tier suppliers and family and friends in my community so it can be shared on a broader level downstream and in multiple channels.'

Suppliers are partners in dialogue. Dialogue can take place on the production floor in a very constructive way. Through the WE project, they learn how to use communication channels and how to structure the internal dialogue in a very effective and practical way so they can work with the worker representatives they elect and develop the dialogue between workers and managers. That leads to more respect between managers and workers, thus growing trust. They realize they can constructively work with each other to build a brighter future for both sides. So this hands-on work on the shop floor results in a shift from control and monitoring to trust and mutual respect, which is, or should be, a key aspect of all CSR communications.

WHAT ARE THE ISSUES FROM A BUSINESS PERSPECTIVE IN COMMUNICATING CSR TO SUPPLIERS?

The key challenge is the structure of the companies' purchasing, their sourcing behaviour. Are they aiming to build long-term relationships with their suppliers, and do they put enough resources into capacity-building and making suppliers their strategic partners who can develop and grow with them? Dealing with this must take place at a very high level. Referring to the WE project with Tchibo, this is working on a micro level. If the structural issue is not solved, I would not be too optimistic about Tchibo's future in the next five to ten years. Why are they not moving ahead after investing all this money into the pilot project, towards more fundamental changes within the company?[3] Hopefully, the time is right now to look into this issue. It is time to shift from short-term purely price-driven sourcing to long-term strategic partnerships.

CAN YOU SHARE ANY BEST PRACTICE EXAMPLES OF CSR COMMUNICATION?

To me, IKEA is just such a best practice example. The key success factor is full engagement with a clear incentive system. They are able to link the performance of suppliers with the size of production orders. For a good performance you receive an extra 10 per cent each year, for an excellent performance it may be even more. This is based on a transparent, digitized system, based on concrete data, so everything is quantified. If you are below the benchmark, you will eventually be out. But IKEA gives these suppliers sufficient time, support and space to improve. Their iWay training is ongoing, and costs are shared between suppliers and IKEA. They use hands-on practical touring for key personnel at the supplier factory level, which is very much appreciated. For factories which are short of skilled labour, they provide tutoring. If suppliers do not know about quantified management IKEA, will train them in processing data so that they report to IKEA.

IKEA has the size to be able build and run such a worldwide knowledge-sharing platform, identify best practice and disseminate it within the group. They are a benchmark for other brands.

---

3   The original interview was conducted in 2010. Meanwhile, as Best Practice Case 5 in Chapter 12 shows, Tchibo has moved on, and the positive outcome of the pilot phase led to the company decision to roll out WE to all strategic supplier factories by the end of 2015. Currently, 175 factories are in the process of qualification.

WHAT DO YOU CONSIDER TO BE KEY SUCCESS FACTORS OF EFFECTIVE CSR COMMUNICATION FROM A SUPPLIER PERSPECTIVE?

I think I would try to tell true stories to end-customers, as it proves destructive when you give people false expectations. People do not understand what sustainability implies on the factory floor, they are too far away from the situation. They do not have the comprehensive understanding of local labour laws, working hours or overtime wages, and it may not be practical to pass on this information. But this information needs to be conveyed so that consumers do not blindly follow some NGOs which lead them to participate in some kind of movement which results in the workers on the factory floor suffering even more. Stories about constructive steps forward have not been told – what has been done so far, what should be done, what is possible – with the aim of changing peoples' mindset. While problem-focused stories exist, solution-oriented ones are missing. We need to tell consumers what their role can be, what they can do. Perhaps we can try to educate them through CSR communication and tell them how they can adjust their purchasing behaviour and support the efforts that are being made.

Key Messages in a Nutshell

Table 3.2   Chapter 3 key messages in a nutshell

Expectations of suppliers towards CSR communication	Consistency Clarity Truthfulness Accuracy Transparency Dialogue Win–win mindset
Roles of suppliers in the context of CSR communication	Sustainable innovators Setting sustainability standards Enabling transparency
Issues of CSR communication to suppliers	From spot-market to long-term supplier agreement
Key success factors for communicating CSR to suppliers	Accountability Honesty Engagement Partnership Measurable Results

4 Communicating Sustainability – the Employee Perspective

For CSR communication [to employees] to be effective all aspects of the 'What's in it for me?' factor need to be clearly articulated.

Erica Jones, Walmart

If being authentic is one of the key success factors of effective CSR communication, then ensuring that your own employees speak positively and enthusiastically about what your company is doing in terms of sustainability and CSR will be of pivotal importance. Employees know the inside story, they can see through the spin, and they observe how the company's representatives really behave. So if they believe and understand, they will be good ambassadors, an important part of a company's external communication.

What do you associate with CSR and CSR communication?

AMBIGUOUS BUZZWORDS

Former Aetna VP and now executive coach Linda Spevacek's first reaction to the term 'CSR' is:

Everything that has to have an acronym in it begs the question: what's behind the whole idea? I would not call it CSR, but rather: why is it that companies should care? Do they care, or is it more of a marketing tool? What is the rationale?

To Veronica Scheubel, who developed and ran Nokia's community involvement programme, CSR is an outdated notion:

We used it in Nokia in 2001, and by 2003 we had moved to CR. Nowadays it is sustainability. I go with what Nike calls it: business innovation and sustainability. Often you now hear 'corporate sustainability'. CSR is too limited to explain social involvement, and in the US it is unfortunately mixed up with philanthropy. Having said that, when I communicate about it on the Internet and I want to reach a wider group of people, I use 'CSR' as most people still use it.

I spontaneously associate everybody's fear of communicating CSR with CSR communication. This is because everybody is scared they'll get it wrong. At Nokia we said: let's only talk about 'community involvement', then we are safe. The moment we start talking about other things we are doing well in, we will be opening a can of worms – people will be pointing out all the things we do not do well enough yet.

She mentions Vodafone, with its 'we said, we have, we will' approach, and Marks & Spencer's Plan A as positive examples of being more courageous and transparent by mentioning the challenges of CSR programmes.

Linda Spevacek makes the point that it is important to create a connection and to explain why companies are actually engaging in CSR and sustainability, especially to employees. Cause-marketing executive Maria Kalligeros of New York-based Kalligeros Communications comments that there is a surprising amount of confusion about these terms, even among people you would expect to understand. She feels it 'encompasses social and environmental responsibility, good corporate citizenship and the awareness companies have of their impact on the world around them', while Lesa Ukman of IEG, Chicago, simply states: 'I hate CSR. Acting correctly, ethically, it is like a mandate. Enron could tick all the boxes, but in their DNA they were shit. It is the imposition of some group's idea of what is socially responsible, but it has nothing to do with how companies behave.'

What are the expectations of employees regarding CSR communication by companies?

ABOVE ALL, AUTHENTICITY

Connect emotionally

More than other stakeholder groups, employees expect CSR communications to 'reach them on an emotional level', according to Linda Spevacek: 'CSR communication needs to be warm and fuzzy, you have to connect with them.' However, if it is just 'warm and fuzzy', they will see through it: 'You need to connect it to the bottom line as well, otherwise there will be cynicism and there may be statements like "Why do we give to this or that cause? I would rather get a pay raise!"' So she points out that it is the role of leadership to make employees feel good about what the company is doing in CSR and sustainability, but at the same time to explain convincingly to them why engaging on these topics is good for the company economically.

Be ethical inside out

Lesa Ukman emphasizes that employees are very much like consumers – because they are consumers as well. That is why they expect their company to be ethical inside-out. Linda Spevacek calls that being authentic: 'Any inconsistencies are very quickly noticed,' because obviously employees pick up on those inconsistencies much quicker than outsiders. So employees may very well be the acid test for the authenticity and consistency of CSR communications. On the other hand, if employees are convinced, if they feel that their company is behaving consistently, walking the talk, they become spokespeople and start representing from the 'inside out'. Lesa Ukman says:

We are moving away from campaigns to movements when it comes to CSR communications. You see that, for example, with the innocent Big Knit campaign – that has become a movement. It happens when people feel 'this is the right thing to do', and for the company or brand, that implies earned media; there is no need to pay for expensive media placement because – in the innocent case – they are talked about on knitting and charity websites. Employees are people, and a lot of people nowadays want to be involved and they want their companies to be socially involved. The social media trend shows that.

She reiterates that the key to getting employees involved in being part of such a movement is the authenticity of the effort the company makes.

Best Practice Case: SKF BeyondZero

Figure 4.1   This SKF E2 bearing was developed in the context of the BeyondZero programme, and helps to reduce environmental impact

Source: Reproduced courtesy of SKF Group.

Award-winning Swedish ball bearings, seals, mechatronics and lubrication company SKF illustrates the benefits of the 'inside out' approach. The 40,000-strong company, which operates in 50 countries, makes sustainability look easy. How did it get this right?

First, it recruited a 'Tiger Team' of 200 trainers throughout the organization – young, and of multiple nationalities. The team set the company a very ambitious goal – not only to reduce its negative impact on the environment, but to do so by striving for a positive one.

During 2005–10, SKF managed just that. This started with awareness training, expanding it within two years to include all the countries where they operated. They set up a Code of Conduct for suppliers, contractors and contributors and won an innovative energy saving award. They increased profits by developing reduced-friction technology, and did so through making work more meaningful, making staff proud of the company they work for.

This was achieved through seeing staff themselves as ambassadors and footsoldiers for their brand. The programme was authentic, not just box-ticking. Employees connected emotionally to it, the process was open and transparent, and there was genuine involvement. SKF identified four kinds of staff: the Passionates, the Business Operatives, the Followers and the Resisters, pointing out that if you get 80 per cent of staff with you, that's pretty good.

Now a regular on both the Dow Jones and European Sustainability Indexes, SKF has established five 'campuses' where employees can learn more about sustainability – an investment which has paid off not only in workforce motivation, but in increased productivity and profits.

For the full Best Practice Case 7, see Chapter 13, page 199.

Open and transparent engagement

The significant expectation of companies' CSR communication with employees is engagement, or 'being fully relational', as Veronica Scheubel puts it. 'All stakeholders are very interested in having an exchange with companies, especially employees, who have a very strong relationship anyway.' There is a lot of emphasis on this point regarding external stakeholders, but obviously it needs to start 'at home'. Scheubel identifies fear as a major obstacle to transparency and interacting with key stakeholders, particularly companies' own staff. 'The book that needs to be written is the book about fear in corporations – that could almost be a chapter in this book on CSR communications! Companies are scared of talking to stakeholders, and they are scared about potential conflict.'

What is the role of employees in the context of CSR communication for companies?

EMPLOYEES FIRST – CONSUMERS SECOND

Brand ambassadors

'Employees are your footsoldiers, spreading the word about reputation,' says Maria Kalligeros, who ran the domestic violence education and awareness programme for her client fashion brand Liz Claiborne Inc.: 'The Liz Claiborne "Love is Not Abuse" programme positively enhanced the company's reputation, increased staff loyalty and attracted potential recruits, because if all things are equal, employees show a preference for joining a company that embraces social programming.' This statement is consistent with the results of *Hand in Hand*, a research study published in 2007 by brands & values management consultants on corporate volunteering as a tool for organizational development.[1] The quantitative research among employers as well as employees found that if the key aspects of a good job (positively challenging assignments, attractive remuneration, good working conditions) were equal, the ethical standing of a company and its willingness to offer corporate volunteering opportunities would increasingly make a difference in staff retention and loyalty, as well as in the perceived desirability of the employer brand.

Communicators and multipliers

Veronica Scheubel underlines the importance of employees, citing Vineet Nayar's groundbreaking book *Employees First, Customers Second: Turning Conventional Management Upside Down*:[2]

> *My take is that once again you do not get very far with the communications push, because people are overwhelmed, so the only thing that works is a participatory approach. We tried it at Nokia – it was amazing. We had the annual quality awards and people could make suggestions for improvements. When we opened that to CSR in 2003/2004 the number of submissions went up by 25 per cent and 30 per cent of all submissions were CSR-related. Engage your employees – because there are so many ideas and thoughts in your company, in the minds and heads of your employees. Have them involved in creating solutions, because that creates ownership.*

This is very much in line with the observation that employees expect authenticity and involvement. Scheubel adds: 'In terms of talking about it, employees will be passionate multipliers if they are personally involved and if they have a reason to stand up for it and talk about it.'

What are the key issues from a business perspective in communicating CSR to employees?

BEING COMMITTED TO CREATING REAL INVOLVEMENT

Willingness to invest in employee engagement

The main concern is how to ensure that management meets the stated expectations of authenticity, active participation and involvement of employees. Add to that the ever-present cost argument, which, as Maria Kalligeros observes, depends on the depth and complexity of your programme. The more active the involvement, the more working time is required, which results in higher opportunity costs. Kalligeros adds that whether these opportunity costs are covered is a gamble that management has to take, among other measures, that employees will feel a compelling and emotional connection to the company, resulting in higher loyalty and better retention.

1   M. Blumberg and V. Scheubel, *Hand in Hand: Corporate Volunteering als Instrument der Organisationsentwicklung* ('Hand in Hand: Corporate Volunteering as an Instrument of Organizational Development') (Bremen: brands & values GmbH, 2007).

2   Vineet Nayar, *Employees First, Customers Second: Turning Conventional Management Upside Down* (Boston, MA: Harvard Business School Publishing, 2010).

Creating real involvement

If management is convinced about the benefits and thus willing to invest, the second challenge is how to actually create the kind of involvement that employees appreciate and that has the desired motivational impact. Veronica Scheubel shares the IBM–achordus.com example:

Achordus.com, the IBM values jam, is a really interesting case study. It is a classic now in the management world about employee engagement and participation and an alternative way of creating value. IBM used the achordus technology and included ten thousand employees in their values conversation for two weeks. The application of the technology meant that it was a well-facilitated conversation. After the two weeks, CEO Sam Palmisano said, 'We are going to read this now,' and brought together the 200 most active jammers for a workshop, picking 20 of them to distil the new values formulation. They came up with not just words, but three sentences. They now have everything that is needed and everybody feels really included and involved. This [achordus] technology is ideal to apply to big workshops, platforms or conversations within the sustainability and CSR arena for companies and corporations.

Best Practice Case: IBM World Community Grid – Technology Solving Problems

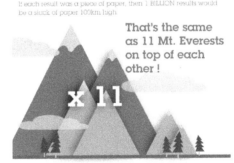

Figure 4.2   IBM's World Community Grid makes a significant contribution to important scientific research by leveraging unused computer processing resources

Source: Reproduced courtesy of International Business Machines Corporation.

With its 'Smarter Planet' and 'Big Green' vision, IBM has truly focused on its core business in applying technology for the betterment of society and the environment, in the process discovering 'a new way of doing volunteerism' which has also offered staff a perfect way to introduce themselves and engage with potential customers.

They can do this when people express curiosity about their imaginative screensavers, giving them a chance to talk about the incredible simplicity but huge impact of the World Community Grid, which is harnessing people's unused computer downtime to lend to vital medical and scientific research.

Managers speak proudly about IBM's 'talent, technology and services', and say there have been no questions within the organization because it not only makes sense, but is a great way to distinguish IBM from competitors. In a lot of countries, staff involvement is 70 per cent, and in some it is over 90 per cent; there is a global team of more than 100 working on the programme. It also encourages innovative thinking, as people are encouraged to explore what could come out of the way IBM's technology is applied and how and where services are offered.

Along with the company's huge investment in research and development and business-related results have come unanticipated benefits to society. One of the key lessons to take away is that there are 'low hurdles to engagement', and that there has been particular value from marketing through social media, with a lot of excellent feedback and increased motivation and retention of employees. So the clear link to IBM's bottom line, a 'computationally rich approach resulting in new data to help resolve longstanding problems', is one which people cannot dismiss as merely marketing. It makes sense in every way.

For the full Best Practice Case 8, see Chapter 13, page 206.

Cutting through the clutter

Another potential difficulty is information overflow. Employees have to process such large and diverse amounts of information in their jobs that they need to be selective. How do you get through to them with the sustainability or CSR message? Or as Scheubel puts it: 'How do you get around the communications push, and how do you get some mindshare, and ideally, heartshare?'

Winning over the cynics

A further challenge is internal scepticism and cynicism. Coming from a consumer context, Antonio Bertone, Chief Marketing Officer of fashion and lifestyle brand Puma, encountered some of that cynicism when trying to introduce an innovative sustainable packaging format, the Clever Little Bag (see Chapter 6). One of the things he learned in trying to involve the organization in this innovative project was that: 'If you are really passionate about change, you have to be OK with being really unpopular. To people who are already 'onboard' and support the project, you can be really committed –

but sometimes someone has to be the leader and run with it.' He says that being authentic and inclusive may sometimes not be sufficient; you need managers and leaders that boldly step forward and believe in sustainability and take decisions, even though they may not always be popular. Antonio Bertone sees the reason for unpopularity among many employees as resistance to change: 'People do not like change. That goes for employees as well as for customers.' And by 'customers', he is not referring to consumers who actually love the 'Clever Little Bag', but to resellers, key accounts, some of which threatened to de-list the entire Puma line if it stuck to the innovative and more consumer-friendly and environmentally friendly packaging format.

Can you share any best-practice examples of CSR communication?

Table 4.1 shows the brands and programmes that were mentioned in the interviews.

Table 4.1   Brands and programmes referenced in the interviews

Brand, company, programme	No. of mentions
Vodafone	1
Estée Lauder	1
Hartford Financial Services	1
Aetna	1
Liz Claiborne	1
Starbucks	1
Pepsi	1

In the community involvement area, Linda Spevacek names Hartford Financial Services due to its extensive involvement supporting the arts in the community, but also in community farming, 'where people go and get their hands dirty to plant crops that are then donated to those who may not have access to fresh produce'. She also mentions insurance giant Aetna, with similarly structured initiatives. Maria Kalligeros singles out Estée Lauder, where company leaders and employees are passionate about breast cancer research.

For Veronica Scheubel, Vodafone in 2004–2005 was a good example, and two other brands that are at the forefront of her mind are Starbucks and Pepsi, but without naming specific programmes.

How do you define 'greenwashing'? Examples?

BUY YOURSELF A REPUTATION – AND CREATE CYNICISM

Veronica Scheubel defines it as 'the attempt to buy yourself a reputation and the opposite of putting your focus on impact'. It is actually shifting the focus from maximizing impact to 'How many dollars do we have to invest to have an impact?' – or minimizing the budget for a defined (minimal) impact. Maria Kalligeros points out the damage that greenwashing does:

> It creates consumer scepticism, media cynicism, and ruins it for companies that approach CSR with integrity. These programmes must be more than window dressing – they must address real social needs, be built upon solid research and include genuine partnerships with advocates who are the true experts about your cause.

What do you consider to be the key success factors of effective CSR communication?

ENGAGEMENT – AUTHENTICITY – INTEGRITY – CONSISTENCY – CONNECTING EMOTIONALLY

All interviewees were in agreement that actually getting employees involved and engaged is the key success factor for effective CSR communication. 'Research shows that in any typical workplace only 29 per cent of all employees are fully engaged and 15 per cent are explicitly disengaged, which has a massive negative cost impact,' notes Linda Spevacek. 'Conversely, increasing engagement will have a huge economic benefit.' The other key success factors mentioned are prerequisites for employees to become engaged: 'authenticity, integrity, consistency' are the ones Spevacek specifies. She adds that the way to get through to employees and get them on board is for leaders to be fully engaged themselves and to communicate using 'personal, emotional and connective language – that is why testimonials from other employees can be so strong and effective'. She reiterates that from a motivational point of view, it is crucial for management to convincingly state why what the company is doing in terms of CSR and sustainability is actually good for business.

Interview with Erica Jones, International Corporate Affairs Manager, Walmart

WHAT DO YOU ASSOCIATE WITH CSR COMMUNICATION?

Use of the term 'CSR' is a relatively new approach at Walmart. We have long been engaged in activities such as environmental sustainability and community giving that are typically thought of as CSR, but it was not until early 2012 we began to position these activities as 'responsibility' and message them as such to our associates. Internally, we refer to our CSR activities as 'Live Better' initiatives, a reference to our mission of 'Saving people money so they can live better'. Our CSR efforts, such as hunger relief, women's economic empowerment, environmental sustainability and healthier food, help us deliver on our mission of helping our customers, communities and associates live better.

WHAT ARE YOUR EXPECTATIONS REGARDING CSR COMMUNICATION OF COMPANIES?

CSR communications are an important part of our overall internal communications strategy to keep our associates informed about what their company is doing. CSR communications are positive messages, and have a positive impact on our associate engagement.

WHAT IS THE ROLE OF EMPLOYEES IN THE CONTEXT OF THE CSR COMMUNICATION OF COMPANIES?

Our associates are a key audience in our CSR communication, and we are active in sharing the company's efforts. Many employees select employers during the recruitment process because of their commitment to sustainability or community initiatives, and to keep these employees engaged, you need to keep them updated on your activities. Our associates are often the subject of our CSR communications. In many cases, we are telling a success story an associate helped to innovate or execute. By highlighting the associate, we are putting a face to our communications for internal and external audiences, providing people with someone to rally around. In other cases, we are making an ask of our associates – such as volunteering in the community, supporting a fundraiser, or looking for ways to be more environmentally sustainable. Our associates are a valuable channel for our CSR communication.

WHAT ARE THE ISSUES FROM A BUSINESS PERSPECTIVE IN COMMUNICATING CSR TO EMPLOYEES?

One of the main issues is the cost associated with CSR efforts. For example, when a foundation grant is announced, most associates take pride in knowing their company is making a positive difference in the community. However, there is a possibility for negative sentiment from associates, so the key is to provide an outlet for associates to share their point of view.

CAN YOU SHARE ANY BEST PRACTICE EXAMPLES OF CSR COMMUNICATION?

Walmart releases an annual Global Responsibility Report (GRR) which tells the story of our accomplishments and challenges in achieving our three aspirational corporate sustainability goals, outlining the work we do to support our communities through our foundation and the opportunities we offer to a diverse workforce. This report centralizes our CSR story for both external and internal audiences to ensure we are providing a transparent record of our initiatives. In regard to associate communication, another best practice is using storytelling as a recognition and engagement tactic. When an associate is involved in driving a sustainability innovation or leading a community project, we highlight their story on The Walmart Green Room blog, our company intranet and in our corporate magazine. Not only does it make the associate feel as though their contribution is valued by the company, but it serves as a way to tell the story to other associates.

WHAT DO YOU CONSIDER TO BE KEY SUCCESS FACTORS OF EFFECTIVE CSR COMMUNICATION FROM AN NGO PERSPECTIVE?

For CSR communication to be effective, it needs to be authentic and transparent. All aspects of the 'What's in it for me?' factor need to be clearly articulated – what is the business return for the company, what is the benefit for the community or environment, and why should associates care? The tone should be conversational and not read like a press release, and should acknowledge the role the associate(s) played in making the project a reality. A meaningful communication about CSR should also point to additional resources for those who are curious to learn and share more, as well as encourage associates to be brand ambassadors by telling fellow associates, customers, family and friends about the great things their company is doing to improve the community or environment.

Best Practice Case: Walmart 'My Sustainability Plan'

Figure 4.3   Walmart 'My Sustainability Plan' logo
Source: Reproduced courtesy of Walmart Corporation.

Walmart initiated its 'My Sustainability Plan' (MSP) in 2010. Walmart associates from 15 countries around the globe were involved in defining personal sustainability goals through 12 focus areas in the three categories 'My Health', 'My Planet' and 'My Life'. Walmart created an online tool which can be licensed royalty-free by any organization within and outside Walmart.

Overall, 100,000 Walmart volunteers have signed up so far and created personal sustainability plans for themselves, and 35 external organizations, including United Parcel Service (UPS) and Unilever, have enrolled since the release in September 2011.

Within Walmart, the international business units with the highest level of staff enrolment are Chile, with about 50 per cent (20,000), and Brazil, with more than 62 per cent (50,000).

Key Messages in a Nutshell

Table 4.2   Chapter 4 key messages in a nutshell

Expectations of employees towards CSR communication	Connect emotionally Be ethical inside out Open and transparent engagement
Roles of employees in the context of CSR communication	Brand ambassadors Communicators and multipliers
Issues of CSR communication to employees	Willingness to invest in employee engagement Creating a real involvement Cutting through the clutter Winning over the cynics

5 *Communicating Sustainability to Customers and Consumers*

Simplicity despite complexity is required.

Michael Kuhndt, CSCP

The broader term describing this key stakeholder group is 'customers', rather than 'consumers'. Focusing just on consumers implies ignoring customer relationships in earlier stages of the value chain. These relationships are often called 'business-to-business', or BtoB. While there will be more attention to (end-)consumers, we will also explore CSR- and sustainability communications between suppliers and their BtoB customers.

What do you associate with CSR and CSR communication?

WE PREFER TO TALK ABOUT SUSTAINABILITY AND SUSTAINABILITY COMMUNICATION

There is a clear preference to substitute sustainability or corporate sustainability for CSR. 'I dislike the term "CSR". While we do all have a responsibility to behave in an appropriate way, I much prefer "sustainability", which is what we are trying to achieve at innocent,' says Jessica Sansom of fruit smoothie company innocent. Gavin Neath of Unilever agrees: 'CSR to me is somewhat flaky: a mix of philanthropy, employee volunteering and corporate sponsorship. All very worthy, but not much help to the business.'

Jessica Sansom agrees that this was the traditional view – a (boring) conversation between companies and their investors in which the company tries to demonstrate its responsibility: 'I associate CSR communication with an annual report which is churned out by big companies, normally to coincide with the annual general meeting. Usually bland, not very revealing, and quite self-congratulatory.' However, in her view, it is now much broader, as it is brought into the consumer arena with a much stronger advertising and marketing approach. While it used to take the form of a printed report, it now comes in all shapes and sizes – on packaging, on websites, in social media, in books as well as in those printed reports. Also, it has moved from just companies communicating about their performance to many people talking about other people's performance. Companies have lost control of their CSR or sustainability communication due to the advent of social media.

Uwe Kleinert of Coca-Cola points out the difference between 'classical' PR and corporate communications and CSR communication, and claims that CSR requires more care and more attention to detail as there is now much more critical scrutiny and there is an expectation that companies will be more self-critical: 'You have to *do* a lot more than you can communicate when it comes to CSR.'

What are the expectations of customers and consumers regarding the CSR communication of companies?

HONEST – ACCURATE – TRANSPARENT – INTEGRATED – ENGAGING

Be honest

'It is incredibly important to be honest – that is the obvious answer, but it really is key to be as honest and transparent as possible.' This statement of Jessica Sansom's was echoed by nearly all other interviewees. Honesty also means being totally accurate, well documented and not leaving out the difficult truths, avoiding spin. Honesty and accuracy also imply 'really good clarity around the contribution of the CSR stuff to the core strategy and how it influences strategic decision-making', according to BP's Nicholas Robinson.[1]

Be accurate

Accuracy means that CSR communication needs to be quantitative rather than just anecdotal, and should include scientific research. It implies the provision of proof for claims, and that they should be complete – 'no spin and no whitewash', according to Uwe Kleinert.

Be transparent

Michael Kuhndt of sustainable consumption think-tank the Centre on Sustainable Consumption and Production (CSCP) explains what he means by 'as much transparency as possible': 'It means to report on the most important points of a company. Companies should examine their hot spots, both organizational and product-related ones. Those should then be communicated. There is no need to report on everything, but there should be a focus on the really important aspects.'

Be integrated

Another key expectation is integration. Former longtime Disney CSR executive Jeff Hoffman says:

> CSR needs to be, and will be, more integrated into the messaging of the company so that when the CEO is talking about business performance, CSR performance will be part of the conversation rather than issuing separate business and CSR reports. It is all part of how a company does business.

---

1   Nicholas Robinson was Head of Corporate Reporting at BP at the time of the interview and until 2011 and since January 2012 has been General Manager, Customer Insight, Marketing and Communications at Contact Energy, Wellington, New Zealand.

Gavin Neath supports that notion, and goes one step further: 'In an ideal world there would be full integration of sustainability and financial reporting. Both the social and the environmental dimensions are an integral part of business performance.'

Be engaging

Last but not least, CSR communication needs to be engaging, relevant and interesting – 'Basically, less bullshit and more getting to the point, which may mean that companies make what they say a lot shorter and less grand,' says Gavin Neath – while Ed Gillespie of Futerra states:

> *We are on record at Futerra as saying frequently that CSR reporting must die. To paraphrase Winston Churchill, 'Never in the field of human history has so much been written by so many and read by so few.' Just reporting data in the form of CSR reports is not enough. You need to derive insights from that data and do something with it, otherwise it is not taken seriously internally and will remain in a CSR bucket.*

Best Practice Case: The innocent Big Knit Campaign

Figure 5.1   innocent's Big Knit campaign with Age UK involved all ages with a 'headwarming' idea

Source: Reproduced courtesy of innocent.

From its inception, the innocent brand has been notably ethical, and its involvement in 'The Big Knit' has certainly cemented the brand's positioning in that part of the corporate landscape.

In 2003, the company became conscious of the fact that around 150,000 elderly people had died in Britain from cold-related illnesses during the winter since the year 2000. The company therefore approached Age Concern (now merged with another age-related charity to form Age UK), an NGO which was running a 'Fight the Freeze' campaign to draw attention to this scandalous problem. The charity recruited the knitting volunteers, and innocent's 'Big Knit' was born, getting people to knit little hats for the innocent bottles. They enlisted the support of prominent chemist/pharmacy group Boots and Sainsbury's, the grocery retailer, which ensured that 50 pence from every innocent smoothie purchased went to the campaign to help insulate elderly people's homes and to ensure they received at least one hot meal a day.

The campaign expanded with celebrity involvement in 2005, and then in 2007 Sainsbury's helped run the 'SuperGran' campaign with innocent and Age UK. By 2011 the eighth year of the campaign, £1 million had been raised, and they began to expand it to Germany, Austria and Switzerland.

The quirky aspect to the campaign was not only that consumers could indirectly give money, but that they could be involved – it was both fun and creative, which is the way innocent sees itself. Sainsbury's staff held competitions, as did knitting magazines. Grocery shopping was made much more interesting, with the little hats bringing smiles to people's faces. innocent developed a 'Big Knit Hat' tag on Facebook, and encouraged people to put pictures of the hats they knitted on Flickr. A blog was launched with a 'Hat of the Week'.

innocent saw a large increase in sales of its smoothies, 11 per cent year on year. There were 94 per cent more 'Big Knit' hats created in 2009 than in 2008, which indicated huge loyalty, and in 2011 alone 65,000 hats were knitted.

In all, 55,000 older people have benefited, not only through insulation of their homes and the provision of hot meals, but through assistance in claiming their winter fuel allowances and the funding of shuttle buses for shopping. The company believes that it has brought young and old people together, strengthening communities, and by thinking outside the box, has created something both 'delightful and surprising' which reflected their core values.

For the full Best Practice Case 10, see Chapter 14, page 221.

What is the role of customers and consumers in the context of CSR communication for companies?

'THEY ARE THE ONES THAT KEEP US ALL ON OUR TOES' – JESSICA SANSOM, INNOCENT

Broadly speaking, customers – and specifically the kinds of customers that most respondents have in mind, end consumers – are first and foremost recipients of CSR or sustainability-related communication. Michael Kuhndt of the UN Environment Programme-affiliated CSCP points out that this implies that consumers these days receive a lot of 'sustainability spam'. By that he means 'a lot of words that are supposed to depict the positive', a lot of unsolicited information that confuses the consumer.

Constructive challengers

From that perspective, he states that companies should offer less rather than more information to those who are supposed to purchase their products. Uwe Kleinert of Coca-Cola feels that consumers should play a constructive role by being informed and personally acting on what they learn about what companies do. If they notice that companies are trying to cut down on packaging, consumers should make sure they put the remaining packaging in the recycling bin and not waste the products themselves:

> If we want to have a good environment in fifty years' time, we all need to join in. If there was more openness to the information and arguments put forward by business that would be helpful. It is OK for consumer associations and NGOs to be critical but always just saying 'this is bad, this is greenwashing' results in no dialogue.

So, according to Kleinert, one key role of NGOs, consumer associations and consumers themselves is to actively and attentively listen as the recipients of the information, treating the company's messages with respect and being prepared to enter into a dialogue.

Jessica Sansom agrees: 'I would like them to be open to actually listen to what companies actually have to say and to ask questions, but also to be receptive.' But she also goes a step further by saying that consumers really need to actively request information on the issues they care about.

Decision-makers

Kuhndt wants consumers to take a more active role than that of just recipients – 'The consumer as stakeholder should be part of deciding on what is important' – a view that is shared by Gavin Neath, who argues that 'in traditional CSR communication there is no role for the consumer', alluding to CSR and sustainability reporting. Companies need to include consumers in deciding what is important to them in terms of sustainability and CSR. The key term is 'benefit orientation' – companies should use the conversation with the consumer to identify 'positive benefits which may interest him or her'. Michael Kuhndt asks the question, 'To what extent do consumer needs actually play a role?', and argues that in many cases consumers are not involved in the stakeholder dialogue early enough in the process. NGOs and media are consulted, but usually not consumers: 'Companies need to focus on the value added by sustainability in their external communication.' He adds that quite clearly, this is a major challenge, as consumer-directed communication is usually the most aggregated form of communication, hence the danger of misunderstanding and confusion. Advertising and point-of-sale communication can usually only transmit very few messages, and he suggests providing more in-depth information on the Internet.

Nicholas Robinson, formerly of BP and now with Contact Energy, makes the point that it is not only facts that count; consumers' emotions and feelings about businesses and their sustainability messages play a major role. He observes that consumers may not want to listen to companies, but rather to thought-leaders in the media and among NGOs, and therefore suggests it is companies that need to listen to consumers, instead of vice versa, to 'get a sense of the sentiment and then be able to communicate specifically with that sentiment in mind'.

What are the key issues from a business perspective of communicating CSR to customers and consumers?

CONVINCE THEM WITH RELEVANT MESSAGES

Relevance

The first key issue may very well be lack of relevance to the product or service in question. 'Historically, we have trained brand managers to look at the brand exclusively through the eyes of the consumer,' says Gavin Neath, who implies that 'relevance' these days may be defined a little more broadly:

> But now they may benefit from taking a slightly wider perspective, that is, not merely looking at the consumer as a user or purchaser of a product which you try to sell them but as a citizen who has an opinion about social or environmental issues which your brand might be able to address.

Complexity

The complexity of the topic of sustainability is another challenge for companies and brands that want to communicate to consumers. Nicholas Robinson states:

> It is like opening Pandora's box, all these interlinked stakeholder perspectives. You try to 'do engagement' in a succinct manner, but the sheer complexity is a barrier and it is hard to do justice to the detail of the issue. Therefore companies need a strategy and plan on how they engage and communicate these issues over time.

CSCP's Michael Kuhndt agrees: 'Simplicity despite complexity is required. You need to aggregate and thereby simplify and at the same time offer to break it down into more detail to those who request more information.'

Lead or be led

'We made a conscious decision not be consumer-led, and rather to lead consumers in our sustainability work, and that we would work in the areas that we believe were the right ones and that would deliver best against the overall sustainability agenda and its requirements,' says Jessica Sansom of innocent. She touches on a key point: it is not always 100 per cent clear what 'the' consumer wants in terms of sustainability. On the other hand, a brand or company can only then come across as convincing and credible if it has an idea about what it believes in. Being a sustainability leader may very well involve both – listening to what the target audience says and thinks, but at the same time acting on your convictions. Still, Sansom continues: 'If you lead your consumers, one challenge is how to explain simply the actions you have taken and how to communicate that back to the consumer.' It is clear that one of the consumer's needs is to be informed, and that is where the above-mentioned challenge of complexity she mentions comes in again: 'There is an awful lot of grey in sustainability and that is what frustrates consumers. They want to be told! They want an easy decision matrix when they go out to buy – but there is no easy decision matrix!'

Best Practice Case: Max Burgers – Climate on (the) Menu

Figure 5.2   Max Burgers was the first fast-food restaurant chain in the world to let customers know the climate impact of their menu choices

Source: Reproduced courtesy of Max Hamburgerrestauranger AB.

Max Burgers, Sweden's first hamburger chain, is a family-owned company founded in 1968. CEO Richard Bergfors along with the rest of his family bore the cost of initiating the 'Climate on the Menu' programme because of their commitment and belief, even before it was apparent that it would be economically beneficial to the company. The meat industry itself is responsible for 18 per cent of the world's entire greenhouse gas emissions. The leadership of Max Burgers, which had already demonstrated its commitment to social responsibility through its proactive policy of employing disabled people from 2002, started to think seriously about the environment.

Max Burgers became the first restaurant chain to add carbon labels to the different selections on its menus, which became known as the 'Climate on the Menu' programme. In partnership with The Natural Step, it developed a comprehensive approach, with voluntary carbon offsets throughout its supply chain, supporting reforestation in Uganda and Mozambique along with agro-forestry and ecosystem services and developing entrepreneurship. It is very difficult to obtain meat from farms which are carbon-neutral, though as Max Burgers discovered, it could reduce methane emissions if farmers used different feed, and similarly it could encourage them to reduce fossil fuel use. Max Burgers would also like to encourage more recycling of farm waste rather than the burning that tends to go on, but apparently laws have made this somewhat difficult.

The company's goal is to eventually make its entire operation fossil fuel-free, and all of its restaurants, of which there are 88 in Sweden and now two in Norway, are powered by 100 per cent wind energy.

Max Burgers has incorporated sustainability leadership training for managers and cashiers into its staff development, creating a culture of sustainability from the inside- out. Year after year, Max Burgers has won awards and prizes too numerous to mention, citing it as one of the best green companies globally – in one year there were over 100 articles about the company in the international media, including *Time* magazine. There have also been television programmes about Max Burgers' approach. It aims to inspire and educate customers to think about environmental issues and to be the best fast food restaurant chain for concerned customers. In 2010, it managed to totally offset its climate impact by planting 60,000 trees in Africa, and its profits have increased by 500 per cent since 2003.

For the full Best Practice Case 11, see Chapter 14, page 228.

When talking to customers who are not consumers, for example for those supplying consumer goods to retailers, the issue is not so much about managing complexity. This is because these customers often have a fairly good grasp of sustainability issues themselves. But that may be the exact reason why, as suppliers, companies need to be confident about their own approach and be able to convince them about it. 'The challenge is to make room for the communication/conversation to work towards the right solutions together,' in Jessica Sansom's view. She adds:

> Because our approach is very commercial, we focus on the balance between business and planet and are flexible. Therefore we get respect for what we are doing. As an example we manage packaging as a portfolio, trying to balance customer and sustainability needs. We will then try to improve performance in other areas of the portfolio instead.

In that context, she stresses that you cannot share certain aspects of sustainability data as it can be closely linked to cost, and passing on that information may affect your competitiveness. Being open about that fact is accepted and respected in most cases.

Reputational risk

'Managing risk has to be at the heart of all these things. It is managing negative reputation and supply chain risks, but also core business risks,' states Ed Gillespie of sustainability communication experts Futerra. Uwe Kleinert adds that it is a specificity of sustainability communications that stakeholders may be more likely to be monitoring them more closely than other corporate communications-related topics. One of the key risks is if there is an imbalance between what a company does and what it communicates to consumers or the general public. 'If the good that I do only relates to 1 per cent of my turnover, it should not be communicated in a way that creates the impression that everything is "good",' says Michael Kuhndt. He adds that 'lighthouse projects' – projects that showcase a more general principle with a concrete example of execution – do make sense. However, there are many examples of companies that have gone public too early and remain in the 'lighthouse stage'. Often communication requires two or three years of hard groundwork and investment upfront. That is why a long-term sustainability strategy is so important. He likens sustainability to capital investment projects which, with a high upfront investment, are supposed to have a long-term payback. Reputational risk is best reduced by a long-term, well-planned approach that allows for consistency and relationship development.

Can you share any best practice examples of CSR communication?

Table 5.1 shows the brands and programmes that were mentioned in the interviews.

Table 5.1   Brands and programmes referenced in the interviews

Brand, company, programme	No. of mentions
Top 5	
Marks & Spencer (UK, Retail)	4
Unilever (excl. Ben & Jerry's, incl. Lipton, PG Tips, FMCG)	3
Ben & Jerry's	2
REWE (Germany, Retail)	2
Novo Nordisk (Denmark, Pharmaceutical)	2
Single mentions grouped by industry:	
(Fast-moving) Consumer Goods (including Top 5)	13
Walkers, Häagen Dazs, Method, Ecover, Cadbury's Green & Black, Nike, Tetra Pak (Consumer Goods Packaging), Lipton, PG Tips, Fairtrade	7
Retail (including Top 5)	11
Kesko (Finland), IKEA, Walmart, dm (Germany), GEPA (FT retailer, Germany)	5
Industry (Primarily BtoB)	
BASF, GE, Anglo American, Rio Tinto	4
Food Service	
McDonald's, Starbucks	2
Cars	
Audi, BMW	2
Financial Services	
Co-operative Bank (UK), Standard Chartered Bank (UK)	2
It/Telecom/Internet	
Deutsche Telekom	1

Again, the most frequently mentioned best practice example is Marks & Spencer. 'M&S is probably the best example in the UK at the moment,' says Hugh Burkitt of the Marketing Society. 'They have done a lot with consumers, but also right up the supply chain, which is one of the most difficult aspects.' Jessica Sansom agrees, and adds that '"Plan A" has done a great job to raise awareness for sustainability issues.' This is also a view that Unilever's Gavin Neath shares – he acknowledges that there has been a notable consumer response to M&S's sustainability and CSR communication.

Runner-up is Unilever, mentioned three times. One could even argue that as Ben & Jerry's is a Unilever brand, Unilever is actually the top best practice example, ahead of M&S. Hugh Burkitt says: 'Another very good example is Unilever. Overall they have probably done more good work across their whole company [than most others].' Obviously, Gavin Neath of Unilever has to agree. But he also provides a useful example that illustrates the effect the Brand Imprint process had on two of Unilever's major food brands, PG Tips and Lipton:

> *Ethical sourcing of tea was one of the issues that emerged from the Brand Imprint study on Lipton. We recognized that the tea supply chain is unbalanced and unjust. The packer and marketer of tea get most of the benefit while the tea pickers do not get enough. Once you start correcting the imbalance, it is interesting to see how the consumer responds. Rationally, he recognizes that there is a company that keeps in mind the concerns of people who grow and cultivate this tea. The emotional response is that consumers make a link in their own mind that because the tea is carefully cultivated, it will taste better.*

Maybe it is not surprising that the majority of mentions in the customer and consumer section are of retailers and FMCG brands and companies. What is interesting is that there are two groups of brands: brands that have sustainability and CSR as part of their core proposition, like Ben & Jerry's, Method (cleaning products), Ecover, Green & Black and German fair trade retailer GEPA and the growing number of mainstream brands that integrate sustainability into their communication. Michael Kuhndt observes about one of the main German retailers that 'REWE is catching up, moving mass-market. While it is a challenge for them, they are getting there.' He also points out where the future of best practice consumer-oriented sustainability will be:

> *Traceability is the future. Generally, traceability is already an established concept, but not in the arena of environmental and social aspects. To integrate ordinary supply chain traceability with sustainability will be the next big topic, which is also a risk management issue, as retailers have the legal responsibility for the origins of products they sell. Therefore, the integration of supply chains will increase, there will be less outsourcing, in order to be able to better monitor quality issues and reduce risk of liability.*

Kuhndt mentions that he discussed sustainability issues with Walmart's CEO at the Davos World Economic Forum and gained the impression that the world's largest company 'is moving in the right direction, is beyond greenwashing. However, the engine is not changed.' By that, he means that what is still missing is the move to new, more sustainable business models rather than trying to modify the existing model or 'engine' to be a little less unsustainable. Then again, those companies that develop new, more sustainable business models do not seem to make it into the mass market, like German Fairtrade retailer GEPA, which remains niche.

Examples from other industries include Japanese consumer goods manufacturer Panasonic. Michael Kuhndt praises the electronics brand for its attempts to explain what sustainability means to it on a product level: 'They arranged an exhibition in Tokyo which communicated their impact very openly and honestly, and with which they very transparently explained where they are going.' What he criticizes about Panasonic is that it does not take a global approach, but focuses on Japan and Asia, something that he calls a missed opportunity. The example on the other end of the scale is Nike: 'They do a great job talking to youth through products and stores, making issues relevant, locally, nationally and globally,' says Nicholas Robinson.

When it comes to talking to customers who are not consumers, sustainability reporting can play an important role. Novo Nordisk was mentioned twice as a role model, because 'they are always heading in the same direction', according to Nicholas Robinson. He adds that Starbucks is a good example in how it communicates its sustainability efforts to its consumers, even through reports. While overall reports tend to be quite similar, in his view there are some strong ones in the industrial area, specifically in mining (Rio Tinto, Anglo American), but also in retailing, where he feels that Finnish retailer Kesko comes across as a real leader in transparency, despite its report being 'boring and low-key'.

Other examples which are not just mentioned but commented on (the following examples were referred to by Jessica Sansom) were Co-operative Bank, Häagen-Dazs with its 'Honey Bees' campaign, Ecover, 'which has not done a lot around communications, but the whole brand resonates CSR', and Walkers, 'who did a great job on communicating the carbon footprint of their potato crisps with a wonderful website'.

Best Practice Case: Cadbury Dairy Milk Goes Fairtrade

Figure 5.3   Iconic chocolate brand Cadbury Dairy Milk goes Fairtrade and gives people a reason to smile

Source: Reproduced courtesy of Mondelez International.

Cadbury's decision to make its Dairy Milk bar, the world's biggest chocolate bar brand, Fairtrade was hugely significant, in the same way as McDonald's moving away from buying apples grown with pesticide use in the US. As such a big brand, it ensured that the rest of the market took a quantum leap so that sustainability has become mainstream, and all the big chocolate brands have climbed on the bandwagon.

Cadbury had been in Ghana for a hundred years, and in assessing the landscape, realized that the cocoa farmers were poor, and the yield had dropped to 40 per cent. Cadbury began working with the farmers to turn the situation around in 2005, recognizing that there might be a risk to the supply of cocoa, not only due to the low incomes of the farmers, but because of the departure of rural young people to big cities and poor productivity overall. Therefore, it established the Cocoa Partnership in 2005, investing £45 million to improve productivity. It decided to go with Fairtrade rather than developing its own certification scheme, as Fairtrade is recognized in the UK consumer market as well as among producers in Ghana and is seen as independent and trustworthy. The programme set out to guarantee a minimum price to farmers and provide them with secure and sustainable livelihoods.

In July 2009, the first chocolate bars came out in the UK, with three more markets added in 2010, Canada, New Zealand and Australia, then South Africa in 2011. During the August 2011 Fairtrade Fortnight in the UK, 20 per cent of the profits from the sale of Dairy Milk went towards funding solar power projects in Ghana. Then another brand, Milk Buttons, also qualified for Fairtrade certification.

Along the way, issues of child labour and gender empowerment have arisen – 30 per cent of the partnership communities are run by women. Cadbury alone accounts for the involvement of 10,000 farmers in 100 communities, whereas Fairtrade overall works with 55,000 farmers in 1,300 communities, so Cadbury's participation has quadrupled the volume of cocoa sold under Fairtrade terms. An additional £2.3 million in Fairtrade social premiums have gone towards mobile clinics, farm skills training and equipment.

Cadbury estimates that it received £1.9 million worth of PR value in the UK alone, that it has reduced the risks of higher costs and supply issues, and it is proud to have leapt from being the 25th most admired company in the UK in 2008 to the fourth. Sustainability has been truly aligned with its brand values, and the creative communications celebrating Ghanaian culture have been joyful rather than moralistic.

For the full Best Practice Case 9, see Chapter 14, page 215.

How do you define 'greenwashing'? Examples?

COMMUNICATION WITHOUT SUBSTANCE

'Often greenwashing is not intentional. I would estimate that between 40 per cent and 70 per cent [of sustainability-related communication] is in this category,' claims Michael Kuhndt. 'It is not out of ill will, but many have not done their homework. They do a thousand things, much of which is not the right thing to do and communicate those. So it is a lot about communicating the wrong thing.' Gavin Neath adds that it is very prevalent, as the area of sustainability is a fashionable one for marketers to explore. There is therefore a lot of talk about greenwashing and interest in the subject: sustainability communications experts Futerra's *Greenwash Guide*, published in 2008,[2] had been downloaded 80,000 times by 2010.

Jessica Sansom has the impression that things may have improved – 'haven't seen any for a while' – but finds greenwashing aggravating. She was particularly irritated by a claim of sustainability best practice Marks & Spencer came up with: 'All our oranges are handpicked' – because *all* oranges are handpicked! This she calls manipulation for marketing purposes – 'as if the marketing department has said "Yes! Sustainability can be my brand differentiation," and then launches irresponsible communication'.

What it comes down to is communication without substance. Jeff Hoffman, previously at Disney, warns:

> *Companies have to be careful. Environmental stewardship should be an important part of how a company does business, but companies must be fully aware of their carbon footprint before talking about how wonderful they are at protecting the environment. Full-page ads in the New York Times or the Wall Street Journal can blow up on you!*

Gavin Neath calls claims that are not well substantiated 'a terrific temptation'. As brand managers have been taught to make competitive claims, there is a need for good internal controls: 'They need be made aware that facts and integrity are very important.'

It is a bit like the ethical marketing of pharmaceuticals: it has to be done with integrity and scientific rigour. Facts should be king, not the desire to produce catchy slogans and tag lines. Brand teams need a lot of training in this area. Figure 5.4 shows the 10 signs of greenwash.

---

2   Futerra Sustainability Communications, *The Greenwash Guide*, www.futerra.co.uk/downloads/Greenwash_Guide. pdf (accessed 10 June 2013).

1.
Fluffy language

Words or terms with no clear meaning,
e.g. 'eco-friendly'

2.
Green products v
dirty company

Such as efficient light bulbs made in a factory
which pollutes rivers

3.
Suggestive pictures

Green images that indicate a (un-justified) green
impact e.g. flowers blooming from exhaust pipes

4.
Irrelevant claims

Emphasising one tiny green attribute when
everything else is un-green

5.
Best in class?

Declaring you are slightly greener than the rest,
even if the rest are pretty terrible

6.
Just not credible

'Eco friendly' cigarettes anyone? 'Greening'
a dangerous product doesn't make it safe

7.
Gobbledygook

Jargon and information that
only a scientist could check or understand

8.
Imaginary friends

A 'label' that looks like third party endorsement …
except it's made up

9.
No proof

It could be right, but where's the
evidence?

10.
Out-right lying

Totally fabricated claims or data

Cut out and keep

Figure 5.4   Ten signs of greenwash

Source: Reproduced courtesy of Futerra Sustainability Communications.

What do you consider to be the key success factors of effective CSR communication?

SUBSTANCE FIRST – VALUE FOR MONEY PLUS – CONSUMER EMPOWERMENT – HOLISTIC INTEGRITY

Substance first

'There needs to be the right balance between communicating and doing. We prioritize the doing, communicating is the icing on the cake,' says Jessica Sansom about innocent's approach. Doing 'business as usual' and then communicating about sustainability is a recipe for disaster, according to Ed Gillespie. The same goes for 'optimizing, doing a bit of housekeeping and increasing efficiency – you still hit the wall, just later, prolonging the inevitable crash'. The only long-term viable option, according to Gillespie, is that companies 'redesign for resilience'. He goes on to explain what that may imply: 'Look at your business, interrogate your core business, and dramatically innovate. This gets suppliers more excited because it opens up new opportunities for them. Some who are propping up the current business model will be less excited, of course.'

Value for money plus

Sustainability-related activities or product traits will in most cases not be the primary benefit of a product or service for consumers. It is more likely that they will be an added value that will potentially help to differentiate it from a competitive offering. Gavin Neath puts it like this:

> Most consumers will not be prepared to pay more and will not accept less quality or less convenience. It has to be a great product at a competitive price. But if you add on a dimension that makes consumers feel that the brand is meeting their broader social or environmental aspirations it can serve as a differentiator and add value.

In other words, if a product or service delivers well on providing the benefit consumers primarily purchase it for at an attractive price – if it offers value for money – then, and only then, will sustainability performance be perceived by some consumers as a positive differentiator. What does not work is to compensate for a deficit in value for money by adding a sustainability dimension. Taking coffee as an example, most consumers would not purchase coffee primarily because it was Fairtrade especially if the taste was substandard. However, if the quality of coffee meets expectations and the price is perceived as good or decent value for money, the fact that it is Fairtrade will provide an added value, at least to some consumer groups or market segments.

Holistic integrity

'Whatever perspective you take, honesty and integrity is the only thing you have in this area,' claims Gavin Neath. Uwe Kleinert warns that in communicating CSR, you need to show the whole picture and should not give in to the temptation to only show selected 'lighthouse projects'. If you do not take the holistic approach, you may face greenwashing claims.

'Holistic integrity' implies that you make transparent what you do as a company and how you do it, as well. 'CSR has to be an integral part of how you think and act on an everyday basis in your daily business,' Kleinert adds. But for CSR communication, we have to realize that there is news each day or each week that is necessarily relevant for the media, as it is just day-to-day business:

> So we need to realize that consumers are more likely to assess successful CSR by that fact that they do not hear anything negative rather than that they hear a lot of positive news. And that is more of a challenge from a communications standpoint, because it is not easy to relate what we as a company [Coca-Cola] are doing on a day-to-day basis, for example in terms of reducing water usage.

Consumer empowerment

Consumer empowerment starts with making yourself understood. Or, as Jessica Sansom suggests : 'Consumers need to understand what you are talking about – the language you use is crucial, you need to tailor the language to the right audience.' What she means by 'empowerment' though, is that through the way you inform them, you enable consumers to make a choice. For the innocent brand, sustainability is one of the key brand promises: 'We get a lot of different responses from different target audiences because they have very different needs.' So communication that meets a consumer need that they understand and by which they feel understood is a prerequisite for what is labelled 'sustainable consumption'.

Interview with Hugh Burkitt, The Marketing Society

WHAT DO YOU ASSOCIATE WITH CSR COMMUNICATION?

CSR to me is an old-fashioned idea of how companies should behave but it is stuck somewhere in the Corporate Affairs Department. We in the Business in the Community (BitC) team looking at this feel we have moved on, we think CSR has been discredited because it was seen as a kind of sideshow. Companies need to move towards sustainability in total. Therefore, we are now talking about sustainable marketing. To explain this concept, we as The Marketing Society together with BitC, supported by ad agency RKY&R [Rainey Kelly Campbell Rolfe Young & Rubicam] have published a pamphlet called *How Can Marketers Build Sustainable Success*?[3]

What I associate with CSR communications is hard to answer, it is such big question, I'm not really sure where to begin. I suppose that increasingly, all companies feel the need to have a point of view about this whole subject. They realize that their customers will have a point of view and they need to talk about it in a way that will reflect well on their brands. Of course, it is also the CSR report, Cause Related Marketing and so on. However, as mentioned above, it should concern the whole subject of sustainability.

---

3   *How Can Marketers Build Sustainable Success?* (2010), www.bitc.org.uk/our-resources/report/how-can-marketers-build-sustainable-success (accessed 10 June 2013). See also *Influencing Consumer Behaviour: A Guide for Sustainable Marketing* (2011), www.bitc.org.uk/our-resources/report/influencing-consumer-behaviour-guide-sustainable-marketing (accessed 10 June 2013).

WHAT ARE YOUR EXPECTATIONS REGARDING CSR COMMUNICATION OF COMPANIES?

Firstly, transparency and honesty. If companies are not, they will be found out, that is the great virtue of the Internet: you are quickly found out and quickly punished. On the more positive side, the right sustainability policies can make a brand more attractive. An example is Marks & Spencer, who have made their brand more attractive by 'Look Behind the Label', 'Plan A' and now 'Doing the Right Thing'. This is a good example of communicating what they are doing quite effectively to create competitive advantage. Another great example is Cadbury's making Dairy Milk Fairtrade. Immediately, Mars responded by associating Galaxy with the Rainforest Alliance. And I have noticed that meanwhile, Nestlé has moved Kit Kat Fairtrade as well. So within a very short space of time two of the biggest chocolate manufacturers have moved to Fairtrade and the third to Rainforest Alliance. I remember forty years ago, when I was working with Oxfam, the big chocolate manufacturers did not want to know about Fairtrade. It seemed to be a law that the rich countries exploit poor countries. Now there is a significant change. Even though all these manufacturers are not buying all their chocolate this way (Mars seems to have committed to move to 100 per cent!), it is a good change

WHAT IS THE ROLE OF CSR COMMUNICATION IN THE OVERALL COMMUNICATION OF COMPANIES?

Sometimes it is the centrepiece, as in the case of P&G's Ariel 'Turn to 30' campaign, where the brand and consumer benefit is combined with a huge environmental benefit. Many of the utility companies in the UK, both gas and electricity, are putting the environmental issue forward to make their brands more attractive. On the other hand, Marks & Spencer talk about 'doing the right thing', about environmental aspects of their brand. But their biggest product category is clothing, which people buy to look good and be fashionable, so its sustainability is not central. Even the exclusively Fairtrade Nestlé brand Café Direct needs to be delicious first before being Fairtrade.

WHAT ARE THE ISSUES FROM A BUSINESS PERSPECTIVE IN COMMUNICATING CSR TO CONSUMERS/CUSTOMERS?

It might not be relevant and not the primary benefit in a given market, and it may therefore not be the right thing to talk about. Another issue is whether it is true and absolutely justifiable what you are doing. Marketers need to consider whether CSR or sustainability may make their product less attractive, for example by making it more expensive. Consumers like sustainability, but they are not prepared to pay a lot for it. Also, marketers will have to consider that different consumer segments have a different point of view on CSR. I have a Marks & Spencer case study in front of me that will be published later this year [2010]. They start by drawing a picture of how 'green' people are in the market: 10 per cent of consumers are really enthusiastic (so called 'Green Crusaders'), 35 per cent are willing to be green if it does not cost anything, 35 per cent are 'Defeatist', with a 'What can I do? – It doesn't make any difference' attitude, and the remaining 20 per cent are hostile, absolutely not interested.

CAN YOU SHARE ANY BEST PRACTICE EXAMPLES OF CSR COMMUNICATION?

Marks & Spencer is probably the best example, they have done a lot with consumers, but also right up the supply chain, which is one of the most difficult aspects. Another very good one is Unilever. Overall, Unilever have probably done more good work across their whole company. They have a process which they call Brand Imprint which they put all their major brands through – how various stakeholders see it, and then make appropriate changes. They have been less noisy about great campaigns. They reduce waste, and are very much concerned about food sourcing, for example fish/MSC [Marine Stewardship Council]. The Co-operative Bank is also very impressive. It is quite small compared with other major players. But they have had an ethical investment positioning and policy for a long time and have done well in the financial crisis, while commercial banks have behaved badly and their performance has reflected this.[4] Audi, the German car company, have done some good work even though car companies have issues due to the nature of their business itself, as it is inherently 'unsustainable'.

HOW DO YOU DEFINE 'GREENWASHING' AND COULD YOU NAME EXAMPLES?

It is claiming that a company or brand is green when it fundamentally is not. In areas like cars and flying, it is easy to over-claim as the process or business model itself is inherently damaging to the environment. I am not aware of recent behaviour that has rebounded, fortunately they do not come to mind. I am a little sceptical of the Rainforest Alliance. You give them money and they give you a badge – but that is more of a suspicion rather than based on hard data. These are organizations that can prosper because companies have to present themselves. Maybe when I see it in relation to Mars chocolate or PG Tips I am not sure how much it actually affects their whole production. If I were a keen environmental journalist, I would like to explore this.

WHAT DO YOU CONSIDER TO BE KEY SUCCESS FACTORS OF EFFECTIVE CSR COMMUNICATION FROM THE CUSTOMER OR CONSUMER PERSPECTIVE?

In an absolutely ideal world, companies will make more profit and encourage consumer behaviour to change in a way that benefits society and the environment – win–win between societal and business objectives. What good marketers have to realize is, if you take a really long-term view: there are product categories in which consumption needs to be limited. Technical improvement can be made to reduce negative impacts, but they will have to be looking for alternatives. They will be moving to selling services rather than just selling things, products. Mass consumer marketing grew up selling people more stuff and things. As we now have all those basic necessities of life, we are moving towards an emphasis on services and experience, also moving to different business models: 'Street Car' for example is an interesting 'car brand' in the UK. They offer short-term hire, you only use it when you absolutely need to, like using public transport.

---

4   In June 2013 this much applauded example of a responsible commercial bank got into trouble over a £1.5bn black hole allegedly related to its acquisition of building society Britannia.

Key Messages in a Nutshell

Table 5.2   Chapter 5 key messages in a nutshell

Expectations of customers towards CSR communication	Be honest Be accurate Be transparent Be integrated Be engaging
Roles of customers in the context of CSR communication	Constructive challengers Decision-makers
Issues of CSR communication to customers	Relevance Complexity Lead or be led Reputational risk
Key success factors for communicating CSR to customers	Substance first Value for money plus Consumer empowerment Holistic integrity

6 *Sustainable Consumption and the Social Responsibility of Marketers and Advertisers*

Marketing is one of the last domains of commercial enterprise to face up to issues of sustainable development. On both the environmental dimension of resource limits/pollution and the social dimension of wellbeing, marketing has significant impacts and is deeply implicated in the current challenges of unsustainable consumption and production. Yet at the same time, and I simplify, while marketing got us into this mess, it may be that marketing can get us out. We need to harness the creativity and the sophistication of marketing, and its methodologies, for human health and environmental sustainability.

Ed Mayo, Chief Executive, National Consumer Council, September 2005[1]

There is a lot of debate about greenwashing in the context of CSR communication, about the need to communicate substance only. Indeed, there are voices in this debate claiming that business should just act and let its actions speak for themselves. Many times the critics have a point, particularly when talking and communicating become the main objective. 'Perception is reality' is a frequently quoted *bon mot* – so let's focus on creating a positive perception of what we do out there. Sustainability and CSR are then located in the marketing or PR departments and are downgraded as topics on the communications agenda.

Three observations may be relevant in this context:

1. Slightly simplified communications, particularly brand advertising and sustainability, seem to be a contradiction in terms. Either you act sustainably, or you market, advertise and communicate. Or you act unsustainably, and you market, advertise and communicate well. This is because looking at some of the consumer-directed sustainability campaigns, one can gain the impression that sustainability and inspiring, high-quality, creative and witty advertising do not go together. You either have great, inspiring advertising, or you have sustainability-related messages.

---

1   Anthony Kleanthous and Jules Peck, *Let Them Eat Cake: Satisfying the New Consumer Appetite for Responsible Brands* (London: WWF-UK, 2006), http://assets.wwfcmsuat.rroom.net/assets/downloads/let_them_eat_cake_full.pdf (accessed 10 July 2013), p. 2. Ed Mayo is now Secretary-General of Co-operatives UK.

2. A large number of consumers (some studies suggest more than 50 per cent[2]) are CSR- or sustainability-minded and claim that social and environmental considerations influence their purchase decisions.
3. Sustainable products and brands are still niche in most markets (organic or 'bio' in Germany had a 3.3 per cent market share in 2010, according to a GfK/IRI survey[3]).

There is a discrepancy between what consumers say they want to do (purchase sustainable products) and their actual behaviour. If over 50 per cent of consumers actually had a preference for products with socially or environmentally friendly attributes, like organic, Fairtrade or generally sustainably sourced, these products would not be niche any more, but a mass-market phenomenon. What is the reason? Is it a supply issue, are there not sufficient sustainable products available in shops? Or is it a demand issue after all? Do consumers only claim that they have a preference for sustainably sourced, ethically traded, environmentally friendly products, whereas in fact they don't really care when it comes down to making the actual purchase? If that is the case, there is nothing retailers and brand owners or consumer goods manufacturers can do.

If we take a look at what the barriers to ethical consumption are, then, not surprisingly, price comes out on top. However, it is accompanied by a lack of knowledge and a lack of trust in the marketing claims of sustainable products. Lack of availability of such products is only in third place.[4] From this we learn two things:

1. Consumers are generally not prepared to pay a (significantly) higher price for sustainably produced product. They want to have their cake and eat it too. If all else is equal, with the quality and delivery of the product as well as price, then sustainability attributes may lead to a preference.
2. Consumers do not feel sufficiently well informed about those sustainability attributes, and they do not trust manufacturers or retailers enough to believe that the sustainable products they offer are actually ethically produced or traded.

In other words, there are two key challenges to marketers of sustainable products and brands: the first is that they need to inform consumers better about sustainability and the sustainable quality of their products because consumers simply do not feel they have the knowledge required. While this first challenge is the rational one, the second challenge is

---

2   Figures vary between research programs and countries. In Germany in 2009, in the middle of the financial crisis, 55% of consumers (out of a representative sample of 6,600) could be classed as sustainability-minded, while 45% were sceptics and rejected the notion of sustainability as a driver of their purchase decisions. The US-based Natural Marketing Institute, which runs the LOHAS (Lifestyles of Health and Sustainability) Global Consumer Trends database covering 10 major markets, found in 2010 that between 10% (Japan) and 18% (Brazil) could be categorized as LOHAS (very concerned with sustainability), while between 69% (US) and 78% (Germany and Japan) were 'sustainable mainstream', and only between 8% (Germany) and 17% (US) very completely unconcerned.

3   GfK-Compact, GfK Panel Services, Consumer Scan Haushaltspanel (sample 20,000/30,000 households), www.gfk-compact.de/files/1110_bio_downloadcharts_101012_final.pdf (accessed 10 June 2013).

4   brands & values, *Ethical Brand Monitor 2009* (Bremen: brands & values, 2009); IGD, *Ethical Shopping in Europe* (Radlett, Herts.: IGD, 2008). Even though these results have a geographical bias and the IGD study shows that there are differences between markets in terms of attitudes to sustainable consumption, we feel these results may be valid for other markets outside Europe as well. While things may have changed since 2009, more recent research shows that consumers increasingly take into account the sustainability qualities of brands when making purchase decisions.

emotional. Consumers generally distrust information about sustainable attributes: 'I do not believe that these products are actually ethically (that is, socially and environmentally responsibly) produced'. They are suspicious, which is not good news for the brands in question. Cases of greenwashing which have been exposed most likely account for some of this low level of trust. The conclusion is that there are both risks and opportunities involved, but most certainly, marketers have a big job on their hands when it comes to sustainable consumption.

WWF-UK initiated the discussion about the social responsibility of marketers and advertisers with its publication *Let Them Eat Cake: Satisfying the New Consumer Appetite for Responsible Brands*,[5] which was based on very solid and substantial research among marketers and advertisers. This report convincingly argued the case for a need to move towards sustainable consumption from a resource point of view, and also exposed the 'six myths of sustainable marketing':

- **Myth 1** – 'The objective of business is to encourage sustainable consumption.' Wrong! Brand managers and marketers are offered incentives to increase sales and market share, not human well-being; new incentives are therefore required.
- **Myth 2** – 'Marketing cannot drive sustainable consumption.' Wrong! Marketing and brand communications can make a major contribution to meeting the biggest challenges of our age.
- **Myth 3** – 'Mainstream consumers do not value responsible brands.' Wrong! There are huge market opportunities waiting for canny marketers who tune in to deep shifts in societal values.
- **Myth 4** – 'Marketing professionals do not understand sustainability.' Wrong! Many marketers are just waiting for 'permission' and an appropriate framework in which to engage with sustainability issues, even if they aren't familiar with the language and concepts of corporate responsibility.
- **Myth 5** – 'Media owners should enforce a strict separation between editorial and advertising departments.' Wrong! If anything, editorial and advertising policies need to be more closely aligned.
- **Myth 6** – 'Agencies are barristers, not beacons of consumption.' Wrong! There is unmet latent commercial potential for more responsible brands; helping clients to spot and exploit that potential is part of the essential function of agencies.

---

5   http://assets.wwfcmsuat.rroom.net/assets/downloads/let_them_eat_cake_full.pdf (accessed 10 July 2013).

Best Practice Case: Puma's Clever Little Bag

Figure 6.1   The Clever Little Bag, designed by Yves Béhar, uses 65 per cent less cardboard than a standard shoebox and is a lot more useful
Source: Reproduced courtesy of Puma SE.

The 'Clever Little World' now being put together by Puma shows how successful the combination of creativity and sustainability can be.

Back in 2008, Puma decided to conduct an audit and lifecycle assessment which resulted in 're-engineering the box' – developing a substitute for the easily identifiable Puma reddish-orange shoebox. This case shows that marketers and advertisers can indeed encourage sustainable consumption, balancing the consumer's need for information with the requisite trust in the brand. The usual assumption is that it's a question of sustainability versus brand advertising and marketing. Why not do it together? Inspiration doesn't always have to conflict with worthiness – you can be both at the same time! Not only that, there is an unmet commercial potential in mainstreaming sustainability.

Puma's goal was to reduce water, energy, paper and fuel consumption while at the same time reducing waste and CO_2 emissions. To do this, it not only involved designers, but warehouse people, and tested what worked and what didn't in the production and supply chain. That meant that it 'lost' nearly two years when the preferred design proved unworkable, but by 2010 the Clever Little Bag emerged, along with Puma's five-year environmental and sustainability plan, and the bag was launched at London's Design Museum in the same year. More products have been developed, including the Clever Little Hanger and EcoCradle packaging, leading Puma to envisage a 'Clever Little World'. The following year, Puma won a design award, and in 2012 it was already at work on 'Bag 2.0', to be launched at the end the year.

In the words of Puma's Director of Marketing Antonio Bertone: 'Sustainability is part of the brand atmosphere.'

For the full Best Practice Case 13, see Chapter 15, page 241.

In their survey of UK advertising and marketing professionals, the authors of *Let Them Eat Cake*, Anthony Kleanthous and Jules Peck, prove that marketers feel they have a responsibility as well as the ability to positively influence consumer behaviour towards sustainability.

In late 2010, the sustainability consultancy brands & values along with marketing weeklies *Werben & Verkaufen* (Germany) and *HORIZONT* (Austria) ran a similar survey in Germany and Austria, polling nearly 1,000 marketing and advertising professionals (readers of the online versions of the two publications) on whether and how they felt responsible for sustainable consumption. The survey results were published in both *Werben & Verkaufen* and *HORIZONT*. In Germany, the survey results were among the top 10 downloads from *Werben & Verkaufen*'s portal in 2011, proving the high level of interest in the subject. The survey was repeated in both 2011 and 2012 in Germany, and ran in Austria in 2011.

The majority of respondents (66% in 2010, 72% in both 2011 and 2012) agreed that sustainability has a high or very high importance for brands, marketing and communication; nearly all felt that its importance will increase over the next few years (95% in 2010, 91% in 2011 and 93% in 2012). Even more importantly, they agreed that they had a responsibility in the context of developing sustainable consumption. Fifty per cent of the respondents considered this responsibility high or very high (59% in 2010, 54% in 2011).

Asked whether they felt they were doing a good job ('How attractive would you consider product-related sustainability communication?'), over half (53%) considered sustainability-related communication to be unattractive. Forty three per cent of respondents from the client side and 40% from the agency side stated in 2011 that they were currently working on sustainability-related communication.

What do marketing people consider to be the main barriers to sustainable consumption? Interestingly enough, they do not hide behind the price barrier. Seventy nine per cent (versus 64% in 2011) believe the main barrier is lack of information; just 70% (up from 60% in 2011) consider lack of trust in the actual ethical quality of products to be barrier number two. The proportion of respondents who believe price is a major barrier sharply increased to 59% (it was 45% in 2011 and 50% in 2010). In other words, the job of communication is to remove the two main barriers. Actually, the price barrier could also be a communication issue in disguise: when consumers say 'too expensive', they actually mean 'not sufficient value for my money'. But if sustainably-produced products deliver at least the same basic value as their 'unsustainable' equivalent plus sustainability in the way they are made and brought to the consumer, they are actually providing a higher value to those consumers to whom sustainability is relevant (that is, at least 50% of them). However, the fact that they are not buying the products indicates that they are not aware of that added value. Hence, it is the job of marketing and advertising to tell them about it.

This is why marketing people are convinced that sustainability-related communication needs to start at product level. It is not primarily about brand image or promotion, but about the product's attributes and about the way it is made.

What is in it for the product or brand? Marketers believe that sustainability can primarily have a positive impact on brand trust, the perception of how innovative it is and its emotional proximity.

The bottom line is that while sustainable consumption is not the exclusive responsibility of marketers and advertisers, they do share this responsibility. The good news is that they accept it and are aware of it; the bad news is that there is still a lot to do before sustainable consumption moves mainstream. What exactly is the job at hand? It is to leverage and to unleash the power of marketing full-force, taking the bull by the horns, pulling out the stops, just as with the products or brands we believe in. Sustainable marketing and advertising needs to become state-of-the-art marketing; it needs to become the pinnacle of creative advertising and communication.

We will illustrate this with a parable. In 1971, McDonald's launched its restaurant, its products and its brand into the German market. By 2011 it was the largest and most successful food service business in Germany, with over 1,400 outlets and a €3.2 billion turnover. This incredible success illustrates the power of marketing. Had McDonald's made product test results the basis for its market entry, it would most likely never have gone into the German market. The hamburger is everything German taste buds do not like: white, soft buns instead of crusty and chewy German bread rolls, combined with slim, rather bland burger meat that could never compete with the chunky, well-seasoned *Frikadellen* you can buy at every street corner. Nor did McDonald's invent fast food in Germany – there were *Bratwurst* outlets all over the place. Yet it created restaurants that people flocked to, and a brand that despite all the negative publicity about the unhealthiness of American fast food became both loved and a legendary success, not least through witty, tongue-in-cheek advertising. If it is possible to sell products that consumers neither need nor particularly want with the power of brilliant marketing and advertising, why should it not be possible to 'sell' sustainability and sustainable products to mainstream consumers?

This is the challenge to marketers and advertisers if they take their responsibility seriously. We need to market sustainable products and services with at least as much conviction, passion, zest and creativity as McDonald's marketed its seemingly unattractive offering, not just in Germany, but in nearly every country and culture across the globe. The power of marketing needs to be unleashed in the sustainability arena, and that implies that product- and brand-related CSR and sustainability communication need to be emotionally appealing, attractive and not just informative. True, information is required, research has pointed that out quite clearly. But information alone does not inspire and motivate consumers. Information alone leads us down the wrong track. Marketing and advertising, along with traditional and social media, need to inform people about how unsustainable our lifestyles are and talk about more sustainable alternatives. But more importantly, they need to make sustainability 'sexy', desirable, cool. This is the role of sustainable brands, because brands have this power. And if their sustainability is substantial, they are credible and will be trustworthy as well as loved.

Two examples showcase what can be done. Swiss retailer Coop, regarded as a global leader in sustainable retailing, shows that sustainable product brands drive business, create differentiation and build the reputation of the retail and corporate brand. The Coop case also shows how a corporate campaign can drive awareness of sustainability if the brand enjoys high trust and credibility. Leisure and sportswear brand Puma, as mentioned earlier in this chapter, provides a great example for how sustainability can be a driver of innovation and design. Its 'Clever Little Bag' illustrates how resource efficiency can be cool and attractive, because the clever solution to saving a lot of packaging material actually provides an added functional benefit to the consumer.

Best Practice Case: Coop Switzerland Sustainability Brand Communications

Figure 6.2   **'For all who come after us' – sustainability is the message of Coop Switzerland's own brand, oecoplan**

Source: Reproduced courtesy of Coop Switzerland.

As a retail chain with a magazine read by 60 per cent of Swiss households, Coop Switzerland enjoyed brand recognition and had for many years been developing its own-label products, known as 'competence brands', with an emphasis on sustainability. However, Coop wanted the retail or umbrella brand itself to reflect this investment, and it needed to reach young people who didn't necessarily read the Coop magazine, *Coopzeitung*. Coop chose this target group because it believes that the youth of today are the ones who will be dealing with the impact of the older generation's misuse of the Earth's natural resources. So the focus was on general awareness about environmental issues rather than what the company was doing. Coop thought this was the right approach as it felt the competence brands were already serving that purpose.

The company had launched its own-brand sustainable cleaning products range as far back as 1989, followed by both food and organic cotton in 1993. By 2007, it was offering sustainably produced meat and eggs. So its youth-focused communication campaign from 2009 onwards involving Stress, a Swiss rapper, built on very solid foundations. This relied on both TV and online advertising, in addition to print ads in the *Coopzeitung* as well as in other mainstream media. There were opportunities for interaction through a schools competition, and teachers found the project very useful. Coop spokesman Dr Thomas Schwetje observes that this sort of approach is helpful, mentioning the distribution of wildflower seeds in a previous campaign, where those planting the wildflowers and sending pictures of them in once they'd grown were able to enter a competition.

After the first adverts with Stress the rapper in 2009, another one was released in 2010, which gained excellent sales for the CD and a Swiss Music Award for the rap artist. Coop Switzerland also ensured that its employees were able to act as ambassadors, introducing various training programmes, and at one stage even hosted a conference for 1,800 staff. Coop Switzerland was not only perceived as the market leader in sustainability following this campaign, whereas it is normally head-to-head with its main competitor, it was named the world's most sustainable retailer in 2011.

For the full Best Practice Case 12, see Chapter 15, page 235.

Of course, there are more great examples of mainstreaming sustainability in an attractive way, some of which are featured elsewhere in this book, such as Cadbury's Dairy Milk moving to Fairtrade, Marks & Spencer's 'Look behind the label' and Plan A or Unilever's Lifebuoy. Overall, however, it seems as if retailers are the ones leading the pack when it comes to making sustainability mainstream, not the big brands. The interview below with Werner Lampert, whose brainchild, Ja! Natürlich, is retailer Billa's[6] highly successful eco-brand in Austria, may help shed some light on the reasons for this development. Lampert

---

6   A major German retailer belonging to German retailer REWE-Group.

is also behind discounter Hofer's[7] innovative 'Zurück zum Ursprung' ('back to the origin') organic brand. However, as Dr Thomas Schwetje, Head of Marketing at Coop Switzerland puts it, while advertisers and marketers have a social responsibility, it is not solely the responsibility of business to create awareness of sustainability and the challenges that lie ahead: 'To create this awareness is primarily the responsibility of governments and of media.' And the prerequisite for effectively accepting that ethical responsibility to drive sustainable consumption for businesses is authenticity: 'Only ethically sound companies should actively communicate in the sustainability area. Others will be exposed by both the traditional media and social media.'

Interview with Werner Lampert, Prüf Nach!

COULD YOU TELL US HOW ONE OF AUSTRIA'S MOST PROMINENT RETAIL AND SUSTAINABLE PRODUCT BRANDS, 'ZURÜCK ZUM URSPRUNG', CAME ABOUT?

The idea came up around 2006/2007, the Year of the Mountain Farmer. The mountain farmer produces a quality that no other farmer can achieve today. We have made this quality the centrepiece, and thereby the work of the mountain farmer and his products have become the backbone of our project. That way, when we talk about sustainability we talk about a new quality dimension. There are things in life you cannot buy, like love, attention, faithfulness, friendship. What the mountain farmer provides when he supplies his milk cannot be weighed up with money. When you see the mountain farmers working at 1,400 metres altitude, how the whole family collaborates, you think of biodiversity. Reflecting on mountain farmers has taught me that biodiversity is not only a moral concept, but that organic bio-products and biodiversity are dependent on each other. What that means is that when we think of dairy products and meat, only if the gene pool is kept wide, only if there is a diversity of herbs, different types of grass and animals of all kinds will there be this exceptional product quality.

In 2008, we brought the concept of craftsmanship into the project. We tried to integrate the quality of the traditional craftsman, his experience, knowledge and heritage.

In 2009, we added CO_2 labelling, which is the first pillar of our sustainability labelling. This is a total success story. It was not our intention to get to this point. When I ran my first project for a retailer in 1994,[8] it was something that was attractive to people. Every day we received letters full of praise and excitement from schools, from young people, mothers. But linking 'Zurück zum Ursprung' with CO_2, with something that young people today are really interested in, has made the product sexy and attractive. As I said, that was not our intention, it just happened.

COULD YOU EXPLAIN TO US THE 'ZURÜCK ZUM URSPRUNG' CONCEPT IN MORE DETAIL?

The key element is the regional aspect. Today, people say, 'This is milk from around here' – and it is appreciated. Milk is a regional product. But if you then see that animal feed is

---

7   Owned by Aldi, a major German discounter.

8   Ja! Natürlich is the organic brand of the supermarket Billa, an Austrian subsidiary of REWE-Group.

brought here from all over the world to feed the cows and they then talk of 'regional brands' it makes you feel nauseous. Ours is a holistic regional concept. That means that animal feed and everything that is connected with the product is sourced from the region. And that means that the value-creation remains in the region. Because of that and the prices we pay, people do not leave the region, the infrastructure can be kept intact.

The second pillar of the concept is transparency. It occurred to me that someone who buys a car knows more about the car and where it comes from than consumers who buy food products. We talk a little bit about transparency, but most of it is smokescreens. With any 'Zurück zum Ursprung' product (there are over 220 now), the consumer can learn everything about the production process through the batch number on the pack that he can enter online on our website,[9] or scan it with an app on his smartphone. Also, we declare any and all additives, and we only use those that are classed as organic. In terms of cattle feed, we have completely given up on using soy products, improving quality and our CO_2 footprint at the same time, and quality is another important key element for us.

HOW DO YOU COMMUNICATE 'ZURÜCK ZUM URSPRUNG' TO CONSUMERS?

We start at the point of sale and in Hofer's leaflets. The website plays a central role. We run advertising campaigns on TV and outdoors, and we do print PR. For two years we have had a very fruitful collaboration with Greenpeace. Because we focus on the benefit to consumers, we were not affected by the financial crisis. While ordinary organic products really lost out, the opposite happened to us: we registered massive growth. I firmly believe that many people only go to Hofer[10] because of 'Zurück zum Ursprung'.

WHAT IS YOUR ROLE FROM HOFER'S PERSPECTIVE? ARE YOU LIKE ANY OTHER SUPPLIER?

We are not suppliers to Hofer. What we provide are all services related to the brand: product development, quality management and communication. Hofer buys products from farmers or producers when we have signed them off quality-wise. The farmers or producers have licence agreements with us, and when we provide our sign-off they can supply to Hofer. We work extremely closely with Hofer; we are in touch on a day-to-day basis.

YOU AGREE FIXED SUPPLY CONTRACTS WITH THE FARMERS IN WHICH YOU DETERMINE PRICES AND VOLUMES. DOES THIS REDUCE THE PRICE PRESSURE FROM THE HOFER PURCHASERS?

I do not know how other purchasers work, but in our case, quality requirements are factored into the pricing decision. Quite clearly there are price points which we know we must not exceed, experience tells us that, because consumers will not buy at that price.

---

9   www.zurueckzumursprung.at.

10   Hofer is the number one discounter in Austria, owned by Aldi.

DOES HOFER CARRY PRODUCTS THAT ARE DIRECT ALTERNATIVES TO THE 'ZURÜCK ZUM URSPRUNG' RANGE?

There are conventional, non-organic alternatives. And these products are certainly cheaper, about 30 per cent. However, if the price difference gets too big, it influences purchasing decisions. Hofer's USP [unique selling proposition] is the perfect value equation. And our products are more reasonable than other organic products, despite our standards, which are outperforming the European Union regulation EEC no. 2092/91.

WHAT ARE THE RESULTS OF 'ZURÜCK ZUM URSPRUNG'?

On a societal level, our project created a lot of buzz and debate. People felt encouraged because they saw that it is possible to do things differently. And we found that there was a consumer potential that is responsive to this holistic, consistent and radical approach. Bio, conventional organic, products on the other hand have become pure marketing. They do not communicate content any more, but only marketing gags.

The regions benefited economically. Our mountain farmer approach seemed pretty odd. We were working with people who did not have much hope or who felt they had no prospects. That changed quickly. The self-confidence and the knowledge that there is a demand for products of an exceptional quality and that people are prepared to pay for that quality brought about a paradigm shift.

For us, it is an economic success. We do not know whether it is an economic success for Hofer as they do not share any figures. Internally, however, we know that the project has had an enormous effect. The Hofer people are proud to have such an interesting project, to get so much positive attention. This is something they can talk about privately, with their friends and family. And if you are proud, that motivates you. And they have made this change from a discounter you used to go to once a week to a retailer where you can meet all your daily needs. That has brought them increased footfall, I am convinced.

WHAT WOULD YOU SAY ARE YOUR KEY LESSONS FROM THE 'ZURÜCK ZUM URSPRUNG' PROJECT?

The brand has an enormous amount of content, that is a strength. But there is danger when you have so much to talk about and we fell into that trap initially, of trying to pack too much into our communication. You need clear and simple messages that people understand and can relate to. We learned that even when things are complex and multifaceted, the key is to simplify and to reduce.

Traceability is not there as a gimmick. It only makes sense if it is combined with clear guidelines. Traceability plus verifiable guidelines is the way to go. The two principles of traceability are (a) fairness towards farmers and primary producers and (b) fairness towards the consumer: if you buy something, you can see where it comes from, who has made it and under what conditions it was made. If you see how consumers are treated, how they are conned, it is about time to introduce fairness towards the consumer into the sustainability concept. That is what we have tried to do.

HOW WILL 'ZURÜCK ZUM URSPRUNG' MOVE FORWARD?

Our main job is to work on quality, to continuously improve it. That is the most difficult challenge of all, to make quality the core topic. Thus, we are working on a sustainability standard for fairly produced products called 'Fairify'.

The concept of quality has been misused, taken advantage of over the past few years. I think that consumers' knowledge about quality is very fragile. We have products that are exceptionally good. We had a vision for this range, and it turned out great. And we have seen them grow and evolve every day, come rain, come shine. It is extremely encouraging if products turn out great in terms of quality. Then their success cannot be stopped.

7 *Communicating Sustainability – the Shareholder Perspective*

What we are looking for is a company that clearly understands what the risk factors are as they pertain to their particular business.
Robert Talbut, Royal London Asset Management

The concept of 'shareholder value' has reigned for three decades and is still prevalent. 'The business of business is business' thinking considered shareholders the only truly relevant stakeholders. While the stakeholder perspective has been a part of the centuries-old 'honourable merchant' mindset, there has certainly been a renaissance in the context of terms like 'CSR', 'corporate citizenship' and 'sustainability' gaining increasing prominence in boardroom conversations and business school curriculae. Sometimes it seems the opposite has happened in 'CSR circles': shareholders are not always considered when speaking of stakeholders, even though they remain the owners of businesses. Shareholders are investors who are expecting a return on their investments, whether they are individuals or large institutional investors who often are investing the savings and pension provisions of individuals. Obviously, the stakeholder group of shareholders includes cutthroat speculators and hard-core capitalists – the stereotypical enemy of campaigners and NGOs. However, the larger proportion of shareholders are themselves responsible corporate citizens and fulfil important societal roles. There has been much debate about the growing importance of government funds, like the Norwegian Government Pension Fund, which since 2011 has been ranked as the largest ethical government fund globally.

We have spoken to UNPRI, the United Nations-backed Principles for Responsible Investment Initiative, an international network to which institutional investors can sign up in a similar fashion to the UN Global Compact, agreeing to the six Principles for Responsible Investment,[1] and also to institutional investors,[2] including banks, investment funds and insurers, and experts on sustainable investment, like the providers of the Dow Jones Sustainability Index (DJSI), and Sustainability Asset Management (SAM).

---

1   '(1) We will incorporate ESG (Environmental, Social and Governance) issues into investment analysis and decision-making processes. (2) We will be active owners and incorporate ESG issues into our ownership policies and practices. (3) We will seek appropriate disclosure on ESG issues by the entities in which we invest. (4) We will promote acceptance and implementation of the Principles within the investment industry. (5) We will work together to enhance our effectiveness in implementing the Principles. (6) We will each report on our activities and progress towards implementing the Principles'; UNPRI, 'The Six Principles', www.unpri.org/about-pri/the-six-principles/ (accessed 10 June 2013).

2   A request for an interview with the Norwegian Government Pension Fund was unfortunately declined, which we regret as we would view this fund's sustainable investment policies as for the most part exemplary.

What do you associate with CSR and CSR communication?

CSR OR SUSTAINABILITY MUST NOT BE AN ADD-ON

'The key term is "integration" versus add-on and "just reporting". The core business "plus" philanthropy is old-school CSR. What I like is the definition of the World Economic Forum,' says Professor Neil Eccles, responsible investment expert and head of the Institute for Corporate Citizenship at the University of South Africa, referring to the declaration that 'Corporate Citizenship has to be part of a company's business model.'[3] In his words, it is 'the responsibility that companies have to make contributions to the community in which they operate through their core business'. Nancy Baxter of US bank Wells Fargo (now with Profitable Philanthropy LLC) sees integrated CSR as a win–win approach: 'We look at [CSR] as an investment process within our communities, those in which we work and where our employees live. Investing in positive ways for positive outcomes is a smart business practice in terms of the long term sustainability of our businesses and our communities.'

Elliot Frankal, former Communications Director of UNPRI and now Director of ESG Communications, observes CSR communication happening on two levels:

> On one hand it is about outputs such as sustainability or CSR reports, websites, community or environmental initiatives and – still – a lot of philanthropy. On the other hand it should be a central driver of corporate strategy. A company should make sustainability the driver of its business and not just an add-on which it then tries to communicate loudly.

Swiss-based Sustainable Asset Management recognizes an evolution in CSR communications. While it started off as being primarily marketing and PR, CSR is increasingly integrated into corporate strategy. Nevertheless, from the perspective of the Dow Jones Sustainability Index, communication still plays a key role. DJSI membership is promoted widely, and there are even innovative consumer-oriented campaigns like that of KLM/AirFrance, which want to print the DJSI logo on all their boarding passes. Neil Eccles is less positive about CSR communication:

> I associate PR, greenwashing and spin with it – at least in the South African context. CSR communication is part of corporates' reputation management. I still have to come across sustainability communication that moves away from just spin. While you get those who are better and those who are worse, the main focus continues to be to put a company in a good light for shareholders and other stakeholders.

He tells his students to look for indications of good news and bad news, because there will always be tradeoffs, and those tradeoffs should be made transparent. He mentions Nike as a positive example of a company that has communicated difficulties, things that went wrong, and then shown how they have improved on it.

---

3   'Corporate Citizenship has to be part of a company's business model. An enterprise must balance the expectations of its wide range of stakeholders'; 'Global Corporate Citizenship', World Economic Forum, www.weforum.org/issues/corporate-global-citizenship (accessed 10 June 2013).

In the financial community, the dominating term is not 'CSR', 'CR' or 'sustainability', but 'ESG' (environmental, social and governance), which is why Jeremy Kent of Allianz SE-owned investors Allianz Global Investors UK[4] defines CSR communication as 'efforts made by a company to inform relevant stakeholders of activities, strategy and performance on material ESG-related items. This communication can come via annual reports, press releases or stakeholder meetings.'

What are the expectations of shareholders regarding CSR communication of companies?

MATERIALITY – IMPACT – HONESTY – TRANSPARENCY

Materiality

'When an investor picks up a report, he wants to know what is in there that is material, which means financially viable, and how does a company handle ESG issues,' according to Elliot Frankal. Neil Eccles underlines this point by saying that 'investors want to see companies supply the financial implications of sustainable development issues, in a way that shareholders can interpret.' Jeremy Kent calls it relevance, and advises companies to try to focus on relevant information rather than 'dumping every bit of information into a several hundred-page report'. As Neil Eccles puts it: 'It needs to be important, and not what the company is good at.'

Impact

'Demonstration of impact is my key expectation,' argues Neil Eccles. 'What has the company actually done to meet the challenges? It is demonstration of impact versus bluff.' Nancy Baxter agrees – she expects communication around what the company is doing, how it can improve: 'It implies an ability to make suggestions, to identify opportunities, to continue to enhance and to implement those.'

Honesty

Honesty means communicating both the good and the bad, in Neil Eccles' view. Or as Elliot Frankal puts it: 'Honesty is great! If you have not managed to reduce your carbon emissions yet, say it and talk about how you are going to change it.'

Transparency

From the ratings perspective, transparency is key. 'If companies have a crisis, they are not necessarily excluded from the index, but we look closely at how transparent they are in dealing with it. If we feel they are covering something up, that may be critical,'

---

4   Part of Allianz Global Investors, a subsidiary of Allianz SE, the German insurer Allianz Global Investors was founded as Rosenberg Capital Management in 1970.

says Claudia Wais, Sustainability Asset Management (SAM).[5] Jeremy Kent concurs, and emphasizes that data and information should be transparent in source, nature and scope. Furthermore, they need to be measured in a consistent manner and reported annually.

What is the role of shareholders in the context of CSR communication or companies?

CHALLENGE COMPANIES TO BRING SUSTAINABILITY CENTRE-STAGE

Challengers for materiality

The key role of shareholders is to challenge companies that communicate regarding the materiality and honesty of their communication. 'They should expect communications to be honest and real. They should be demanding the same quality in CSR reporting as in their financial reporting – it should be fact-based, rigid and less flowery than it often is,' argues Neil Eccles, and adds: 'Right now, sustainability reporting is not aimed at shareholders.' Jeremy Kent agrees, and points out:

> If shareholders are acting as trustees to the ultimate shareholder, then CSR communication should be treated as other financial and operational information disseminated by the company is. That means that shareholders should incorporate this information into the framework of their analysis of a company in order to determine if the investment is suitable for the beneficiary.

Challengers for real sustainability

However, Elliot Frankal feels that the role of shareholders in CSR communication has been limited so far, which he sees as a perception problem among investors themselves:

> They have a core role in communicating to most companies' boards that sustainability should be central to their business plan. Why? Because sustainability is actually a proxy for good management, implying that the company is risk-conscious. Take, for example, climate change or how a company manages sustainability in the supply chain. If there are issues in those areas, the shareholders' role is to point that out to the company. One lesson from the financial crisis is that society is looking for shareholders to be good stewards of the companies they invest in. Certain investors, like pension funds, which are long-term investors, have a clear interest in the long-term risk management of their investments because they know there is a real business case for sticking with an investment. It is very expensive to get out of an investment, so the rationale is rather to stay in and engage. An example is the large public pension fund NYSTRS,[6] which had a large investment in Cracker Barrel, a restaurant chain, which was taken to court because of discrimination against homosexuals. NYSTRS stuck with them through a ten-year court case and worked with them on implementing lessons learned from the issue.

---

5   Claudia Wais was Regional Director at SAM during the time of the interview and until July 2011. Since August 2011 she has been Senior Product Specialist at Zürcher Kantonalbank.

6   New York State Teachers' Retirement System, the second largest retirement fund in the state of New York, among the top 10 US pension funds.

What are the key issues from a business perspective in communicating CSR to Shareholders?

NOT MEETING INVESTORS' EXPECTATIONS

Expectations of materiality

The way Neil Eccles sees it, the issues are very closely related to expectations – often CSR communication, especially reporting, does not cover material issues, is not honest and transparent in terms of relaying both the good and the bad (risks!), and does not always include third-party assurance. Rather than merely reporting, Elliot Frankal recommends talking directly to investors about sustainability in the context of 'normal' investor relations: 'Sustainability is a really important part of the overall communications, and investors would anyway not base their investment decisions on a report.'

Continuously raising the bar

Another issue is the one that SAM's Claudia Wais points out – that what was impressive yesterday may be mandatory and boring today, as rating agencies like SAM continuously raise the bar. Only a best practice company can be a super sector leader in the DJSI[7] – and responsible investors want to invest in those benchmark companies, not in the laggards.

Best Practice Case: Novo Nordisk Integrated Reporting

novo nordisk
annual report 2011
Financial, social and
environmental performance

Figure 7.1   Novo Nordisk's award-winning 2011 Annual Report, integrating financial, social and environmental reporting
Source: Reproduced courtesy of Novo Nordisk A/S.

---

7   SAM appoints benchmark companies (where they exist) in all major industries and calls them 'super sector leaders'.

At Novo Nordisk, sustainability is not seen as something separate, it is 'how we do business', according to Susanne Stormer, VP for Corporate Sustainability. The Danish company is the global leader in diabetes care. It doesn't make a distinction between shareholders and stakeholder interests either.

In 1994, it started with an environmental report; in 1999, this included a social dimension – the company's obligations to employees and to society – and by 2004, it published its first integrated report, fully incorporating the triple bottom line approach into its financial reporting.

Novo Nordisk's mission, 'Defeat Diabetes', is enacted through the brand message 'Changing Diabetes', which manifests itself in three goals: to develop products promoting better health care for those with the disease, to encourage early diagnosis, and finally, to prevent diabetes through communicating about healthier lifestyles and making people aware of the risks. This may seem counter-intuitive for a company selling diabetes-related products, however Novo Nordisk points to China as an example. The company first became involved there in educating doctors and helping to create awareness as well as an infrastructure, working with the Chinese Ministry of Health. Only after this did Novo Nordisk start to promote its products, and it now has a 70 per cent share of the Chinese insulin market.

The purpose of its integrated reporting is to 'enhance financial valuation and explore the role between financial and non-financial performance'. Novo Nordisk believes that it is vital to improve the metrics used to measure non-financial performance as well as to 'speak the language of the CFO', to focus on growth, return on investment, risk management and the quality of company managers. The company believes that integrated reporting has given clarity to help shareholders make better management and business decisions through better measurement and better information. Accountability and transparency are vital at all stages, which in Novo Nordisk's view leads to increased market trust, and while it cannot 'unambiguously' say this has led to the increased earnings it has demonstrated, it does believe that the benefits in terms of reputation, employee engagement and level of innovation have been contributing factors.

Not only was Novo Nordisk top of the corporate Knights Global 100 Leaders in Sustainability in 2012, its 2010 annual report was lauded as the best integrated report at the Corporate Responsibility Reporting Awards in the same year.

For the full Best Practice Case 14, see Chapter 16, page 249.

Can you share any best practice examples of CSR communication?

Table 7.1 shows the brands and programmes that were mentioned in the interviews.

Table 7.1   Brands and programmes referenced in the interviews

Brand, company, programme	No. of mentions
Vodafone, CSR strategy, stakeholder engagement	1
Novo Nordisk	1
SASOL (petrochemicals, South Africa), sustainability report, stakeholder engagement	1
BMW	1
Roche	1
PepsiCo	1
DSM	1

Jeremy Kent explains:

> *Vodafone has done a quality job in developing their CSR strategy, initially seeking feedback from shareholders and stakeholders to develop a CSR approach that is relevant to the business and delivers what stakeholders are interested in. The next phase was driving performance improvement on internal metrics used to track CSR or sustainability. And most recently, the company has transitioned to leveraging the sustainability strategy to drive business opportunity.*

Elliot Frankal's favourite is Novo Nordisk:

> *Their core mission explains how sustainability promotes their business. They are the largest manufacturer in the world of insulin, but their core mission is to eradicate diabetes. Sounds crazy, but by having that as their main mission, they get the best scientists, have very good staff retention rates and tend to work very well with governments and civil society organizations. Their market share is very high – sustainability powers their business.*

Neil Eccles shares a rather unlikely South African example:

> *SASOL, a South African petrochemicals company has all sorts of problems, was fined in the EU for price fixing. But they present the bad news story, too, they balance the good and the bad. Therefore, they are really best practice. Their sustainability report is balanced, they see the challenges, they provide targets. They are very brave, and put their CEO on a critical NGO platform – that is the kind of bravery I would like to see more of.*

For SAM, its supersector leaders exemplify best practice in a given industry. For example, in 2011/12 these were BMW in Automobiles & Parts, PepsiCo in Food & Beverage and DSM in Chemicals. Finally, Nancy Baxter defines best practice companies very concretely as those that have a:

continuously updated, easily identifiable spot on their home page so you can click through and find greater detail, for example to see national statistics, break it down regionally and bring it down to the local level, as many CSR activities are very local and that is where it matters. This detail is really important, as well as aggregated data. As a shareholder, I would hope I would be able to walk into any company office or location and experience the ethos of the company. I want to hear and see the talk walked at all levels of an organization.

How do you define 'greenwashing'? Examples?

COMMUNICATING WITHOUT COMMITMENT

Nancy Baxter visits companies Wells Fargo plans to invest in, and recommends that investors and shareholders need to be good observers, looking behind the communication and gaining a firsthand impression of what is going on in the organization. Greenwashing for her is 'a star showing up at the Oscars or another award ceremony with a rented Prius so they look like they are environmentally conscious'. Elliot Frankal names UK retailer Tesco as an example: 'They were selling renewable energy lightbulbs in the UK, and promoted them by giving away free Air Miles on the Tesco Club Card – which is a bit like giving away a free pack of Marlboro with a Nicorette pack.'

To Jeremy Kent, greenwashing is:

an attempt to create the appearance that ESG issues are an important feature in the strategy of the business when in fact these do not feature as a core focus for the business. This can manifest itself in several ways: a sustainability or CSR team that sits in isolation from the rest of the business (used as a marketing tool), hundred-page sustainability reports stuffed with case studies, but little in the way of data or strategy information.

Neil Eccles takes a similar view when he explains that it implies:

using reporting mechanisms to paint a picture of greenness, to paint a picture of being benign, socially positive, but without substance. A classic example to me is the UN Global Compact – possibly the accessory to greenwashing. No evidence of commitment is required, but the criteria for removal are very weak. The amount of kudos related to being a signatory is comparatively huge. One could call it 'bluewash'.

What do you consider to be the key success factors of effective CSR communication?'

INTEGRATION AND SUBSTANCE – INTERACTIVITY AND ENGAGEMENT – RIGOUR AND EXTERNAL PRESSURE

Integration and substance

'Making it the core of your business' is how Elliot Frankal of UNPRI puts it. 'And instead of having a CSR report, integrate it into the financial report. Show the actual impact you are having in an environmental and social as well as in an economic sense.' Substance means 'encapsulating the expectation that [sustainability] happens', adds Neil Eccles. Furthermore, it implies taking a long-term perspective and working at it continuously and consistently – or in other words, sustainably, as Claudia Wais says, based on the conviction that in the long term sustainable companies outperform unsustainable ones.

Interactivity and engagement

While openness and honesty are 'base camp' and a mandatory requirement, a key success factor from the shareholders' perspective is that companies talk to them. Jeremy Kent explains:

> The Vodafone example is useful in describing this. A company should interact with stakeholders and internal parties in order to determine what it is that should be communicated. This information should be presented regularly and in a format that can be readily accessible. Also, strategy should be constantly evolving with input from shareholders (and other stakeholders) in order to give insight on the direction of the business.

Shareholders want to be involved in the sustainability element as much as in the financial aspects of the companies they own.

Rigour and external pressure

Neil Eccles emphasizes the point that there needs to be more impetus from the outside – primarily from governments, alongside activists and the media – to ensure that companies implement sustainability significantly:

> Trusted verification needs to be developed. Some of those tools are there, like AA1000 and the standards which exist. However, enforcing the application of those standards comprehensively is key. What are needed, therefore, are more externally imposed standards, just like in financial reporting, where the assurance and verification is a lot more robust than in the CSR or sustainability field. Sustainability reporting needs to become mandatory and it needs to be policed – expecting it to be voluntary is expecting too much.

From the perspective of companies that take sustainability very seriously and have integrated it into their core business, this simply means being a step ahead in terms of rigour. If reporting becomes mandatory, nothing will change for them. For those that are only starting out, the scenario of 'policed reporting' implies that there may be a good case for aiming to catch up with the best practice examples.

Interview with Robert Talbut, Royal London Asset Management

WHAT DO YOU ASSOCIATE WITH CSR COMMUNICATION?

CSR or ESG are non-financial risk factors, and I associate with CSR and CSR communication how companies monitor and manage those risks and communicate what they do. There are a range of sources from narrative to the annual report and actual meetings in which they relate to us how they perceive significant risks, which for us in turn may imply upsides or downsides with respect to our investments. We will then talk to other commentators, including NGOs and media, trying to understand the way in which management are safeguarding the company assets and managing them to provide an attractive return to us. The way in which they identify and manage those non-financial risks is an important signal to us about the quality of the management and the quality of the investment. There are different types of risk depending on where the company is located and on the industry. There are not necessarily the same risks for all companies, even in one industry, so we are looking for substantive risks as they relate to that particular company in that particular industry in that particular country.

WHAT ARE YOUR EXPECTATIONS REGARDING CSR COMMUNICATION OF COMPANIES?

Sounds like mum and apple pie. I want the best of all possible things in the best of all possible situations. What we are looking for is a company that clearly understands what the risk factors are as they pertain to their particular business, and we are interested in understanding what they are doing about those risks. Increasingly, what we want to see is that the company's attitude towards risk in general and their specific risks are reflected in the way in which their executives are rewarded.

WHAT IS THE ROLE OF SHAREHOLDERS IN THE CONTEXT OF CSR COMMUNICATION OF COMPANIES?

We have a few different roles. Part of our role is to ask the right questions. Another part is to evaluate the answers we receive and to voice an opinion. We start off expressing it privately, but if we do not believe we are getting traction with a particular company on an issue that we think is particularly important, we do reserve the right to make that concern known publicly.[8]

WHAT ARE THE ISSUES FROM A BUSINESS PERSPECTIVE IN COMMUNICATING CSR TO SHAREHOLDERS?

That is about convincing our investors that we are providing the appropriate degree of oversight to our clients' money. In managing a client's money, it is not only about the upside, but the downside risks. I believe that increasingly, clients will expect us or want us to do more to convince them that we are a good guardian of their assets.

CAN YOU SHARE ANY BEST PRACTICE EXAMPLES OF CSR COMMUNICATION?

Some of the best engagements that we actually have would be with companies in the extractive industries. The reason I say that is, yes – they get a bad press, but they themselves realize that these are important issues, in terms of their own reputation, and

---

8   'Robert Talbut, Head of the Association of British Insurers' investment committee said "companies would be wrong if they believe 'no' votes simply reflect poor communication, when in fact they reflect calls for fundamental reform"'; *Sunday Times*, 6 May 2012, Business Section, p. 1, in the context of shareholders revolting against executives' remuneration packages.

therefore they are prepared to spend more time and effort in engaging with us in trying to convince us they are aware of and managing those risks appropriately. Some of the companies exposed to these bigger risks are companies that do engage better on these topics than some others. Intuitively, people might not think Apple would have an issue with respect to CSR, but it is only when you start burrowing into the company and going back to the supply chain that the issues become apparent. These things can crop up in the most unusual places, and it is not a straightforward process.

WHAT DO YOU CONSIDER TO BE KEY SUCCESS FACTORS OF EFFECTIVE CSR COMMUNICATION FROM AN NGO PERSPECTIVE?

I think it is management taking responsibility on these issues so they are owned by the board and not delegated outside the board. The clearest thing to us is that we want to see the board take this responsibility, that its members properly understand the issues, and as I mentioned earlier, increasingly we want to see these types of things being a factor in remuneration.

Key Messages in a Nutshell

Table 7.2   Chapter 7 key messages in a nutshell

Expectations of shareholders towards CSR communication	Materiality Impact Honesty Transparency
Roles of shareholders in the context of CSR communication	Challengers for materiality Challengers for real sustainability
Issues of CSR communication to shareholders	Expectations of materiality Continuously raising the bar
Key success factors for communicating CSR to shareholders	Integration and substance Interactivity and engagement Rigour and external pressure

8 *Communicating Sustainability – the Media Perspective*

Do first, then communicate. I do not want statements of intent.
Volker Bormann, Financial Times Germany

Media people traditionally take a critical view of business and CSR or sustainability. The interviews with this stakeholder group confirm this. What was disappointing, though, was the lack of willingness of the (traditional) media even to talk to us. One cannot help but feel a little cynical about the fact that journalists, who normally seek interviews, are extremely reluctant to grant the same favour. The BBC, for instance, which we felt was potentially a true best practice example in terms of its annual report and the general CSR grapevine, gave us some very terse, monosyllabic one-line responses to our questionnaire. However, even these were only obtained after several years of email and telephone pursuit, including via the attention of one of the candidates for the new Director General – a disgrace if you consider that one of the authors has been paying licence fees to this honourable institution for almost 30 years. Others, like the Mirror Group, simply declined or did not even respond.

It is for this reason that we place more of an emphasis on social media and agencies that deal with the media – simply because they were a lot more generous and helpful in providing us with their views and insights. The book on the social responsibility of the media is still waiting to be written.

What do you associate with CSR and CSR communication?

COMMUNICATION DRIVES CSR

'I have always been worried that CSR is more marketing than conviction,' declares Volker Bormann of *Financial Times Germany* (FTD).[1] 'A lot of charity promotions and less responsibility, too much fun, too much focus on producing an effect rather than on action.' Janine Wood of Armadillo Consulting Group agrees: 'CSR should be part of the business model but many companies use CSR as a PR and marketing tool and do it because they want to look good. They do not do it for all the right reasons, for the desire to make a change for the better.' Former Shell Executive Vice President Communications

---

[1] Business daily *Financial Times Germany* was regrettably discontinued on 7 December 2012.

Björn Edlund, now Chairman of Edelman EMEA, associates the UN Global Compact and the triple bottom line concept with CSR. He remembers:

> When we started using the term, it became more sophisticated …. However, CSR is also something where the whole sustainability idea is in danger of becoming diluted, as there is a lot of activity in the field that is driven by consultants with a reputation management agenda as well as academics who make things too complicated.

For Greg Schneider of CSR social media platform 3BL Media, CSR communication is the 'belief and the requirement that companies need to pay attention to and work towards a triple bottom line'. Sustainability blogger Fabian Pattberg associates 'doing business responsibly' with CSR, and adds that 'every business has its responsibility in society and CSR is the management approach to act on this responsibility'.

Tim Samuels of UK media production company Tonic Productions feels that CSR communication tends to fall into one of two categories, 'the over-earnest bore-you-to-death, or the over-slick don't believe a word of it,' while the BBC's Alec McGivan associates it with honesty, transparency and relevance. Volker Bormann believes there is the dangerous temptation to make CSR a marketing tool:

> It is like cackling before you have laid an egg. With CSR communication I associate a lot of reporting, and sometimes I wonder whether creativity gets lost in this desire to report, this standardization of reporting. Huge quantities of paper, incredible amounts of energy that could have been invested better elsewhere. At least that is how I feel. I have never been able to really indulge with relish in a CSR report, they always begin so pompously.

'Historically, CSR has been driven through a communications perspective, and it is thus not intrinsically driven,' argues Fabian Pattberg. 'When you get more content that you can back up with facts and figures, that changes. Unfortunately, most CSR communications is still not fact-driven. Actually the trend is even negative. There was best practice before the financial crisis, now (2010) there is a trend to copycat.' Greg Schneider considers the voluntary nature of CSR communications, that they are not mandatory, to be key: 'Most important is disclosure and transparency.' Björn Edlund agrees, and feels that reporting what companies do is extremely important: 'However, if it becomes a different way of doing PR, it is wrong. CSR communication has to be about performance and behavior.'

What are the expectations of the media regarding CSR communication of companies?

ACTION PRECEDES TALKING – ABOVE ALL, TRANSPARENCY – BE YOURSELF – DO IT WELL, AND MAKE IT CONTEMPORARY

Action precedes talking

'Companies need to do their homework before communicating,' stresses Fabian Pattberg. Volker Bormann thinks along similar lines: 'Do first, then communicate. I do not want statements of intent.' 'First you have to be able to measure and report on your activities,' adds Björn Edlund.

Above all, transparency

If the action is there, the mantra is transparency. Or as Volker Bormann puts it: 'Open your mouth. You will see when there is a crisis whether this transparency has any value.' He cites the example of mail order giant Otto, which had problems in its supply chain but did not want a documentary report about it:

> Good corporate communications require talking openly about problems, too, and ideally before they arise. But this is so rare, because of the salesman reflex of only talking about opportunities, never about problems. This tendency to whitewash is a disease that afflicts business people. If I choose to talk about problems, I have a serious advantage because I can choose who I talk to and make sure that those people I choose to talk to actually understand what I want to relate to them. The likelihood that they will expose you is then very limited.

Be yourself

'Do not try to be something you are not,' warns Fabian Pattberg. Trying to please hurts companies' credibility, and the media usually see through it. The way CSR is communicated needs to resonate with the company culture and identity because credibility is key, often more important than the actual message. This is particularly important in the social media context: 'Being sincere is the most important aspect, plus a basic understanding of how social media works. You notice that a company is sincere if it is not pushing too much. Centrica is a positive example. They gained reputation due to their long-term stakeholder engagement approach.' Being yourself also implies knowing what subjects actually can or should be communicated, because some things should be taken for granted. 'There are things that are beyond communication,' argues Volker Bormann:

> Some things are so natural, so self-evident, that they are not worth talking about. Being decent to your staff – you can make a big story about it, but certainly not with the intention of covering up other problems. And to be true to yourself, what you communicate needs to be relevant to you and your business. That is what I very much dislike about certain charity initiatives, because they do not seem relevant.

Do it well, and make it contemporary

Doing it well and being contemporary implies doing it well technically, in terms of the framework, but also in terms of the media employed. When it comes to reporting, Björn Edlund expects companies of a certain size to adopt GRI (Global Reporting Initiative) guidelines, and explains why the way you communicate on sustainability has significant financial relevance:

> It shows you are taking a stakeholder approach. You signal that you decide on what depth of data you want to disclose, and as a big enough organization you may want to break it down by country. On top of quantitative reporting, you have to do qualitative reporting, 'What is my

negative impact in the world?', 'What is my role as a company?', the purpose of being in business and the need to find your CSR that matches your business. In the case of an oil company, you look at your environmental impact and the impact you have on local communities where you operate; your overall impact on the climate, as well as how you work with people who use your product. You aim to develop a CSR directive along your whole value chain, that is the ideal model. Once you have done that, you have to work with the tension between shareholders and other stakeholders. Today we have moved away from the Friedman paradigm that the business of business is business, and shareholders are now seen as 'another stakeholder group'. However, shareholders and other stakeholders are closely connected, because when critical stakeholders start acting against a big business, it soon becomes a customer issue, and after that a shareholder issue. When you talk to shareholders, you have to translate CSR aspects into risk. Let me give you an example from Shell to illustrate this, the Sakhalin project. Shell built a huge gas complex in a joint venture with Japanese companies and Gazprom. When this was being built in 2003/2004, there were protests from environmental groups that the projected pipeline would run through the breeding waters of the Pacific grey whale. In the end, an expert panel re-routed the pipeline from offshore to the island, which cost more than $300 million. When this was reported at a quarterly meeting, an investor commented that 'each whale must be worth 3 million'. The CFO gave him an excellent answer: 'It is about preserving rare species, not only in Sakhalin, but also in other places around the world, and if we drill further not taking the whales into account, we won't be able to operate at all.' The point is that you cannot look only at the additional cost of the pipeline in comparison to the whales which are still there, but you have to translate CSR language into financial language. It is a different way of looking at things, and the SRI [socially responsible investment] concerns are becoming more and more mainstream and there is a convergence between the concepts of financial performance and non-financial risk. Put differently, CSR or sustainability performance is understood by the financial community as taking a long-term perspective on financial performance.

The BBC's Alec McGivan expects CSR communication to be 'regular, accessible communication that is engaging and informative'. Tim Samuels of Tonic Productions agrees, and feels that to be engaging, companies need to raise the bar in terms of the way they apply creativity and imagination in their CSR communication:

If companies really are doing good stuff and not just paying lip-service then they need to up their game, as it is generally pretty dire at the moment. I expect companies to execute the same creative standards that they would be employing when communicating any other messages. They currently spend on written materials so I would hope that they embrace the contemporary communications world of social media, too.

'No engagement, no conversation,' is how Greg Schneider puts it. And this is where social media comes in:

More C-suite officers need to be representing their brands and beliefs and their CSR in social media. For instance, write a consistent blog, including video coverage of what you are doing internally. Make those stories available. Change the one-way communication to conversation. The danger is, however, always there that organizations will be inclined and tempted to restrict conversations, but that quickly leads you back to old-style one-way communication. Fear is without reason if there is nothing to hide! The benefit is that they find so much feedback in social media about their brand and their CSR. It is a leap of faith that CEOs and board members have to take if they want to engage.

What is the role of (social) media in the context of the CSR communication of companies?

REFEREE – CATALYST – COMMUNICATION CHANNEL

Referee

'The role of media is to provide balanced, impartial, truthful information in the public interest,' states Alec McGivan of the BBC. 'For media, it is vital to report honestly, to ask the right questions, and to ensure they are not abused as a marketing tool,' declares Volker Bormann of *Financial Times Germany*:

> *In the context of CSR, media should have been driving the debate to a greater extent than they have done. Journalists should give an account, they should report, and they should not act themselves. But by asking the right questions, you can inspire and stimulate a debate. Take the issue of financial regulation after the crisis. It is our job as media to breathe down the necks of politicians and financial players, reminding them of it! Or take BP and the Gulf disaster – it is so quickly forgotten, even though there has not been any improvement.*

Catalyst

Björn Edlund sees the media as a catalyst in the context of sustainability and CSR:

> *It is the same as everywhere else – the media should make important things interesting. A key role of the media is to drive sustainable consumption! They need to make CSR and sustainability issues interesting, exciting, to reflect them in discussions, getting everybody involved in this field, making these topics relevant to people who are consumers and make them ask themselves the question, 'How can I live a comfortable life without contributing to social or environmental problems?' Overall, the media's role is under-played. They did a great job leading up to Copenhagen.[2] Copenhagen was a failure, but it helped many more people understand about climate change. The role of the media is not to be a cheerleader. It is the job of companies to make stories so interesting that they make it to the front page. Very often, the way to engage the media is via a conflict or a complaint or looking at the glass being half empty. Companies that have experience with the media won't worry much about that!*

Tim Samuels makes a similar point:

> *The media generally see business as evil, which is unfair as there is a lot of good going on. Arguably, though, companies have not been good at communicating what they are doing well.*

---

2   'Copenhagen' refers to the 2009 United Nations Climate Change Conference that took place in Copenhagen on 7–18 December 2009.

The media needs access to these stories, and thus companies need to smarten up in terms of how they tell them.

Communication channel

The role of social media is more that of a communication channel than traditional media – in the other direction. 'Social media provides the opportunity to listen to stakeholders and facilitates engagement at different levels of commitment,' argues Greg Schneider:

While Twitter is low-commitment, LinkedIn, for instance represents a higher level of commitment. Obviously, no social media tool takes the place of sitting down and having a personal encounter. But compared to traditional media, social media allows brands or companies to get a real-time sense of how they are perceived, and thus supports decision making.

Janine Wood of Armadillo Consulting Group warns of 'shoehorning existing content into social media': 'Social media has to be from the heart and not marketing blurb. In the CSR context, it offers a good opportunity to talk about the issues that are there and give the company a voice that is more human.' While it offers new opportunities for communication, Fabian Pattberg is convinced it is not the remedy for everything. It can help if it is applied correctly and based on substance and facts:

If you get things right internally, people will feel that you are sincere, and in this credibility and sincerity are key. Take Novo Nordisk as a positive example. Their online and social media communication is not amazing, but the more you get into it, the more substantial it gets. That is credible. An example from the other end of the scale would be Pfizer, which had problems in terms of its community involvement. They now focus on it more, but you get the sense they do not mean it as they say it. In the retail sector in the UK, M&S are doing great, but not as many people believe Tesco. And a lot of people would not believe Chevron if they claimed they were investing in renewable energy.

Best Practice Case: SAP Community Network

Launched in 2003 as the SAP Developer Network, a subsidiary of SAP Communities and Social Media, it was renamed the SAP Community Network (SCN) in 2007. It began as a technical integrated platform enabling developers and IT people to interact, and now has more than two million individual members as well as thousands of businesses involved in over 200 countries. This is social networking writ large in the 'geek' community, as they themselves would describe it.

SCN focuses on three areas: (1) the public online communities, including the SAP Developer Network, the Business Process Experts Community, the SAP Business Objects Community and the University Alliances Community; (2) the Eco-Hub, which SCN describes as an online app store and solutions marketplace, and (3) SCN's physical events, conferences and seminars.

At the forefront of the social media and Web 2.0 world, SCN encompasses social intelligence, social innovation, social commerce and social insight, and this puts SCN squarely in the arena of exploring how CSR and sustainability can relate to software and business processes, with an emphasis on efficiency, interconnectedness and speed.

SCN sees its community network as 'facilitating the ability of people to inspire others'. One way in which it does this is through advising the top 10 companies on the Dow Jones Sustainability World Index on ways to use technology to monitor and improve their sustainability management and reporting. SCN believes this means it adds value 'on and offline', maintaining active management of its online communities and always aiming for the highest technical quality.

For the full Best Practice Case 15, see Chapter 17, page 257.

What are the key issues from a business perspective in communicating CSR to the (social) media?

TELLING STORIES WELL – BUILDING RELATIONSHIPS WITH THE MEDIA – EMBRACING SOCIAL MEDIA

Björn Edlund stresses the point that CSR and sustainability needs to be related to the media in a way that is relevant:

> *Make the stories attractive to journalists. Any story being told needs to have a beginning, a middle and an end. It requires a protagonist, a point of view and a moral. It cannot be just an addition of facts – otherwise it will not be perceived as interesting. Make sure they can track your progress. Be very open and easy to understand. Companies often underestimate the importance of being understandable, rather than being perfect. To be interesting, stories need to be personal and at the same time globally relevant. Companies need to learn what constitutes news. Signing up to the Global Compact is not news, but maybe what they are going to do after signing up is!*

Storytelling links the 'what' and the 'how'. Björn Edlund's message is: you need to choose relevant content and you need to package it in a format that is engaging. And stakeholder engagement is the buzzword when it comes to the 'how'.

In the case of the media, stakeholder engagement is not new. You have always needed to build relationships with the media to be effective in corporate communications. The point Volker Bormann makes is that you need to see things from the journalists' perspective and support them in what they need to do:

> *The most important is that you present what is really relevant to the company and that you do it in a way that is attractive to journalists, that they can 'sell well'. But obviously it needs to be substantial, because if he figures out it was only a smokescreen, you have not made a friend.*

You need to gain his trust by communicating honestly. Then there are not many journalists who have a deep knowledge of sustainability and CSR, so you need to educate them, help them raise their game in this area. That is why a lot of communication between companies and the media needs to go on behind the scenes. This requires patience, it is more about the conversation and the relationship with the journalist than about that article you want him or her to write. But having that patience is part of responsibility and sustainability.

'Social media allows you to spread information immediately among key influencers, so it is very powerful,' claims Greg Schneider of 3BL Media:

Companies and brands need to embrace social media because it allows them to act, and not just react. Someone who has realized that is Jeff Schwartz of Timberland, who is very active and accessible in social media. More top executives need to realize the potential of social media. What hinders them may be the fact that social media cannot be easily manipulated.

A prerequisite to using social media successfully in the CSR context is not doing it half-heartedly and not seeing it as just another media channel. 'It is simple and straightforward – you only need to be honest and open,' Janine Wood is convinced – and at the same time she clarifies that 'it requires resources, you need people to respond. That is why you need full commitment to social media.'

Can you share any best practice examples of CSR communication?

Table 8.1 shows the brands and programmes that were mentioned in the interviews – each of them only once.

Table 8.1   Brands and programmes referenced in the interviews

Brand, company, programme	No. of mentions
Retail	7
Marks & Spencer, John Lewis, dm, tegut; Migros; Otto, Tchibo	
(Fast-moving) Consumer Goods	2
(Unilever, Nestlé)	
Accountancy	2
KPMG, PwC	
Others	5
Novo Nordisk, Shell, GE/ecomagination, Jamie Oliver Group; Michelin	

'I have not seen anything recently that could not be further improved,' says Volker Bormann. He mentions German retailers Otto and Tchibo, but feels they could do even better. Fabian Pattberg mentions Novo Nordisk and its online communications, which despite being far from brilliant, 'get more substantial the more you get into it'. Björn

Edlund used to be responsible for Shell's global corporate communications, and says that the oil giant was a forerunner in social media, starting 'Tell Shell' which today one might call a blog, as early as 1995 after the Brent Spar disaster. Shell also ran an energy dialogue in conjunction with the Copenhagen summit, focusing on climate change. Other topics included Nigeria and local communities.

The other examples Edlund cites are General Electric (GE) with its ecomagination programme, focusing the company strategy on sustainability-inspired goals, and Unilever, which he considers 'excellent in how they look at the real world and their sustainability impact on the world in the context of sourcing ingredients'.

For Tim Samuels, there are the 'obvious ones like Marks & Spencer and John Lewis'. However, he feels:

> Companies like KPMG and PwC are doing some amazing work in communities. Probably the best example is the Jamie Oliver Group where each of Jamie's companies are connected to the Jamie Oliver Foundation, are informed of its objectives and are fully engaged – the spirit of social engagement permeates throughout the organization.

However, Greg Schneider also offers an example of a public company, greenopolis.com, set up by the public waste management authority in Houston, Texas, because of the way they quite boldly applied social media as part of their overall communication.

Janine Wood feels that social media is actually a lot older than most people think:

> The Michelin brothers started the trend over a hundred years ago with their definitive guide to road travel with the implicit motive of selling tires! The guide was considered useful, was interactive as readers were invited to provide suggestions, and it was, at that time, available free of charge at petrol stations.

Another example she mentions is an initiative geared to supporting the poorest people around the world, the so-called 'Robin Hood Tax'.[3] The site gained more than 70,000 members over the first few days, campaigning for the taxation of financial transactions to help alleviate poverty around the world.

How do you define 'greenwashing'? Examples?

EXPECTATIONS > PERFORMANCE

'There is this wonderful formula PwC came up with: "Trust = performance – expectations". Greenwashing is when you just play in the expectations bit and under-perform,' says Björn Edlund of Edelman. Interviewees agree that the most overt greenwashing goes on in the energy field, particularly the petroleum sector: 'The biggest baddies are the oil companies – Shell, Exxon. They blatantly stated they were doing good things, but Shell even funded groups that denied climate change. They sold off their solar energy business because it was not profitable,' observes Janine Wood. Volker Bormann cites BP: 'They gave themselves a green image with "Beyond Petroleum" while not calculating the very

---

3   See www.robinhoodtax.co.uk.

great risk to their core business.' Ex-Shell manager Björn Edlund agrees that BP's move towards 'Beyond Petroleum' was a huge mistake:

> they were over 95 per cent in oil and gas in 1998, and continue to be today. They should have known that as in energy, it takes a new source thirty years to become 1 per cent of the energy mix. So they were talking about what people wanted to hear rather than what was true.

Alec McGivan provides a succinct definition of greenwashing: 'an attempt to portray a company as sustainable using marketing and PR when in fact it is not'. Volker Bormann agrees with that definition, but feels that the trend towards greenwashing has subsided, and speculates that 'perhaps the popularity of the term has led to greenwashers communicating less'. Greenwashing has become more subtle – you do not have anything relevant to talk about in the context of sustainability, so you decide to talk about something else: 'which essentially implies misleading (the) media and the general public'.

What do you consider to be the key success factors of effective CSR communication?

TRUTHFULNESS – INTEGRITY – EXCELLENCE IN EXECUTION

> *Truthfulness and integrity.*
>
> *Alec McGivan, BBC[4]*

Truthfulness

Björn Edlund points out that truthfulness 'starts with companies having a clear understanding where they stand in society – no illusions about what they contribute. At the same time, understand that the media live on stories that are relevant to people.' To Volker Bormann, truthfulness implies honesty and transparency – 'also, or particularly, in a crisis'. And those companies which are good at corporate communications in general will also be good at CSR communication, as the same or very similar principles apply. 'Honesty and authenticity are key,' agrees Janine Wood.

Integrity

Integrity implies authenticity and doing, as well as communicating, CSR for the right reasons. 'It is key that it is not cynical, but part of the very DNA of the company,' in Tim Samuel's view.

---

4   Alec McGivan left the BBC and his role as Head of Outreach at the end of March 2013. http://www.bbc.co.uk/blogs/outreach/posts/Farewell-to-BBC-Outreach (retrieved 7 July 2013).

Excellence in execution

Tim Samuel adds that CSR needs to be 'communicated creatively and in a contemporary way, that the story is told in a journalistic way rather than as PR spin'. Greg Schneider explains how this can be implemented in the social media context:

> First of all, create a set of media assets to talk about what the organization stands for, for instance podcasts, videos and so on. Talk about who you are, what you stand for, why you exist. This is an ongoing campaign that needs to be run continuously, internally and externally. It is the most important part of the message. Secondly, start specific initiatives, like news services, innovation news, new offerings. Thirdly, move to calendar-driven events, for instance CEO presentations, fundraisers, trade shows, showcasing how the company engages with its stakeholders and telling them were they can meet you. And if they are talking about those three all the time, you have success.

Interview with Professsor Peter Kruse, nextpractice

WHAT DO YOU ASSOCIATE WITH CSR COMMUNICATION?

Unfortunately, a kind of eye-catching surface design in a more and more money-focused society. It produces starry-eyed idealism and tends to just change the surface rather than the value system behind it. If mimicry does not work any more, then you get CSR communication. My worst encounters with narcissism I have had in areas where I expected them the least, in the area of socio-environmental topics: so much show that it made me feel dizzy. Big presentations where I wondered why they did not include people, but tried to convince them with presentation after presentation. Global expert panels where the same faces show up again and again.

If you combine CSR and communication, you get CSR communication. Too often I have experienced that professional communication is a substitute for credible values.

WHAT ARE YOUR EXPECTATIONS REGARDING THE CSR COMMUNICATION OF COMPANIES?

Transparency, transparency, transparency – in the true and honest sense of the word. Take Nestlé. Who has forbidden you to talk openly to people? Why do you close down Facebook sites and stop communicating with people? Whoever gets involved with communication on the Internet needs to know what he is letting himself in for. In the ethical area, it can be counter-productive. CSR never communicates beyond the real values in the corporate culture. Therefore, credibility is more important than rhetoric and authenticity, and the willingness to take the risk that comes with transparency has a higher relevance than strategic communication and wordsmithing. People are not stupid, because they continuously check credibility on the net – a whole generation has learned that.

WHAT IS THE ROLE OF (SOCIAL) MEDIA IN THE CONTEXT OF THE CSR COMMUNICATION OF COMPANIES?

We have to realize that we do not have full control any more over what we communicate. CSR communication is now only a conversation with others that simply dissolves because on the Internet there is no professional communication, there is only communication. When power is redistributed via emotional resonance only, a child can produce a video that is downloaded six million times while an expensively produced advertising message is being ignored. Whether something becomes a wave is decided by others, and even substantial reactions can simply go up in smoke very quickly. You need to hit a permanent point of resonance, and the half-life of a hype shows me how system-changing and sustainable the hype is. Social media changes the power balance in communications – once and for all.

WHAT ARE THE ISSUES FROM A BUSINESS PERSPECTIVE IN COMMUNICATING CSR TO MEDIA?

You need to ensure that as many people as possible in your company surf the Internet and become your communication partners. Make sure you are radically oriented towards the changing societal values landscape and that you can ride the waves of this dynamic world. That implies that we need to put cognitive ability and empathy above professional communication. If you are in social media, you are not onstage but in the party room – and if you are at a party and think that everybody needs to listen to you, you are silly. We are not even in two-way communication any more, it is about one to many and many to one, it is a conversation in which millions are involved. I do not talk with a fixed addressee, not with an individual person, but with the totality of the Internet, so it is a blend of mass communication without the dominance of the sender, and I am dependent on the empathy of the individual. This empathy is the basic dynamic of the whole net, the cultural space we call the Internet. Empathy is a fundamental cultural dynamic. There is no word for it – it is not dialogue, but more than that!

CAN YOU SHARE ANY BEST PRACTICE EXAMPLES OF CSR COMMUNICATION?

There are quite a few bloggers who are not just self-absorbed. They are people who summarize patterns that are helpful to others. These people are unpretentious and give a very credible account of what they find important. Most of that content has a high quality, and that quality increases with the recipient and his capacity for resonance. The role of the expert who has expertise on behalf of others has a high level of responsibility. It no longer makes sense to call the sommelier if you want to know how the wine tastes, now you ought to taste it for yourself. All of us need to become appraising experts! This will make us into powerful customers.

There are honest endeavours in companies in the arena about CSR. Duttweiler[5] started very early on, even though Migros today is somewhere else. Mr Wolfgang Gutberlet of tegut[6] is a

---

5   The founder of Swiss co-operative and retailer Migros.

6   A regional German food retailer.

retailer, and he is authentic. Götz Werner[7] is interesting, he is so persistent and he has the courage to promote topics he believes in.

The challenge we have today is to motivate customers to pay more for values. But if we apply discount strategies, reduce prices and margins, there is no innovation. So how do we get people to pay more for items than it costs to produce them? How does Apple do it? Because they make something that is innovative and that people covet. Apple is one of the few brands that people really covet. Another example is Mini. This shows that the basic idea of creating added value is not dead, we have only tried the opposite for twenty years, and now comes the turnaround. CSR is part of this turnaround, because people try to find meaningful components in the world of consumption, they are concerned with sustainability issues. And that is why CSR and sustainability issues become relevant to the profit margin.

HOW DO YOU DEFINE 'GREENWASHING' AND COULD YOU GIVE EXAMPLES?

If you look at how the automotive industry has messed it up by launching 'Blue' product lines (Mercedes, VW) without having the technology to back them up – that really is a con! Cars are never environmentally friendly, regardless of what features you add. The industry blows its chance that way. If they really have something environmental to sell, then sell it to me! But do not take me for a ride. Tesla shows how it is done![8]

WHAT DO YOU CONSIDER TO BE KEY SUCCESS FACTORS OF EFFECTIVE CSR COMMUNICATION FROM A (SOCIAL) MEDIA PERSPECTIVE?

You need to be consistent in your behaviour – otherwise you constantly operate at a superficial level. It is as trivial as saying that lying is the most strenuous thing you can do.

Key Messages in a Nutshell

Table 8.2   Chapter 8 key messages in a nutshell

Expectations of the media towards CSR communication	Action precedes talking Above all, transparency Be yourself Do it well, and make it contemporary
Roles of the media in the context of CSR communication	Referee Catalyst Communication channel
Issues of CSR communication to the media	Telling stories well Building relationships with the media Embracing social media
Key success factors for communicating CSR to the media	Truthfulness Integrity Excellence in execution

---

7   The founder of leading German chemist and drugstore chain dm.

8   Tesla Motors is a California-based manufacturer of electric cars, www.teslamotors.com (retrieved on 7 July 2013).

9 *Communicating Sustainability – the Academic and Expert Perspective*

No one is interested in stand-alone programmes or 'policies' anymore. They want action and then transparent and accessible communications, not large reports that no one reads.

Brendan May, The Robertsbridge Group

There are many experts in the area of CSR, sustainability and related communications disciplines. You could group them into academic experts and practitioners, who are mostly consultants or spokespeople of 'think-tanks'. Some of the practitioners have previously worked in sustainability functions in larger companies and corporations. In this chapter, we attempt to provide a 'bigger picture' and to focus closely on some key topics, among them in particular sustainability reporting.

What do you associate with CSR?

In the long run we have to get rid of CSR as it has the tendency to make permanent an unhealthy dichotomy between business and society.

Karl-Henrik Robèrt

Mallen Baker provides a fairly comprehensive definition of CSR and CSR communication: 'CSR is about how companies manage the business processes to produce an overall positive impact on society, how companies communicate with key stakeholders to facilitate better practice, and how subsequently they communicate about what they are doing to meet their responsibilities.'

Jean-Philippe Renaut, expert in sustainability strategy implementation, previously with SustainAbility, suggests that CSR summarizes all corporate initiatives that improve the sustainability performance of an organization. Céline Louche, Assistant Professor at Vlerick Management School, associates CSR with a change in corporate behaviour, both in terms of consumption and production. She calls this an ideal view, while often the reality is that CSR can sometimes be a way to avoid change:

It's a tool. When it's not well used, there is no change. Just engaging a few people in the company and naming that CSR policy does not suffice. You do not change the core of the company, but you expect to be perceived as sustainable by external stakeholders. Risks and reputation concerns are not enough to call it responsibility. The essence of CSR is active, genuine change and its link with sustainable development to create a bigger picture. It is a mistake to think of the footprint of a company without putting it into the bigger picture and having a holistic approach, as a positive action for the company may not be positive for society.

The integration of business into the overall objectives of society is a point that the founder of The Natural Step, Karl-Henrik Robèrt, emphasizes as well. He argues that CSR may be a good starting point, but is dangerous in the long run: 'As a separate concept, it will support a dichotomy between business and society and lead corporations astray. It may be even more dangerous than having no agenda at all.' Lord Hastings of Scarisbrick, Global Director of Citizenship at KPMG agrees, and therefore suggests changing the terminology:

Personally, I think it is vastly bigger and want to switch the language to 'responsible and sustainable business and corporate citizenship'. CSR is an appropriate description of company-related community activities, but not about the transparent reportable impact of business in society or the way a big company takes on a remit with global issues. CSR may be voluntary, charitable, and as part of a community process is honourable and vital, but does not reflect a mature corporation out in the world in which it works, constantly compelling business to take leadership with responsibility to stakeholders, not just for shareholders.

Tim Callington (Edelman) makes the point that what he associates with CSR has changed significantly over the past couple of years, and the notion has therefore broadened as well:

Now that it is at the heart of the business, everybody at any level has to be aware of it, being engaged somehow, because it is fundamental to the character and reputation of an organization. In the past, it played a more peripheral role, and it now has a much more central and fundamental one to the operation of an organization and it is more linked to transparent corporate behaviour. I am not sure who said it, it could have been Rupert Murdoch, but it fits: 'Basically every company today is a media company.' And that is why ethical behaviour and responsibility are so important.

What do you associate with CSR communications?

Today I associate CSR communications with the wider issue of how a corporate, service or product brand is constructed and how it presents itself to stakeholders.
Hamish Pringle, Strategic Advisor at 23red

Brendan May of the Robertsbridge Group says:

Historically, the PR and advertising of ad hoc 'citizenship' or 'green' programmes has too often been in isolation from the overall strategy and impact of the brand or business. For too long the talk was of 'CSR initiatives'. Thankfully, the term 'CSR' is fast being banished and corporate sustainability is becoming the mainstream driver of business behaviour.

Rita Clifton, most recently CEO of Interbrand, notes that her understanding of it has changed dramatically over the past 10 to 15 years:

I used to associate it with Cause Related Marketing, where a big company gives money to a charity or event, like McDonald's and Ronald McDonald houses, not related to the business strategy and not the core of the business. It is now more subtle and happily more substantial, covering a whole range of things.

Hamish Pringle, co-author of Cause Related Marketing classic *Brand Spirit*, agrees:

Companies nowadays need to subscribe to the idea of the triple bottom line. It is not enough to return profits to shareholders. In addition, companies have to account for their impact on the environment and on society at large. In Brand Spirit we showed how people's expectations of brands have evolved, so they need to have a mix of rational-functional values, emotional-psychological ones and ethical-spiritual ones when attempting to deliver a brand promise. Today I associate CSR communications with the wider issue of how a corporate, service or product brand is constructed and how it presents itself to stakeholders.

Stan Dupré, French sustainability and CSR expert of think-tank and management consultants Utopies, derives two interpretations: 'CSR reporting and institutional advertising campaigns on CSR, focused on corporate rather than on product level.' With CSR reporting, he too often sees untargeted communication. C.B. Bhattacharya, who holds the E.ON Chair in Corporate Responsibility at the European School of Management and Technology in Berlin, takes a different perspective when he remarks that for him, CSR communication:

is a context where a company does not necessarily have control over what is being said. Third-party or media-driven CSR communications can have a totally different kind of impact on stakeholders. It is definitely a complex topic, and there is no easy way to navigate the landscape. Different people have different ideas of what a company is doing in CSR – even just two individuals exposed to the same information may have diverging views about what and how the company is doing.. One and the same initiative may be communicated to various stakeholders in a way which means they will have contrasting views. Managing this so that stakeholders ultimately get a coherent message about what the company is doing is a challenging task.

What are the expectations of academics and experts regarding the CSR communication of companies?

SUBSTANCE – INTEGRATION – HONESTY – HUMILITY – ENGAGEMENT

Substance

'Do or do not, there is no try' – Robert Rubinstein quotes Yoda from *Star Wars*, and adds: 'I am just tired of listening to companies chatting about this.' CSR communication needs to be based on substance, which Jean-Philippe Renaut defines as 'strategy, systems, targets and performance'.

Substance also implies that the information conveyed needs to be relevant and fact-based. C.B. Bhattacharya says that it should

> *emphasize what the company has managed to accomplish, rather than trying to convey a superior image of a very green or socially responsible company. Often we find that they try to convey an image without the facts. NGOs and other stakeholders react to facts, so companies should focus on what they have done rather than what they intend to do or just talking in an abstract fashion about the company.*

He adds that it is not just about money, but tangible societal benefits: 'A lot of companies focus on how much money they are spending, but stakeholders often are more interested in how many lives you have saved, how many times you cut down the CO_2 footprint or have achieved other fact-based metrics.'

Best Practice Case: Research by Professor C.B. Bhattacharya on the Effectiveness of CSR Communication

Something which comes up time and again when evaluating CSR communication is how to attribute value to it and measure it. Professor C.B. Bhattacharya was one of the first people to tackle the challenge of quantitative research in this field with his work on the effectiveness of CSR communication.

In many instances, one finds low awareness among stakeholders, and as a result of that, unfavourable attitudes. Applicable in so many instances is the need to reduce scepticism and to help stakeholders to understand that the issue is tied into the overall reputation of a company. Another universal element is that different stakeholders, which tend to include those making law and writing policy – governments, whether at local national or supranational levels, NGOs, local community leaders, employees and customers – will all have different expectations and will 'consume' their communications through different channels. For example, many audiences do not actively seek to learn about a company's CSR activity, but will be passively exposed to it through the media if a scandal erupts (think of BP), whereas experts, institutional investors and opinion-formers will be actively seeking that information through corporate reporting, for example.

Bhattacharya encapsulates four key factors which companies must think about:

1. intrinsic motivation;
2. convergence between a social issue and the company's business (in other words, the brand synergy);
3. reputation;
4. communications channels.

It is also important to consider positioning, remembering that communications must be tailored for different audiences, that first you need to create awareness, and ultimately that messages about you are better received if they come from unbiased sources – in other words, 'loosen up' for more credibility. Do not try to control social media, be an enabler. Relax (if that is possible). And finally, the lesson which still needs to be repeated: consumers will not compromise on price and quality and accept deficits in the core product or delivery of service just to be perceived as ethical.

For the full Best Practice Case 16, see Chapter 18, page 265.

Robert Rubinstein points out that frequently the metrics can be misleading: 'It is very difficult to get from the dark to the light side. Take the Dow Jones Sustainability Index – the ones who score the highest are the biggest CO_2 polluters, just because they report!'. Yet measuring is where substance becomes, well, substantial, so it is square one. And in order to measure, you need action, 'tangible demonstrations of where actions have been taken', as Tim Callington puts it. 'No one is interested in stand-alone programmes or "policies" any more. They want action and then transparent and accessible communications, not large reports that no one reads,' adds Brendan May of The Robertsbridge Group.

Integration

Very closely related to substance is integration – a point that was made in more detail in the context of associations with CSR and CSR communications. 'It should be a more integrated part of what a company does, its core responsibility: good practice at the core of the strategy, the company's core purpose beyond profit,' says Rita Clifton. And yet, integration also means that CSR and sustainability must be linked to self-interest, otherwise there is no link to core business – or as Robert Rubinstein declares: 'Show self-interest, show the opportunities, show the money flows.'

Honesty

Honesty seems like a pretty clear expectation – if there were such a thing as objective truth, that is. What it boils down to is, as Tim Callington of Edelman emphasizes: 'a straight answer and a straight story. Unfortunately, too much of what businesses do in this space is obscured in corporate language.' So too much communication can easily camouflage the 'straight story', the key message. Honesty also implies transparency, and this in turn means that companies should not just report on the positive, but candidly admit where they may have a negative impact in the world. In the words of Mallen Baker, honesty implies 'a degree of candour about problems, not just boasting about successes'.

Humility

A rare quality in people, yet the sign of great leaders, is humility.[1] Leaders in sustainability communications are companies that do not try to convey the impression that they have made it already. According to Brendan May: 'Any company that claims they have arrived at a destination is deluding themselves and their audience.' This is obviously not always easy, and goes against the old motive of using CSR to improve the corporate image. However, the digital revolution and the development of social media is making sure that 'spin' is becoming an increasingly risky tactic that is more often than not exposed. So one could call humility the sibling of transparency in the context of CSR communication. It implies sticking to the facts, being transparent both about one's motives ('Do we really want to take CSR and sustainability seriously?') and achievements as well as shortcomings. Brendan May's key expectations define the context for humility: 'authenticity, humility, honesty'. Coming across authentically implies that the company really communicates its genuine identity and does not attempt to portray an image that is not consistent with this identity, while honesty implies sticking to facts and not omitting those areas where a lot of challenges remain. Humility demonstrates a hunger to learn, and is the flipside of ambition – or as Jim Collins puts it, 'fierce resolve' – the other sign of great leaders.

Engagement

Substance, integration and honesty relate to what to communicate – relevant and material achievements in the area of sustainability related to the core business, balanced out by the risks. Humility is the attitude, while engagement is the 'how' of effective sustainability communications:

> If [CSR communication] includes engagement, the process improves performance over time. When an organization is seen as accountable over a specific issue, a defined strategy with systems to support it, and metrics and targets well communicated, then over time your stakeholders will steer you in the right direction, or even help you move in that direction.

May's key point is that communication needs to be a process, not a one-off activity. That is exactly why Céline Louche is not so much interested in CSR reports per se, but the process behind them: 'CSR reports are never good enough but the process is extremely important to raise awareness, to increase transparency and accountability. CSR communication on its own is not enough, it depends a lot on how it is used by the company. It is not just about keeping stakeholders quiet. You should stimulate debate on the not-so-easy questions, those where there is no right or wrong answer.'

---

1   Jim Collins, 'Level 5 Leadership: The Triumph of Humility and Fierce Resolve', *Harvard Business Review* (January 2001).

What is the role of academics and experts in the context of the CSR communication of companies?

PROVIDING THOUGHT-LEADERSHIP AND DISSEMINATING KNOWLEDGE

Providing thought-leadership

Karl-Henrik Robèrt feels that the key role of academics and experts is to provide competence to top managers and business leaders and support them in developing suitable strategies. As a professor at a major business school preparing leaders to deal more effectively with sustainability challenges, C.B. Bhattacharya provides a fairly comprehensive answer, because he sees a threefold role: (1) providing thought-leadership, providing a (thought) framework to business leaders in how CSR communication works and how to apply it efficiently and effectively; (2) teaching students, particularly executives, about CSR communication, and (3) disseminating knowledge, research results and experience in CSR communication in publications (journals and books) targeted at practitioners.

Disseminating knowledge

Céline Louche sees her role as an academic as 'studying the evolution of CSR communication and transparency mechanisms as well as to help companies to communicate their data on CSR more efficiently'. This can include advice on how CSR messaging differs according to context, how to comply with the Global Reporting Initiative (GRI) in different countries, and to critically reflect on the communication of companies with a view to improving it. Part of that role is to analyse both actions and communications and to assess the fit. It may even include developing tools to assess communication effectiveness.

What are the key issues from a business perspective in communicating CSR?

TO WHOM, WHAT AND HOW TO COMMUNICATE

To whom

This issue is really at the heart of this book: 'Companies need to communicate to different groups of interest and expectations,' in Céline Louche's words. Different stakeholders, different expectations – and the challenge is how to align them, particularly if they push you. 'It is about stakeholder pressure,' says Jean-Philippe Renaut of SustainAbility, 'increasingly consumers, but to a large extent shareholders, in the form of rating agencies and institutional investors.' Lord Hastings of Scarisbrick gives Nestlé as an example:

> The best example is Peter Brabeck, the Nestlé chairman. He had to undertake a variety of private meetings with shareholders to allow Nestlé to retain a significant level of return in order to invest it in water sustainability, which would have a longer-term impact, telling them, 'Choose to work with me in leading business on water recovery/investment and we can be in the front line but you will have to sacrifice a short term return.'

The Nestle chairman's willingness to forgo the short-term returns in favour of a longer-term impact was made possible because he explained this to the shareholders. This ability to take a longer view might not always be feasible. Some would argue, like Rita Clifton, that when facing conflicting stakeholder pressures there is a need to invest in the area of greatest return. In her opinion this involved 'the need to have a CSR communication strategy, and to define the 'what, when and how to'. According to C.B. Bhattacharya: 'It is a complicated thing: what/when/how is driven by which stakeholders you want to communicate with. Therefore a company needs to think about the business of communicating strategically rather than in an ad-hoc way.'

What

Once you have figured out which stakeholders to communicate and engage with, 'what' will be the content of the message. Remember Rita Clifton's advice that the 'what' has to be determined based on an assessment of which message and communication will provide a company with the biggest return on investment. This may well be the avoidance of cost if you are looking at a risk equation. Another important determinant in choosing the appropriate content is the complexity of the issue. Is it actually possible to get the message across effectively? Céline Louche is familiar with this challenge:

> We have just done a project about nanotechnology. Some companies want to communicate about the risks involved with nanotechnology, but how do you do it when it is such a difficult subject and there is no understanding in society about what nanotechnology is? How can you communicate it in a way that people will understand?

So the content needs to be easy to comprehend, and it needs to be relevant.

How

Storytelling links the 'what' and the 'how'. Tim Callington calls it an opportunity rather than a problem, and illustrates it with examples:

> There is the opportunity for engagement, for gathering a community around a message. An example is 'Filter for Good' with Brita water filters and Nalgene, maker of water bottles, run by Edelman US in 2009. The idea: reduce the amount of water bottle waste (40 billion bottles are thrown away in the US each year, equal to $1 billion worth of plastic). Consumers received vouchers for purchasing Nalgene bottles, people could track the number of water bottles saved. The campaign was run online, and shows the advantage of digital media. It is a channel to engage with people and to create an (online) hub and thereby build a groundswell of interest. What digital does is that is allows people to pull in the content they want to have, which makes it more relevant and it therefore makes more of an impact. It also provides an instant feedback loop on how you are behaving as a company. A good example of this is General Motors when they launched their 'FastLane' blog, a very innovative move for an automotive company. They received instant feedback on design, products, and reputation – and learned fast what people did not like, as well.

This opportunity to engage can be particularly valuable in a crisis, and Callington cites BP:

BP had a global Twitter feed, and when the Gulf crisis broke out it, became a channel for criticizing BP on its handling of the crisis. BP's public relations were not straight and transparent, but it was trying to put a veneer on the issue. So on the one hand the fact that the feed existed meant that BP had a huge online reputation issue to deal with. But on the other hand, it was also a great opportunity.

It was an opportunity, it has to be said, the petrol giant did not take, because it stuck with the 'old' paradigm. Callington concludes:

The opportunity with digital is that you can cut straight into insights into the way your brand is seen. It offers transparency. However, that means not just content, but also tone and language! You have to put the corporate tone and industry jargon to one side and have to want to honestly and directly engage. Transparency, directness and simplicity give you credibility online. It means bringing people to the fore who normally would not be spokespeople. For instance, if we are dealing with a technology client and dealing with the developer community, you need someone who can be technically on a level with them so they want to engage with that person.

The 'how' also implies an understanding that 'single-channel communications no longer work', according to Brendan May:

You need to be deploying every channel, which means all parts of the business need to commit to and understand the sustainability agenda. A good meeting with a regulator is worthless if your brand is being destroyed on Facebook. A nice digital campaign is devalued if you are not talking to NGOs. The challenge is to move from the mindset of 'having a CSR team' to training the board at the top as well as the staff at the bottom about what the company or brand's values are when it comes to corporate sustainability.

Can you share any best practice examples of CSR communication?

Table 9.1 shows the brands and programmes that were mentioned in the interviews.

Table 9.1   Brands and programmes referenced in the interviews

Brand/company, industry/programme	No. of mentions
Top 5	
Marks & Spencer (retail/corporate)	5
Unilever (FMCG/corporate, Dove)	3
General Electric (industry/ecomagination)	2
Timberland (consumer goods)	2
Novo Nordisk (pharmaceutical/corporate)	2
Vodafone (telecoms/corporate)	2

Table 9.1 Brands and programmes referenced in the interviews *continued*

Brand/company, industry/programme	No. of mentions
Single Mentions Grouped by Industry:	
(Fast-moving) Consumer Goods (including Top 5)	8
Nike, Stonyfield, Coca-Cola, SAB Miller, P&G, Alpro	7
Retail (including Top 5)	3
Tesco, Body Shop	2
Financial Services	3
Standard Chartered, Caisse d'Epargne, Triodos Bank	3
Industry/manufacturing	3
Lafarge, Interface	2
Food Service	2
Starbucks, Max Burgers	2
Hospitality	1
Scandic Hotels	1

Marks & Spencer once more leads the pack. 'Plan A by Marks & Spencer is a great piece of communication, packaging together a whole range of complicated things, correlated with their position on the front foot, in a great way and wrapping it up well,' says Rita Clifton of Interbrand. What Hamish Pringle likes about M&S's communication is that it is being thoroughly implemented throughout the supply chain and that the communication is very clear and convincing – so substance and commitment meet executional excellence.

'Unilever, the corporate brand, is now about the vitality umbrella, gradually taking the company down the route of well-being and ethical standards,' adds Rita Clifton, while Céline Louche particularly likes the Dove campaign as 'it says something important beyond the company'.

Another favourite is Timberland, partly due to the way it involves its consumers in grassroots projects like building houses in disadvantaged communities, which, according to C.B. Bhattacharya, has much more impact than traditional, arm's-length mass media advertising, which can be easily lost in the clutter.

Overall, consumer-oriented examples dominate (consumer brands and retailers in particular). Innovative examples include the fourth largest French retail bank Caisse d'Epargne, which has launched a CSR label for financial products as an open source concept.

How do you define 'greenwashing'? Examples?

OVER-PROMISE AND UNDER-DELIVER

Opinions on greenwashing differ significantly. While Karl-Henrik Robèrt does not feel that most cases of greenwashing actually deserve to be identified that way, Robert Rubinstein of TBLI Group states bluntly: 'Most CSR communication is greenwashing.' Rita Clifton and Mallen Baker. disagree with Rubinstein. Baker says:

> Greenwashing is a misused and heavily abused term. It should be restricted to companies that seek to mislead observers into believing that their operations are benign whilst knowing that they are not. It is often abused to describe any company that talks about what they are doing on the environment whilst not being perfect.

Rita Clifton believes that:

> [Greenwashing] is over-used as a term. It is frustrating because often companies cannot go as fast they would like. If a company is doing the bare minimum on the inside and trying to make something of it on the outside, then that is greenwashing, but only that. There is the sheer hypocrisy of people who kick everybody and everything without acknowledging that business has to pay for everything.

Tim Callington is sympathetic to this point, but feels at the same time that there is a moral dimension:

> Fundamentally, it is about dishonesty – to be fair, some organizations find themselves greenwashing by accident: they recognize the importance of environmental impact, and they do not meet the standards of stakeholders, which are very high, while making claims that are not really substantiated. This over-claiming will be found out, credibility is wiped out immediately, and this resulting loss is not a short-term thing, but can define attitudes towards an organization or brand.

So how do you avoid greenwashing? Brendan May offers a very simple formula: 'Always under-promise and over-deliver. Greenwashers do the exact opposite. Greenwashing is over-claiming, dressing poor performance up as "trying to do better" or making nonsensical propositions that a high-impact industry is green because it is doing one or two good things.' Céline Louche picks up on this point:

> Greenwashing may not be lying, but manipulating consumers by providing particular information without including the broader picture, and creating an impression everything is fine. It happens quite easily if you forget what CSR is about and use it as a marketing tool. One example is supermarkets that highlight their activity referring to their policy on plastic bags, stating, 'We are green because we don't give you any plastic bags,' while there is more than enough plastic in the supermarket and they pass on the cost to the consumer.

Jean-Philippe Renaut makes the interesting observation that greenwashing can also be the result of poor service delivery (sustainability promises that do not over-promise, but are completely irrelevant to most stakeholders). It is less that there is a discrepancy between the walk and the talk, but rather an issue about not managing the biggest concerns of your stakeholders:

> *British Telecom is an example – a quasi-monopolistic supplier that wins sustainability awards but is very bad at service delivery: if you search for 'I hate BT' on Facebook, you will find over 200 groups named that – which could become true engagement because these are spaces created by BT's own community, its clients, who quite obviously do not care at all about BT's sustainability reporting. This is not really greenwashing, but more engagement gone wrong. BT did not seem to report on the right material issues, focusing on server room energy efficiency and virtual economy rather than basic service quality.*

So clearly, another way of avoiding greenwashing is to listen before you speak, and to truly engage with stakeholders.

What do you consider to be the key success factors of effective CSR communication?

STRATEGIC – SUBSTANTIAL – TARGETED – ENGAGED – AUTHENTIC

Strategic

For Karl-Henrik Robèrt, it is key that top management learns to define what sustainability actually means to them, as otherwise it is not possible to be strategic. This is of particular importance to shareholders, according to Lord Hastings of Scarisbrick, as they 'need to feel caught up in a journey with the chief executive and the board on sustainable business'.

Best Practice Case: The Natural Step Framework

The man behind Sweden's impressive sustainability drive – perhaps the only country in the world to have sought to engage its entire population in the pursuit of sustainable lifestyles – is a medical doctor specializing in cancer science who was formerly based at the world-renowned Karolinska Instituet.

It was in the course of this work that Dr Karl-Henrik Robèrt began to think seriously about the link between human health and unsustainable behaviour. He concluded that as a global society, we are actually heading backwards in evolutionary terms, through examples such as extinction of species, deforestation, climate change and pollution, and what he terms 'assaults on nature', our dependence on 'linear processes' or linear thinking has put humanity at risk.

He developed a scientific consensus document on the human predicament of continuous linear processes and the self-benefit of being part of the solution rather than the problem. The document, designed as a picture book plus an audio cassette, was sent to all 4.3 million households in Sweden. In forthcoming scientific publications and doctorates, Robèrt and his colleagues then developed four conditions or principles for sustainability. An organization is sustainable when it has eliminated its contribution to:

1. systematic increases in concentrations of substances from the Earth's crust;
2. systematic increases in concentrations of substances produced by society;
3. systematic physical degradation of nature;
4. conditions that systematically undermine people's capacity to meet their needs.

Now based at the Blekinge Institute of Technology, Dr Robèrt is looking at how sustainable development can be applied to all academic fields, and The Natural Step helps governments, communities, schools, colleges, universities and corporations to develop 'blueprints towards sustainability'.

What he feels is vital is that we shift from piecemeal management to long-term strategic plans for future sustainability. The Natural Step's unique approach integrates scientific rigour with simplicity and applicability. Dr Robèrt has shown, theoretically as well as empirically with organizations that are applying the framework, that revolutionary and innovative thinking can open up new markets, reduce risks and increase numbers of customers at the same time as cutting back on waste and energy consumption.

Electrolux is a good example – it was the first white goods producer in the world to phase out CFCs without phasing in other chemicals that had no future, developing new metal strategies from the same sustainability knowledge, and developing a whole new line of new products that would respond to the growing green market demands. Electrolux CEO Leif Johansson recently declared that the company had earned billions from applying the principles to understand – before its competitors – how markets and legislation would change.

For the full Best Practice Case 17, see Chapter 18, page 270.

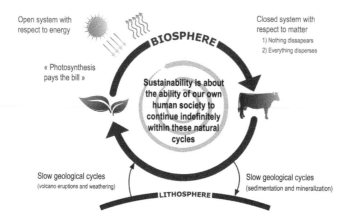

Figure 9.1   The cycle of nature
Source: Reproduced courtesy of The Natural Step.

Substantial

'CSR communication is the same as other communication or advertising. It needs to be rooted in a corporate, service or product truth and then be conveyed convincingly and credibly,' according to marketing and brand expert Hamish Pringle. For Jean-Philippe Renaut, substance implies that the communication is rooted in company strategy and is clearly supported by top management. Moreover, it implies 'having proper management systems in place as well as performance metrics and targets' so that communication can be fact-based.

Substance, in Rita Clifton's view, means that the company as well as the communication is generating value for its target audience – *sustainable* value, that is. The acid test: 'Is the customer coming back to buy your goods and services?'

Targeted

'Really understand who you want to deliver info to and what they expect,' says Stan Dupré of Utopies, repeating a timeless truth of marketing and communication. In the CSR communications context, he feels the need to issue a warning: 'Forget the CSR report and try to think what the best channel for each target audience is.' The challenge is to make sustainability 'attractive to the relevant target audience', adds Jean-Philippe Renaut.

'Engagement' is the key long-term success factor of effective CSR communication, according to Renaut. For Stan Dupré, CSR communication needs to be forward-looking, 'delivering information in a strategic way in order to anticipate future risk, which is the only way to build trust, particularly in the financial community'. However, 'delivering information' does not accurately describe what defines 'engaged' communication, which Tim Callington stresses: 'It implies a willingness to listen – that is the most important part! Be prepared to show some humility, particularly from an executive position, be prepared to engage in dialogue.' Mallen Baker agrees: 'Effective CSR communication is two-way.' 'It needs to create a change and engage employees, consumers, CEOs, NGOs, and make people think,' argues Céline Louche. 'Many CSR issues do not have an easy answer, that is why it is key to be able to change the difficult situations, raise the awareness.'

Authentic

'Authenticity is key – you need to show that [your communication] is really integrated into core business activity, not an add-on!', claims Robert Rubinstein. To Hamish Pringle, CSR communication needs to have 'an authentic human voice, and tell stories'. This implies honesty and openness, but also having the courage, according to Tim Callington, to 'share responsibility with the people on the ground – make them your stars by letting them tell your story'.

Interview with Professor C.B. Bhattacharya, European School of Management and Technology

WHAT DO YOU ASSOCIATE WITH CSR COMMUNICATION?

I associate it with a company not necessarily being in control over what is being said or getting communicated in different forms, so that on one and the same initiative, different stakeholders may have a different view. Third-party or media-driven CSR communications can have a totally different kind of impact on stakeholders than direct communication. It is definitely a complex topic, and there is no easy way to navigate the landscape. Different people have different ideas of what a company is doing in CSR – two individuals exposed to the same information may have a very different view of what and how a company is doing. Managing the complexity so that ultimately stakeholders get a coherent message about what the company is doing is a challenging task.

WHAT ARE YOUR EXPECTATIONS REGARDING THE CSR COMMUNICATION OF COMPANIES?

It needs to be fact-based and emphasize what the company has managed to accomplish, rather than trying to convey a superior image of a very green or socially responsible company. Often we find that they try to convey an image without the facts. NGOs and stakeholders react to facts. So keep CSR communication fact-based, focusing on what you have done rather than what you intend to do. Also, a lot of companies focus on how much money they are spending, but stakeholders are often more interested in how many lives you have saved, how many times you cut down on CO_2 and so on.

WHAT IS THE ROLE OF ACADEMICS AND EXPERTS IN THE CONTEXT OF CSR COMMUNICATION OF COMPANIES?

I would see my role as to try to provide some kind of framework, to conduct research with stakeholders to understand how they interpret and process CSR communication and use that knowledge to come up with frameworks that can offer guidelines to industry, in terms of what to communicate as well as how and when to communicate so that companies are able to use their resources more effectively and efficiently. Another role is teaching students, in particular executives. When these messages [regarding CSR communication] are told to them in different forums, hopefully that makes a difference in their practice, in the roles they go back to in their companies. A third role is to write articles in practitioner-oriented journals, like *Forbes* or *Ethical Corporation* and books that are targeted at practitioners. It is about sharing and disseminating your knowledge with the hope that managers pick on it and improve industry standards in the context of CSR communication, which currently are not very high.'

WHAT ARE THE ISSUES FROM A BUSINESS PERSPECTIVE IN COMMUNICATING CSR?

In general there are three issues: (a) what (the content of the message), (b) when (timing) and (c) how (to communicate). It is a complicated thing if you ask yourself what, when, how, and driven by which stakeholders with whom you want to communicate!

Because of this complexity, a company needs to think about the business of communicating strategically rather than in an ad hoc way.

If we put the question in the context of the relationship between business and academia, we could ask: what can academics and practitioners learn from each other? What practitioners offer to academics is an opportunity to learn. An example: P&G gave me an opportunity. They wanted me to figure out whether their CSR programmes worked in a social and environmental and in an economic sense. Companies can offer a 'playground' for academics, and from playing in that playground, academics can relate back strategies to practitioners so that it becomes a very fertile ground for exchange. However, not all companies see it that way; there could be more opportunities for collaboration.

CAN YOU SHARE ANY BEST PRACTICE EXAMPLES OF CSR COMMUNICATION?

Awareness of CSR communication tends to be quite low, if you talk to consumers at least. Among employees, it is obviously higher. In general, the awareness tends to be higher when consumers are actually engaged in the CSR initiatives themselves. Will you influence the consumers to participate in a programme rather than just giving money or saying, 'We do a lot for the environment'? Timberland is a good example. They invited their consumers to build houses with them and involved them in various kinds of community projects. When consumers work on these projects together, the impact is much greater than mass media advertising, which is easily lost in the clutter. Grassroots-level initiatives tend to end up being more effective than more arm's-length, mass media approaches. P&G's Crest 'Healthy Smiles' campaign, teaching children to care for their teeth in communities, is another good example. Where they work with this programme, awareness of oral hygiene tends to be high.

HOW DO YOU DEFINE 'GREENWASHING' AND COULD YOU NAME EXAMPLES?

Greenwashing happens when a company does not have the facts to back up what they are communicating, when they don't have the stakeholders' best interest at heart, but rather only try to project an image of CSR. Those techniques are not effective in the long term.

WHAT DO YOU CONSIDER TO BE KEY SUCCESS FACTORS OF EFFECTIVE CSR COMMUNICATION FROM AN NGO PERSPECTIVE?

Fact-based. Persistence. You cannot expect just to communicate something once and have people listen to you and know what is going on. Combining communications with direct experience is more powerful than communication alone. If stakeholders have the chance to participate in your CSR programme, they are more likely to remember what the company is about and what they are doing.

Key Messages in a Nutshell

Table 9.2   Chapter 9 key messages in a nutshell

Expectations of academics and experts of CSR communications	Substance Integration Honesty Humility Engagement
Roles of academics and experts in the context of CSR communication	Providing thought-leadership Disseminating knowledge Challenging corporate communication
Issues of CSR communication from academics' and experts' perspective	To whom, what and how to communicate
Key success factors for communicating CSR to academics and experts	Strategic Substantial Targeted Engaged Authentic

The Cases

It needs to have a humble voice, needs to be truly clever, and it needs to hit a
benchmark in terms of environmental performance as measured by an LCA.
Antonio Bertone, former Puma Chief Marketing Officer, for
'The Clever Little Bag' featured in Chapter 15

This section contains 19 cases that highlight good (if not 'best') practice in communicating sustainability in reputation-enhancing, brand-building and value-creating ways. Originally they were supposed to be inserted as illustrative examples into the stakeholder sections but in the course of researching the cases and interviewing some of the key people behind them they grew both in size and depth. They offered such interesting insights and featured such important lessons that we decided to develop them into full-blown case studies and create a 'Part II' of the book. The stakeholder perspectives remain the guiding principle so that the 19 cases cover the full breadth of communicating sustainability as outlined in Part I.

Structure of the Cases

Each case starts off with a summary of the idea and inspiration behind it and provides a timeline as an overview. In a second section the proposition and implementation are outlined, case or campaign specific communication principles described and unique features and points of differentiation highlighted. The third section focuses on the results: how did key target audiences respond? What were the business results of the communication? And were there any tangible societal or environmental outcomes? All cases conclude with the most important lessons learned in the process and key success factors. We hope that this structure will prove useful in particular to those readers who are actively involved in communicating sustainability. As in Part I of the book, the cases are based primarily on interviews with stakeholders responsible for realizing these outstanding examples of effective CSR communication and are brought to life by numerous quotes from their proponents. We are grateful to all that were willing to talk to us and to share their insights.

The Cases – a Brief Overview

- 'Lifebuoy's Global Handwashing Behaviour Change Programme' is a great example of how collaborating with NGOs (and GOs) on a major cause can both touch billions of people's lives and produce tremendous growth for a brand at the same time.

- Fairtrade is a phenomenal success story in many parts of the world and offers a fascinating communication platform to brands. This is illustrated both in Case 2 about Fairtrade itself and in Case 9 'Cadbury Dairy Milk goes Fairtrade' that shows how one of the most iconic and mainstream chocolate brands added a further quality dimension by moving to cocoa sourced 100 per cent Fairtrade.
- Governments can influence the communications agenda and contribute to sustainable consumption – the German Bio-Label (organic label) has proven that impressively since its introduction in 2002.
- 'The French Environmental Labelling Experiment' is a great example of how the dialogue between business and government led to the establishment of a concept that may take the scale of communicating product carbon footprints to consumers to a new level.
- German retailer Tchibo brought about a paradigm shift when starting to talk *with* stakeholders in the supply chain rather than *about* them. The 'Worldwide Enhancement of Social Quality (WE) Project' conducted in collaboration with German development agency GIZ is an innovative approach in which companies work with the employees and management in supplier factories to create a collaborative win–win solution: improved living and working conditions as defined by the employees and their managers themselves on one hand and increased productivity and quality gains on the other.
- Even though fashion label ROMP no longer exists due to the 2008 financial crisis its legacy lives on – an intriguing case which combines high fashion design with full traceability in the supply chain for consumers as well as producing the world's first fully organic leather.
- Increasingly companies are asking themselves how to embed sustainability in their organization. SKF's 'BeyondZero' initiative started as an internal employee awareness building programme that has now resulted in a portfolio of products that helps customers to reduce their carbon footprint.
- With the 'World Community Grid' IBM applies ingenious technology to both leverage unused computer capacity for good and illustrate the power of that technology to employees as well as to a wide group of external stakeholders.
- Communicating sustainability builds brands – fruit smoothie maker innocent shows that with their long-running 'Big Knit' campaign which underpins its core values and further strengthens the already strong emotional connection consumers have with this likeable brand.
- Can a carbon footprint enhance the appeal of hamburgers for consumers? What sounds like a very daring approach to say the least works exceptionally well for up-and-coming Swedish hamburger chain Max Burgers with their 'Climate on (the) Menu' approach.
- 'Sustainability Brand Communications' Coop Switzerland is a great example of how communicating sustainability can contribute to sustainable consumption both by applying a differentiated brand approach – dedicated 'sustainable competence brands' for distinct product areas – and by bold and eye-opening advertising.
- Another way of building sustainable consumption is by creating innovative packaging – Puma's 'Clever Little Bag' does not just save resources but creates a buzz and a tangible consumer benefit at the point of sale, acting as in-home communication for the sports and lifestyle brand.

- Diabetes care world leader Novo Nordisk shows that integrated reporting works and does not need to result in a boring publication but in a credible and inspiring piece of sustainability communication.
- What is the role of media in communicating sustainability? Certainly the media have a much more significant role to play than we are able to explore in this book. SAP's 'Community Network' shows how social media instruments can be used strategically by businesses to drive sustainability related communication and facilitate stakeholder engagement.
- To many practitioners of sustainability communication one of the most central questions is: what works? Why is one piece of sustainability communication ineffective and why does another one deliver excellent results? Prof. C.B. Bhattacharya of the European School of Management and Technology (ESMT) outlines the central principles in his body of research and publications which we summarize in Case 16.
- A cohesive and research-based strategic framework for sustainability can be extremely helpful to structure sustainability communication. This is what 'The Natural Step Framework' provides, created by Swedish former cancer surgeon Karl-Henrik Robèrt.
- In the Part I interviews, the most frequently mentioned example for good practice was UK retailer Marks & Spencer. With its 'Look behind the Label' campaign it took consumer-related sustainability communication to a new level in 2006 and followed it up with a ground-breaking programme and stakeholder directed communication called 'Plan A' that evolved into 'Doing the right thing'.
- Carpet tile pioneer Interface is our best practice example when it comes to communicating sustainability effectively in a business-to-business context. Centering all product related communication on full sustainability transparency, by creating Environmental Product Declarations based on full product lifecycle assessments for all products is bold and innovative and at the same time underpins the company's central communication principle 'Tell the Complete Truth'.

Our intention with the 19 cases is to provide inspiration but also practical application. It can be very helpful to analyse such examples and the lessons learned with the aim of transferring them to a specific communication challenge. We are convinced that taking a closer look at what the featured organizations and brands have accomplished will provide valuable insights for any practitioner of sustainability communication – be it stakeholder oriented, business-to-business or consumer directed.

10 The Civil Society Perspective – Best Practice Cases

Best Practice Case 1: Lifebuoy's Global Handwashing Behaviour Change Programme

IDEA AND INSPIRATION

Idea behind the Handwashing Behaviour Change Programme

Lifebuoy was launched in 1894, William Lever's goal being to help bring affordable hygiene to Victorian England at a time when epidemics of typhoid, smallpox, cholera and diphtheria were a constant threat. It is one of consumer goods giant Unilever's oldest brands, and one of the first truly global brands. Since its launch, the brand has championed the message of health through personal hygiene.

As early as the 1930s, Lifebuoy began running handwashing educational programmes in schools in the UK and the US. The brand has continued running hygiene education programmes consistently throughout its history. The Lifebuoy Swasthya Chetna ('Healthy Awakening') programme reached over 130 million people from 50,000 rural villages in India by the end of 2009, making it the largest hygiene education campaign ever conducted. In Indonesia, working with an extensive network of partners – including national and local government departments, non-governmental organizations, retailers and the media – the Lifebuoy Berbagi Sehat programme, which earned Lifebuoy the Citizen Brand Award, reached more than 1.1 million people by the end of 2008 with better access to handwashing facilities and toilets and hygiene promotion.

In November 2010, Unilever launched the Unilever Sustainable Living Plan. The plan outlines the company's goal to double the size of the business while reducing its environmental impact and increasing the positive social contribution which Unilever makes to society. The Lifebuoy brand is at the very heart of this plan.

Within the Unilever Sustainable Living Plan, Lifebuoy's brand managers have set themselves a breathtakingly ambitious goal: 'By 2015 the Lifebuoy brand aims to change the hygiene behaviour of 1 billion consumers across Asia, Africa and Latin America, by promoting the benefits of handwashing with soap at key occasions, thereby helping to reduce respiratory infections and diarrhoeal disease, the world's two biggest causes of child mortality.'[1]

---

1   Unilever, *Lifebuoy Way of Life – Towards Universal Handwashing with Soap: Social Mission Report 2010–2012*, www.unilever.com/images/slp-Lifebuoy-Way-of-Life_2010-12%20oct12_tcm13-352150.pdf (accessed 2 June 2013).

'Our inspiration is that we want to change people's handwashing behaviour, thereby making a difference to their everyday lives and, by doing so, also build our business,' says Samir Singh, Lifebuoy's Global Brand Vice President. He emphasizes the importance of the fact that handwashing behaviour change is fully embedded at the heart of the Lifebuoy business model, the social mission going hand- in- hand with the brand's growth strategy.

Lifebuoy has now brought together decades of experience in running handwashing programmes, with the latest scientific research, to devise a methodology which aims to achieve sustained behaviour change (for example, see Figure 10.1). This new methodology is now being rolled out globally in the new Lifebuoy Handwashing Behaviour Change Programme, working with partners in order to deliver the brand's ambitious one billion goal.

Changing behaviour

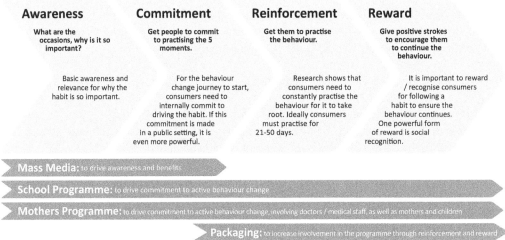

Figure 10.1 The Lifebuoy Handwashing Behaviour Change Model
Source: Reproduced courtesy of Unilever plc.

Lifebuoy attributes the successful scaling-up of the programme from mid-2011 until the end of 2012 to three factors:

1. embedding the programme in the brand's marketing activities, securing the right leadership to ensure that all the marketing teams are on board;
2. developing key partnerships with governments, local NGOs, and Unilever stakeholders (from the top to the bottom of the business);
3. finding ways to drastically cut the cost of implementation to make it affordable for countries to participate.

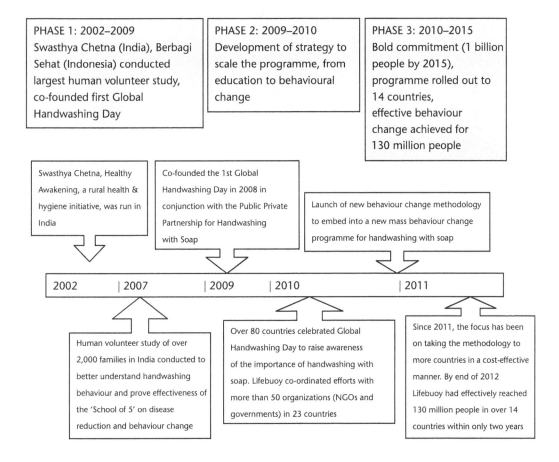

Timeline of the Lifebuoy Handwashing Behaviour Change Programme since 2002

PROPOSITION AND EXECUTION

Concept of the Handwashing Behaviour Change Programme

The Lifebuoy brand aims to make a difference in people's day-to-day lives. Working with public and private sector partners around the world, the challenge is to transform handwashing with soap from a good idea in the abstract into an automatic behavioural pattern at critical times of the day.

Lifebuoy social mission activities involve spreading positive hygiene messages and having an impact on handwashing behaviour. Activities focus on three core areas:

1. handwashing behaviour change programmes
2. skills development and partnerships
3. advocacy

Handwashing behaviour change programmes are central to Lifebuoy's social mission activities around the world, reaching people in everyday situations, promoting the practice of handwashing with soap at five key times: before meals (breakfast/lunch/dinner), during bathtime, and after using the toilet. The programmes are designed to change hygiene habits – driving sustained behavioural change – and have been developed based both on scientific research and experience gained over many years running Lifebuoy programmes in Asia and Africa.

To ensure that the messages make a difference, the programmes seek to engage communities, ensuring that people understand the important role that handwashing with soap plays in keeping people safe and healthy (see Figure 10.2). For example, the Lifebuoy Schools Programme, called 'The School of 5', runs over 21 days and uses a unique combination of comics, puzzles, stories and games to guide children and their parents through the four-step behaviour change process.[2]

Figure 10.2 Poster reinforcing the 'five times a day' message

Source: Reproduced courtesy of Unilever plc.

2   Ibid., p. 20.

Dr Myriam Sidibe explains what makes the Lifebuoy Handwashing Behaviour Change Programme so unique:

Lifebuoy is a brand for the masses, and very affordable for lower-income families, meaning the brand is readily available in homes in the top ten countries for child mortality. In addition, the programme that we have developed is very simple and clear and therefore easy to implement. This enables us to work hand- in- hand with governments and their public health authorities in the countries in which the programme runs – Lifebuoy is increasingly accepted as a partner.

For Lifebuoy, the need for partners who share the brand's vision and goals is crucial to implementing the brand's social mission, and skills development and partnerships therefore play a vital role: 'Achieving the Lifebuoy goal of reaching one billion people effectively, with a handwashing message that will drive behaviour change, is not something the Lifebuoy brand can do alone.'[3]

By sharing skills and experiences with partners, Lifebuoy can help build expertise in communicating the importance of handwashing with soap, developing and implementing campaigns that have a greater impact on promoting positive behaviour change. Lifebuoy partners with both government and NGO organizations in the countries and communities in which the brand operates , and with global organizations, through Unilever partnerships including the PPPHW (Public Private Partnership for Handwashing with Soap), WSUP (Water and Sanitation for the Urban Poor) and the London School of Hygiene and Tropical Medicine. By partnering, Lifebuoy multiplies its knowledge about behaviour change and learns how to adapt communication to local needs and requirements. Only through these partnerships is it possible to drive concerted, cross-sector change. Katie Carroll of NGO FHI360,[4] formerly the Academy for Educational Development,[5] which hosts the Secretariat for the PPPHW initiative, remembers the early days: 'The partnership grew out of collaboration with the WSP, the World Bank Water and Sanitation Project. In 2001 the idea of bringing different NGO, business and public sector partners together to promote handwashing on a large scale came up.' She is very positive about Unilever's involvement:

From our perspective, we are very excited about having a company on board that contributes so much to promoting the handwashing message. NGOs have limited resources, but companies like Unilever have their products, bring incredible market knowledge to the party and can reach so many consumers. This kind of power is very helpful to spread information on a large scale.

Advocacy activities aim to raise the profile and promote the importance of handwashing with soap across stakeholder groups, creating the right environment for investment in behaviour change activities. Despite its clear link to the 4th Millennium Development Goal (to reduce child mortality across the world), the importance of handwashing with soap is still not sufficiently appreciated and integrated into policies, programmes and

---

3   Ibid., p. 9.

4   'FHI360 is a non-profit human development organization dedicated to improving lives in lasting ways by advancing integrated, locally driven solutions'; www.fhi360.org (accessed 2 June 2013).

5   The Academy for Educational Development stopped receiving USAID government funding at the end of 2010 and subsequently sold its assets to ensure that all its programmes were continued. The programmes related to the Handwashing Behaviour Change campaign were taken over by FHI360.

initiatives in many countries and regions. Events such as Global Handwashing Day play a major role in this context, as do other Lifebuoy-branded initiatives like national health symposiums in different countries, helping policymakers to see how the simple promotion of handwashing with soap can tackle some countries' greatest development challenges.

The first Global Handwashing Day was celebrated in 2008, as a means of shining a global spotlight on the importance of handwashing with soap. This annual event was co-founded by Unilever Lifebuoy alongside other private sector companies, UNICEF, the London School of Hygiene and Tropical Medicine and the other organizations that make up the PPPHW. Global Handwashing Day is now celebrated annually by millions of people from more than 80 countries across every continent.

What are the programme-specific communication principles?

Table 10.1 shows the programme-specific principles of the Lifebuoy Global Handwashing Behaviour Change Programme case.

Table 10.1 Programme-specific communication principles – Lifebuoy's Global Handwashing Behaviour Change Programme

Principles	Example
1. Relevance for the target audience	In order to become relevant to children and their mothers (the core target audiences), Lifebuoy has found ways to make hygiene fun, with built-in incentives for changing behaviour. Without working hard to find the 'fun factors' and the right incentives, the programme's communication would not have the desired effect of achieving lasting behaviour change.
2. Focus on sustained behavioural change	The Lifebuoy Handwashing Behaviour Change Programme is not an education programme. It is geared towards sustained behaviour change, based on the results of the human volunteer study carried out in Mumbai, India, in 2007–2008. This study showed that the Lifebuoy programme of hygiene promotion – emphasizing the importance of handwashing at five key occasions during the day and the role of mothers and children – is successful both in terms of reducing illness and sustaining handwashing behaviour change. All programmes therefore feature five 'non-negotiable elements': (1) positive reinforcement to help mothers and children feel good for taking part; (2) mothers and children as dual targets, with mothers reinforcing handwashing with soap behaviour at home; (3) pledges where people make a public commitment to an action in front of peers; (4) 'glow germ' demonstrations that provide a visual illustration of the importance of washing away invisible germs with soap, and (5) a 21-day programme– only with repetition do actions become habits.[6]
3. Product is key	The product plays a key role. In India, for instance, the red Lifebuoy soap bar is very well known and has a strong image. Many people can relate to it through personal experience. That makes it easier to convince people of the behaviour change message. In an interview with the International

---

	Social Marketing Association, Dr Sidibe explains: 'The role of the product is not brought up enough, with its experience of fragrance and the fond childhood memories associated with its use.' In countries where the brand does not have a strong heritage, the connection of consumers with the product has to be built. From a commercial point of view, this is another reason why embedding the handwashing programme into all brand marketing activities is crucial.
4. Easy to apply	The handwashing message is relevant and easy to apply, and demonstrating this ease as well as providing incentives for application is part and parcel of the programme concept. Combined with this is Lifebuoy's affordability, making the financial hurdles low for consumers to participate. In fact, the Lifebuoy team is keen to lower financial hurdles further, and is working on even more affordable solutions. Srirup Mitra, Global Brand Director of Lifebuoy, says: 'I am personally leading an innovation project which seeks to deliver a sustainably low cost bar of soap for low income consumers in Asia and Africa. These are the consumers who need the most protection from germs that cause health problems such as diarrhoea. Sadly, they are also the people who find it the most difficult to regularly afford soap. This innovation delivers a soap bar that provides the best value in usage compared to any other soap available.'
5. Clarity of the mission	Particularly when it comes to partnership, it is imperative to have a clear and straightforward concept that can be easily communicated and understood. With its ambitious target, together with the focus on three core areas – handwashing behaviour change programmes, including the 'School of 5' schools programme, skills development and partnerships, and advocacy campaigns like Global Handwashing Day, the Lifebuoy mission is both clear and memorable.
	Furthermore, Unilever is very transparent about its intentions and its business objectives. Doing well by doing good always means the social benefits go hand in hand with achieving business growth objectives. The company makes it sufficiently clear that it is a commercial operation and not a charity.

Target audiences of the programme modules

The primary target audiences for the behaviour change programmes are schoolchildren and their mothers. There is communication directed at children, working with cartoon characters to relate the message in a fun and motivating way. Throughout the programme, mothers are seen as key to reinforcing handwashing with soap behaviour with their children and establishing good household hygiene habits.

Secondary target audiences imperative to delivering the one billion objective are teachers, partner organizations and governments, key opinion leaders and Unilever employees.

In order to scale up existing Handwashing Behaviour Change Programmes, a 'Train the Trainer' model has been piloted in Indonesian schools in a partnership with local NGOs and the Indonesian government, and will be rolled out to other markets. The model involves Lifebuoy teams training teachers to deliver the Handwashing Behaviour Change Programme, each of them then cascading it to a further three schools to create a multiplier effect.

In the context of skills development and partnerships, dialogue and engagement with local, regional and global partner organizations are the communication focus.

Advocacy initiatives aimed at both the primary target audience and key opinion leaders. In the context of Global Handwashing Day 2012, millions of people around the world – including children, mothers and opinion leaders – made a pledge to wash their hands with soap. Other advocacy initiatives include the Africa Sanitation Conference 2011, where Unilever partnered with the African Ministers' Council on Water and reached over 900 opinion leaders from 65 African countries to raise the profile of sanitation and hygiene in all political and development processes in Africa. The overall objective of the conference was to get Africa on track to meet the Millennium Development Goal for Sanitation and Hygiene (MDG7).

BUSINESS CASE AND RESULTS

Key societal impacts of the programmes

The goal of the Lifebuoy Handwashing Behaviour Change Programme is extremely ambitious: to change the hygiene behaviour of one billion consumers across Asia, Africa and Latin America by 2015 by promoting the benefits of handwashing with soap at key occasions.

What has been achieved so far in terms of reach and actual health impact?

In 2007–2008, Lifebuoy conducted a scientific human volunteer study in Mumbai, India, involving 2,000 families. The study was designed to assess whether using soap at the right times could reduce the incidence of sickness in families. The study revealed that among those families that received hygiene education, the use of soap increased by as much as ten times and led to a 25% reduction in the number of incidences of diarrhoea among children aged five. The trial also showed a 19% reduction in acute respiratory infections, a 46% reduction in eye infections, and a 26% reduction in school absence due to illness. This study methodology and its impact form the basis of the new Lifebuoy Handwashing Behaviour Change Programme today.

By the end of 2012, over 130 million people will have been reached by the Lifebuoy Handwashing Behaviour Change Programme across 14 countries, reducing incidences of diarrhoea and saving thousands of lives.

Ongoing diary studies in Indonesia – involving innovative use of a daily activity sticker diary applied since 2011 – show an 11% increase in handwashing occasions from pre-intervention (September 2011) to six months after programme completion in May 2012, indicating sustained behavioural change. Further quantification of handwashing occasions is expected in 2013 from studies currently running in Indonesia, Kenya and Ghana, applying smart sensor technology. This Unilever-developed technology places smart sensors inside soap bars, enabling researchers to gather accurate data to measure the impact of handwashing occasions unobtrusively at a micro level.

Commercial impact of campaigns on the Lifebuoy brand

The commercial impact of Lifebuoy Handwashing Behaviour Change Programmes is measured using in-home panels, combined with sales data, market share and brand equity tracking data. Unilever's own in-home panels, across thousands of consumer homes in key markets, track general soap category consumption, and specifically Lifebuoy consumption. Full evaluation studies are in place for 2012, but positive results have been recorded from programmes in 2010 and 2011:

- In Pakistan and Vietnam – which started the Lifebuoy Handwashing Behaviour Change Programme in 2010 – increases in Lifebuoy consumption of 8% and 11% respectively were recorded in 2010.
- In Indonesia, soap usage increased overall by 8% from pre-intervention levels in September 2011 to May 2012.
- In India, the multi-brand Khushiyon Ki Doli consumer contact programme – which educated 30 million 'unreachable' mothers in rural India about germ protection – delivered 8% growth in Lifebuoy consumption in 2011 (relative to 1% growth in comparative geographical areas without the programme), in addition to improved brand awareness and endorsement.

Diarrhoea rates have decreased significantly over the last five years, and all trends tend to indicate that there is a direct correlation between commercial growth and diarrhoeal disease reduction.

Internal impacts of campaigns

On 15 October 2012, over 33,000 Unilever employees from 97 Unilever offices around the world joined in Lifebuoy-initiated Global Handwashing Day celebrations. This high level of employee engagement demonstrates the high profile the Lifebuoy campaign has within Unilever and the support the entire organization provides for this crucial corporate initiative, as part of the Unilever Sustainable Living Plan.

KEY SUCCESS FACTORS

Table 10.2 shows the key success factors of the Lifebuoy Global Handwashing Behaviour Change Programme case.

Table 10.2 Key success factors – Lifebuoy's Global Handwashing Behaviour Change Programme

Key success factors	Description
1. Integration into country marketing plans	Internal alignment with each country's management and marketing teams is crucial to achieving programme scale. The Lifebuoy Global Social Mission is fully integrated into the work of the Brand Development marketing team, and they work with their colleagues in regions and countries who are responsible for the local business, to set up formalized agreements to achieve the Lifebuoy Handwashing Behaviour Change Programme targets in a way that makes business sense.
2. Effective partnerships are essential	Partnerships at all levels are fundamental to the success of Lifebuoy Handwashing Behaviour Change Programmes. The brand has pioneered co-investment models both with government organizations and with NGOs. For instance, in Vietnam, Lifebuoy is working with government institutions to make Handwashing Behaviour Change Programmes part of the national curriculum. In communicating with partners, it is important to be transparent about Lifebuoy's business objectives. The Lifebuoy ambition is to do good while doing good business, as without business success, Lifebuoy programmes are not sustainable. Unilever and Lifebuoy do not need to feel guilty about this objective, and therefore will prefer only to work with those organizations which also understand the business context and are not averse to profit.
3. Low-cost model for sustainability	In order to drive behaviour change in hundreds of millions of people, Lifebuoy recognized it needed to find ways to drive down programme costs. For instance, it moved away from expensive promoter-driven models, and instead leveraged networks and partnerships. The brand also incorporated lower-cost digital elements to increase reach.

REFERENCES

Interview with Dr Myriam Sidibe, Unilever-Lifebuoy Global Social Mission Director.

Interview with Eloy Parra, PPPHW (Private Public Partnership for Handwashing with Soap).

Interview with Katie Carroll, formerly AED, now FHI360.

'Lifebuoy Adopts Indian Village', www.hul.co.in/brands-in-action/detail/Lifebuoy-adopts-Indian-village/346573/?WT.contenttype=brands%20in%20action (accessed 2 June 2013).

'Social Marketer Profile Series – Myriam Sidibe on Unilever's Social Mission', by Heather Ray, 26 April 2012, http://i-socialmarketing.org/blog/entry/social-marketer-profile-series--myriam-sidibe-on-unilever-lifebuoys-social-mission- (accessed 2 June 2013).

Unilever, *Lifebuoy Brand Equity*, www.docstoc.com/docs/111031783/Lifebuoy-Brand-Equity---PDF (accessed 10 June 2013).

Unilever, *Unilever Sustainable Living Plan: Progress Report 2011*, www.unilever.com/images/uslp-Unilever_Sustainable_Living_Plan_Progress_Report_2011_tcm13-284779.pdf (accessed 2 June 2013).

Unilever, *Lifebuoy Way of Life – Towards Universal Handwashing with Soap: Social Mission Report 2010–2012*, www.unilever.com/images/slp-Lifebuoy-Way-of-Life_2010-12%20oct12_tcm13-352150.pdf (accessed 2 June 2013).

Best Practice Case 2: Fairtrade Comes of Age

IDEA AND INSPIRATION

Idea behind Fairtrade

In the 1950s, the Fair Trade movement started in the US and in Europe as a partnership between non-profit importers (non-governmental development charities) as a way of alleviating poverty in poorer countries. It was later recognized that small-scale farmers and workers in developing countries were struggling to make a decent living with low market prices. Fair Trade was therefore seen as an opportunity to help them protect their livelihoods. With this legacy, during the 1980s and 1990s, organizations such as Max Havelaar, the Fairtrade Foundation, Transfair and Rättvisemärkt amongst others emerged to seek to transform trading structures and practices in favour of the poor and disadvantaged in developing countries. They created different Fairtrade certification marks in an effort to create fairer trading conditions for producers.

These Fairtrade labelling initiatives came together to form the Fairtrade Labelling Organizations International in 1997, now known as Fairtrade International (FLO). It is the umbrella organization for Fairtrade across the globe. The role of Fairtrade International is to set Fairtrade standards and co-ordinate the development of a global strategy for Fairtrade. In 2002, Fairtrade International launched the international Fairtrade Certification Mark (see Figure 10.3), which appears on products and means that Fairtrade ingredients have been traded in compliance with Fairtrade Standards. From 2004, this included auditing the producers and traders by FLO-CERT to ensure they comply with the standards.

Figure 10.3 The Fairtrade logo has become the symbol for Fairtrade, recognized by most European consumers

Source: Reproduced courtesy of Fairtrade International.

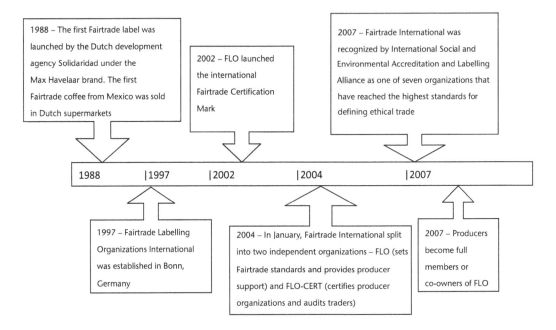

Timeline of Fairtrade

PROPOSITION AND EXECUTION

Concept of Fairtrade

In the early days of Fairtrade, there were people who made jokes about those who purchased and drank fairly-traded coffee. This was because there was a time when the product quality of Fairtrade products was not up to standard, so that the consumer paid a premium for what was considered to be inferior-tasting coffee – for example, consumers had to feel that supporting coffee farmers in Nicaragua or elsewhere was more important than good or great-tasting coffee. Those days are long gone, and Fairtrade has become not just an organization improving the lives of underprivileged producers of coffee, cocoa and many other products, but also a positive model or blueprint and a market success.

Fairtrade is a trading partnership based on dialogue, respect and transparency which seeks greater equality in international trade. It is an innovative supply chain model, and aims to distribute its economic benefits to all stakeholders in a fair way. In terms of communications, Fairtrade organizations engage actively in supporting producers and consumers, awareness-raising, and campaigning for changes in the practices of conventional international trade. In 2002, Fairtrade International launched the international Fairtrade Certification Mark. This is applied to products that meet the Fairtrade Standards, including cocoa, coffee, fruit juices, vegetables, sugar and rice, and non- food products such as cotton and flowers. The objective of launching the Fairtrade Certification Mark was to improve the label's public visibility. To attain the Fairtrade Certification Mark on products, companies have to go through inspections and audits under the Fairtrade certification system. This includes inspections of companies' compliance with Fairtrade Standards to ensure relevant social and environmental standards are met.

Are there any campaign-specific communication principles?

Table 10.3 shows the campaign-specific communication principles of the Fairtrade case

Table 10.3 Campaign-specific communication principles – Fairtrade

Principles	Example
1. Producer partnerships	Producers are not simply beneficiaries, they are also joint partners in Fairtrade. Fairtrade-certified producers jointly own and manage Fairtrade International, and they have the opportunity to be involved in decision-making. Through Fairtrade International's Board, its committees and consultation processes, producers can influence prices, premiums, standards and overall strategy.
2. External communication	The Policy and Communications Department of the Fairtrade Foundation (UK), like any Fairtrade International member, aims to raise public awareness and consumer demand for Fairtrade in the UK. It has launched a variety of programmes and campaigns, including developing local campaigns in towns, churches and schools, media relations and PR, as well as publications. Also, the Fairtrade Certification Mark on products serves as the marketing tool for the producer organizations. The high visibility of the mark allows consumers to make responsible purchasing choices and builds awareness of Fairtrade products.

Target audiences

The primary target audience of Fairtrade since its inception is producers, particularly small-scale farmers and farm workers. There are more than 1.2 million workers and farmers in 66 developing countries in Africa, Asia and Latin America who benefit from Fairtrade. At the other end of the value chain, consumers are the secondary target audience.

Key benefits to Fairtrade target audiences

Fairtrade benefits for small-scale farmers and farm workers include:

- increased power and a more significant role in the trade of their produce;
- producer organizations can request pre-finance from buyers of up to 60 per cent of the negotiated purchase price;
- training from Fairtrade International or partner organizations;
- protection of workers' rights in line with ILO (International Labour Organization) conventions;
- the Fairtrade premium to invest in business development or community projects such as health care and education;

The Fairtrade benefits to consumers include the following:

- Like other ethical labels, the Fairtrade system provides consumers with an opportunity to make ethical purchasing decisions, in line with their values and principles. The Fairtrade Certification Mark provides the assurance that specific criteria have been met in the production and trade of the product.
- Purchasing products with the Fairtrade Certification Mark helps consumers make a (political) statement and feel empowered by playing a small part in addressing global trade inequalities and thus 'doing good'.

BUSINESS CASE AND RESULTS

Key societal impacts of Fairtrade

With the establishment of Fairtrade, marginalized farming communities in the developing world have significantly benefited from fairer terms of trade (see Figure 10.4). In 2012, there were 991 Fairtrade-certified producer organizations in 66 producing countries, which represented over 1.2 million farmers and workers. In addition to other benefits, approximately €65 million in Fairtrade premiums was distributed to communities in 2010–11 for use in business and community development. Fairtrade International estimates that seven million people, including workers, their families and dependents, directly benefit from Fairtrade.

Figure 10.4 A farmer in the Dominican Republic harvesting cocoa with simple tools
Source: Reproduced courtesy of Fairtrade International.

Commercial impacts of Fairtrade

The sales of Fairtrade-certified products worldwide grew by 12% during 2010–11. In 2011, Fairtrade certified sales amounted to approximately €4.92 billion. In 2012, more than 1.2 million producers and workers in 66 developing countries are now benefiting from global Fairtrade sales. In some national markets, Fairtrade accounts for 20–50% of market share in certain products. These are the markets where Fairtrade has managed to move from niche to mass market – something which has not been achieved in all markets as yet.

The most successful move from niche to mass market is in the UK. For instance, Sainsbury's Fairtrade sales increased by 19% to £280 million in 2010 compared to 2009, which implies that one in four pounds spent on Fairtrade in the UK is spent at a Sainsbury's store. Its banana sales rose 10% after changing to Fairtrade. It sells 650 million Fairtrade bananas a year, which is more than all of the other major supermarkets combined, according to Kantar Worldpanel. Sainsbury's banana sales alone generate almost £4 million of Fairtrade premiums a year, benefiting small-scale farmers, farm workers and farming communities in the Dominican Republic, Colombia and St Lucia. During Fairtrade Fortnight 2012, Sainsbury's sold £12 million worth of Fairtrade products, which was a record – an increase of 11% compared to 2011. The retailer expects sales of Fairtrade products to reach £1 billion by 2020.

Brand impacts of Fairtrade

According to GlobeScan's worldwide study among 17,000 consumers in 24 countries, Fairtrade is the most widely recognized ethical label.[7] In fact, this and other studies show that it has managed to become a strong brand rather than just being a label. This sets it apart from other labels and certification schemes. In many countries, it is at least in the top two or three labels with the highest consumer awareness. There has been some success in establishing brands and lines that mainstream Fairtrade. Successful examples include Cadbury's Dairy Milk chocolate, Sainsbury's bananas and Starbucks coffee.

In Germany, the Ethical Brand Monitor, a major research study on the sustainability dimension of brands, found in 2009 that the Fairtrade Certification Mark was perceived as the most ethical brand among 406 researched brands, assessed by a representative sample of 6,500 respondents, with a stronger reputation than even the much-promoted Bio (organic) label.

LESSONS LEARNED AND KEY SUCCESS FACTORS

Lessons learned

These are the main lessons from the Fairtrade case:

1. It is possible for an NGO to create a strong consumer brand without massive advertising spending.
2. Improving the living and working conditions of farmers and farm workers can be

---

7   Fairtrade press release, 'Global Survey Shows UK Leads the Way on Fairtrade', 11 October 2011, www.fairtrade.net/single_view1+M533a992acd9.html (accessed 10 June 2013).

communicated as a consumer benefit that consumers are willing to pay a certain price premium for, as long as the products deliver value for money.

3. The ethical dimension of a brand cannot compensate for deficits in the value-for-money proposition of a product, but needs to be an added-value component. Fairtrade coffee, for instance, needs to be of at least the same quality and taste as any other similarly priced coffee. The Fairtrade Certification Mark signals that the product is an ethically 'good' product.

4. Ethical brands can become mainstream. Fairtrade has achieved this goal, at least in some UK product categories. In other markets and segments, this objective has not been achieved yet.

5. High brand trust and credibility at both ends of the supply chain require a strict and transparent process.

Key success factors

Table 10.4 shows the key success factors of the Fairtrade case.

Table 10.4 Key success factors – Fairtrade

Key success factors	Description
1. Trust between the Fairtrade Certification Mark and consumers	Part of the success of the Fairtrade programme depends highly on consumers' trust in the Fairtrade Certification Mark. According to worldwide GlobeScan research, 64% of consumers say they trust the Fairtrade Certification Mark. This can be attributed to the transparent information given in the Fairtrade certification process. Trust between the Fairtrade Certification Mark and consumers has developed to become a credible trademark of guarantee.
2. Consumer empowerment	Brands effectively convey benefits to consumers by providing them reasons to purchase Fairtrade products. With the Fairtrade Certification Mark, consumers are given information enabling them to make responsible choices in consumption. Also, they are able to help improve the livelihood of people in developing countries, and receive high-quality products in return.
3. Support by public authorities	One of the important factors of market success is the increasing recognition by the public at regional, national and international levels. Some European governments and the European Parliament strongly support awareness-raising campaigns and pilot schemes in Fairtrade. With the support of public authorities, there is more attention given to Fairtrade in the media and among the general public. This has also enhanced the credibility of the Fairtrade International labelling system.

REFERENCES

'An Interview with Rob Cameron, CEO of Fairtrade International', www.accountability.org/about-us/news/cr-leaders-corner/rob-cameron.html (accessed 2 June 2013).

'General Overview of the Fairtrade', www.slideshare.net/fairtrade/general-overview-of-the-fairtrade (accessed 2 June 2013).

Interview with Harriet Lamb, Director of the Fairtrade Foundation (now CEO of Fairtrade International), 4 December 2009.

'What is Fairtrade?', www.fairtrade.net/what-is-fairtrade.html (accessed 2 June 2013).

11 *The Public Sector Perspective – Best Practice Cases*

Best Practice Case 3: The German Bio-label

IDEA AND INSPIRATION

Idea behind the German Bio-label

The background to this was the BSE[1] crisis of 2000–2001, which in Germany culminated in the resignation of the Ministers of Health and Agriculture. It dominated the media for months and caused a massive feeling of insecurity about food among the population. Organic products gained prominence, but there were a vast number of different labels, based on different standards and schemes. An idea to create one simplified label based on the agreed European Bio-Standard came up which would clearly communicate 'organic' to consumers. Products that wanted to carry the label needed to at least conform to the EU organic farming guidelines.

PROPOSITION AND EXECUTION

Concept and development of the Bio-label

The Bio-label (in German, Bio-Siegel) was developed under enormous time pressure, yet a multi-stakeholder approach was applied. Several roundtable discussions with all relevant stakeholder groups, farmers' associations, representatives from the food industry, the animal feed industry and consumer advocacy groups were conducted, because all of these groups were relevant for communications about the label and essential for ensuring buy-in from consumers. Both organic farmers and conventional farmers were involved to create the broadest possible platform and consensus. Consensus was achieved in record time with a little help from the BSE crisis, which provided the necessary sense of urgency to produce results.

---

1   Bovine spongiform encephalitis, commonly known as 'mad cow disease'.

Jan. 2012 – 3,992 companies used the Bio-label on 63,633 products

Jan.–Feb. 2002 – official market launch of the Bio-label. The development and launch of the label took place with unprecedented speed by legislative standards, and was supported by a heavy advertising campaign, created by Hamburg-based Wire Communications

Nov. 2000 – first BSE cases in Germany. Massive media scandal that led to the resignation of two ministers in January 2001

Dec. 2010 – 3,803 companies used the Bio-label on 61,744 products

Dec. 2011 – 80% said it aided awareness (according to a TNS Emnid survey)

| 2000 | | 2001 | | 2002 | | 2010 | | 2011 | | 2012 |

Sep. 2001 – presentation of the Bio-label by German Agriculture and Consumer Protection Minister Renate Künast

Launch of the EU organic label that can be used by products that contain a minimum of 95% of ingredients from organic farming. In Germany, so far it is not used much due to high awareness of the German Bio-label

Timeline of the German Bio-label

The reason consensus was achieved was that all parties gained from the label: all benefited from the reduction in complexity which the label provided (there are 200–300 pages of laws and regulations governing organic farming). The label itself, as a brand, is simple and communicates instantly and clearly the message 'organic' in three letters ('Bio' – see Figure 11.1). Consumers benefited because the label created transparency and was easy to understand. They felt they were able to trust it, as all products and their production processes were externally checked. For producers, it was beneficial as all they had to do was to produce a sticker to put on their packs or modify their packaging design accordingly.

A key difference to the launch of other labels was that the government realized the Bio-label would only gain broad acceptance if it were well known. So the launch of the label in February 2002 was supported by a fully-fledged advertising campaign (see Figure 11.2) with over €15 million of media spend, according to Dr Ingo Braune from the German Federal Ministry of Food, Agriculture and Consumer Protection. His ministry headed up the Bio-label campaign, primarily in the print media, with some TV exposure. The campaign paid off. The label today is used by nearly 4,100 companies on over 65,500 products (as of September 2012) and has an 80%+ awareness level (2010 83%, 2011 80%), which next to the private Bioland label (81%) makes it the most well-known sustainability label in Germany (compared to Fairtrade 48%, Rainforest Alliance Certified 39%, FSC 16% and MSC 13%).

Figure 11.1 German Bio-label logo
Source: Reproduced courtesy of Bundesministerium für Ernährung, Landwirtschaft und Verbraucherschutz (Germany).

Figure 11.2 'One label from Apfel [apple] to Zwiebel [onion]' – stylish advertising to create awareness
Source: Reproduced courtesy of Bundesministerium für Ernährung, Landwirtschaft und Verbraucherschutz (Germany) and Wire Advertising.

What role does the German Bio-label play for Germany and Europe?

Dr Braune states that for Germany, the label has catalysed the breakthrough of organic food, even though it is hard to prove this statistically. It has brought organic out of a microscopic niche and created a market segment. It means that no longer are organic foods only to be found in health food stores, now they can be purchased in any retail outlet, including the powerful discounters. And all organic products in those retail outlets carry the Bio-label: 'Compared to all other food declaration initiatives that we have worked on, including "GMO-free", it has had a more profound impact. The [BSE] situation and the interest of the population were unique.'

The Bio-label has had an influence on discussions at the European level. It contributed to the European Commission's decision to launch a compulsory organic label. However, Dr Braune is critical of the path the Commission has chosen, and is not sure the EU label will have a comparable success to the German Bio-label. 'We focused on consultation, stakeholder engagement, a voluntary approach and the law of supply and demand,' he explains. 'The EU relies on bureaucratic obligations, legislative power and a top-down approach.'

Are there any campaign-specific communication principles?

Table 11.1 shows the campaign-specific communication principles of the German Bio-label case.

Table 11.1   Campaign-specific communication principles – German Bio-label

Principles	Example
1. Substance	The Bio-label is based on very detailed standards and procedures that make the status 'Bio' reliable and trustworthy.
2. Bottom-up	The inclusive 'roundtable' stakeholder consultation approach meant that there was broad buy-in by all relevant stakeholders upfront.
3. Simplicity	The label itself is simple, has good shelf-impact and stands out against other labels.
4. Commitment	The willingness of the German government to provide substantial launch support in the form of a €15 million awareness-building advertising campaign increased the acceptance of the label with companies. The Bio-label became a brand with a positive image and reputation that other brands were willing to put on their packaging.

Target audience

The two key target audiences were companies (farmers and the food industry) and consumers. Communication with companies was primarily directed via industry associations, using the roundtable approach, but there were one-to-one consultations as well. Consumers were targeted directly with the advertising campaign (see Figure 11.3). Indirectly, they were approached via the companies, the label on the products and communication for Bio-labelled products and brands.

How did/does the collaboration with companies/the private sector work?

While the primary partners are the industry associations, there was and is quite a lot of direct consultation by the Federal Ministry of Food, Agriculture and Consumer Protection with individual companies. Dr Braune observes: 'It was always and continues to be a very open and constructive dialogue, which is something of a positive exception.' Obviously, individual dialogue does not mean tailor-made solutions, which the legislature cannot provide. However, it is this open and two-way communication that has most likely made a difference.

Figure 11.3 'Organic products do the trick' – building the value perception
Source: Reproduced courtesy of Bundesministerium für Ernährung, Landwirtschaft und Verbraucherschutz (Germany) and Wire Advertising.

What role does the label itself play in communicating 'organic' to consumers?

'With the label we created a framework, that very soon was up and running and basically did not need any major support,' says Dr Braune. The initial campaign kicked it off, then the companies using the label took over the communication and ran with it. The ministry treats it as a media topic and regularly feeds news into the pipeline, plus it has its own dedicated website.[2] Due to its broad acceptance, the label has basically become synonymous with 'organic' for consumers.

BUSINESS CASE AND RESULTS

Key societal impacts of the Bio-label

The Bio-label has managed to make organic mainstream, to get it out of a very small niche. It has very high awareness (see above), so that everybody, including those who do not purchase organic products, knows about it.

Furthermore, it has helped to build momentum, not just on the demand side with consumers, but as a result on the supply side as well, and more farmers have moved to organic farming. There is wider acceptance of organic farming in agricultural areas – Bio-farmers are no longer the oddballs of rural communities.

How does the Bio-label work commercially for brands and producers? Do they get a sales uplift?

The sheer market growth of the organic segment and the fact that discounters created their own Bio-product lines, indicates that Bio has been a commercial success for all parties

---

2   www.bio-siegel.de.

involved. And Dr Braune cites an interesting research finding from Bonn University, which conducted studio tests of organic products with and without the Bio-label. They were able to show that the Bio-label stimulated the 'reward areas' in the brain and led to higher purchase intent.

LESSONS LEARNED

These are the main lessons learned from the German Bio-label scheme's implementation:

1. The key lesson and success factor was securing the buy-in of all major stakeholder groups upfront. The investment in that bottom-up approach was the basis for the incredible speed to market.
2. The label itself was simple.
3. Government as an initiator is pre-competitive and trustworthy.
4. Transparency and substance are a basis for trust.

REFERENCES

Interview with Dr Ingo Braune, Bundesministerium für Ernährung, Landwirtschaft und Verbraucherschutz (BMELV).

Best Practice Case 4: The French Environmental Labelling Experiment

IDEA AND INSPIRATION

Idea behind the French Environmental Labelling Experiment[3]

Consumption of domestic goods, particularly food, is a major source of carbon emissions. In the effort to alleviate CO_2 emissions, it is crucial to educate and inform consumers about product-related CO_2 emissions and other negative environmental effects in order to change purchasing behaviour. To boost the general public's environmental awareness, the French government and companies like the major retailer Casino jointly founded the Le Grenelle environment multi-stakeholder platform,[4] a very broad roundtable, and initiating the French Environmental Labelling Experiment. The Grenelle Roundtable is based on the Grenelle I law (2009), which stipulates the right of consumers to have environmental information about products. Grenelle II provides the legal basis for the Environmental Labelling Experiment: there was a legal requirement to display carbon and environmental indicators on consumer products on the basis of a trial phase starting on 1 July 2011. The idea of the Environmental Labelling Experiment is to learn about how product-related environmental information can be communicated effectively to consumers and how it can help them to make informed choices based on this additional information, for instance by considering the climate impact of their purchases. The experiment allows participating companies and brands to develop their own labelling concepts and ideas. The French Sustainable Development Ministry will evaluate the lessons learned from the experiment and use them as input for a planned mandatory environmental label for consumer products. The experiment is expected to raise awareness of the relevance of sustainability in the context of personal consumption to pave the way for such a label.

PROPOSITION AND EXECUTION

Concept of the French Environmental Labelling Experiment

From Grenelle I to the establishment of Grenelle II, the Grenelle Roundtable under the leadership of the Ministry of Sustainable Development developed the methodological framework for environmental labelling, called BPX 30-323. It encapsulated the general principles and the general methodological framework for the quantification of consumer products. This was adopted in July 2009 and revised in January 2011, after a test phase with the retailers Casino and E.Leclerc using product category rules (PCRs) defined for nine product categories.

After the Grenelle II law was passed, the experiment started with a call for projects in November 2010. Companies which were interested in taking part in the experiment could apply by the end of the year. A total of 230 applications were received and reviewed

---

3   'Expérimentation de l'affichage environmental' is the official French title. See www.developpement-durable.gouv.fr/-Experimentation-de-l-affichage,4303-.html (accessed 2 June 2013).

4   It is officially called the ADEME-AFNOR Stakeholder Platform, and consists of 670 organizations and over 1,000 experts. It has three sub-platforms: The Methodological Working Group, 13 sub-sector working groups (based on product categories) and the Communication Format Working Group. There is also a Database Governance Committee supporting the platform.

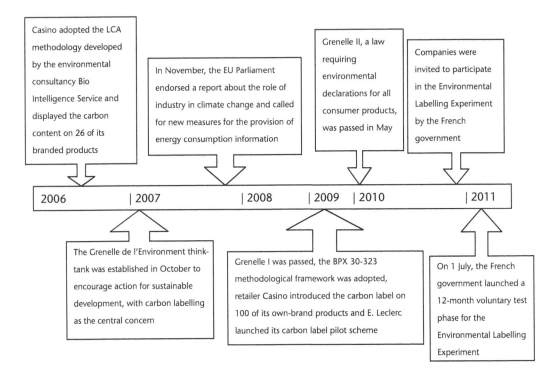

Timeline of the French Environmental Labelling Experiment

by the Sustainable Development Ministry, and a ministerial announcement on 11 March 2011 selected 168 companies to participate in the experiment, based on product type, technical feasibility and the overall quality of their proposals. Projects could start from 1 July to 1 December 2011, and had to run for a minimum of one year. The experiment was ended on 31 December 2012. At the beginning of 2013, the results of the experiment were to be reviewed and the results presented to the French parliament.

The labelling approach was based on product lifecycle thinking, and the environmental product information needed to be based on a lifecycle approach, including both product and packaging, and had to apply more than one environmental criterion – carbon labelling alone was not sufficient. Participating companies needed to adhere to the following terms:

- quantification and communication;
- compliance with the BPX 30-323 methodological framework and LCA approach;
- compliance with the relevant product category rule;
- displaying the carbon footprint in absolute figures;
- displaying at least one other environmental criterion;
- communication to consumers;
- participation for at least one year.

Participating companies had flexibility in the way they communicated the information to consumers, and which additional environmental indicator they chose apart from CO_2.

The Ministry of Sustainable Development and the Grenelle Roundtable supported participants with a public database and an online calculator to help with input data for the LCAs. Also, the LCA approach suggested was a simplified version of a full lifecycle assessment.

The participating companies were large (> 500 employees – 25%), medium-sized (50–500 employees – 45%) and small (< 50 employees – 30%).

The evaluation would be based on consumer reaction, technical feasibility and learning in terms of data, indicators and methods of calculation, brand and corporate image effects, costs, effects on the supply chain and market research results. Companies would receive a self-evaluation form which was common to all participants. Specific sector interviews would be conducted, and there would be control tests conducted by market surveillance authorities. Also, consumer and NGO opinions would be evaluated. Based on the evaluation, the ministry would then prepare a report and recommendation to the French parliament.

What makes the experiment unique from a CSR communication point of view is that the legislative process was based on a very broad stakeholder engagement process and that companies had excellent opportunities to communicate their position. Retailers Casino and E.Leclerc took this opportunity and ran two pilots on carbon labels as part of the consultation process. The results of these pilots were instrumental in defining the methodological and process framework for the national experiment (see Table 11.2).

Table 11.2   Principles of the French Environmental Labelling Experiment

Principles	Example
1. Multi-stakeholder approach	The very broad stakeholder engagement process is the cornerstone of the experiment. It ensures buy-in of all relevant societal groups and provides the experiment with a solid democratic foundation.
2. Legislative basis	The fact that the experiment is based on a national law provides it with the necessary authority.
3. Transparency	The process of the experiment and the data used are made transparent to the public by the Ministry of Sustainable Development website.
4. Lifecycle thinking	Lifecycle thinking is the methodological basis for the environmental labelling in the context of the experiment.
5. Quantitative evaluation	Quantitative evaluation will be the basis for the recommendation to parliament and the subsequent decision on mandatory environmental labelling.

Target audiences

The French Environmental Labelling Experiment had three main target audiences:

1. consumers at national level: their feedback would define what a mandatory environmental label should look like;
2. manufacturers and brands across all sectors, both those participating in the experiment and those watching from the sidelines;

3. retailers which carried the labelled products on their shelves – some were directly involved with own-label products.

Key benefits of the French Environmental Labelling Experiment for the target audiences

Consumers were exposed to a variety of different environmental labelling approaches. They could get used to them, evaluate them and provide their feedback on what worked for them and what did not. In addition, overall consumer awareness of the environmental impact of consumer products was raised and consumers were empowered to take more informed purchasing decisions.

Manufacturers and retailers had an opportunity to gain experience in labelling and feedback the lessons learned to the government. They were involved in and could influence the process of developing the mandatory environmental label.

LESSONS LEARNED SO FAR

The experiment was still ongoing at the time of writing. However, these are some of the first lessons learned:[5]

1. The call for participation in the experiment was a resounding success.
2. Business mobilization and involvement in the process was encouraging.
3. The breadth of ideas and different labelling executions and communications were inspiring.
4. Sector and supply-chain co-operation developed as a result of the experiment.
5. There has been considerable international interest in the French scheme.
6. The biggest challenges were connected to data availability for the product lifecycle assessments.

Casino's Indice Environnemental

'Initially we created the Carbon Index to help consumers compare the carbon impact of several products and support them in making the best choice,' explains Marc Voinnesson, Director of Sustainability Projects at Casino. As part of the Grenelle process, the retailer launched the index in 2008. The index is not an eco-label that implies that products carrying the label have a better environmental performance than those that do not have it. All products can carry the index to create transparency, allowing the consumer to compare and find the product with the lowest impact. 'By allowing customers to choose low-impact products, Casino hopes that this will create a knock-on effect for all manufacturers,' says Marc Voinnesson. In 2011, as part of the national Environmental Labelling Experiment, Casino launched step two, the Indice Environnemental (Environmental Index), which is now progressively replacing the Carbon Index.

---

5   Presentation by Sylvain Chevassus at the 6th PCF World Summit, Berlin, 26–27 October 2011.

The idea behind the Environmental Index is to have one value similar to the nutrition-related Guideline Daily Amount (GDA): the index represents the environmental impact of 100 grams of product compared to the environmental impact of the total daily food consumption of the average French person. The idea is that consumers will be able to relate more easily to the new index if it is displayed next to the nutrition information with the GDA value to which they are already accustomed. The index focuses on three environmental criteria only – greenhouse gases, water consumption and water pollution – and is calculated on the basis of the simplified lifecycle assessment methodology defined by the French government, as described above.

The Environmental Index is displayed on the front of the pack (see Figure 11.4), while on the back of pack there is a QR code that provides consumers with more detailed information on the environmental performance on the dedicated website www.indice-environnemental.fr.

Figure 11.4 Environmental indicators join calorie counts on Groupe Casino's Breton biscuits

Source: Reproduced courtesy of Groupe Casino.

'The Index needs to be displayed on the front of pack,' says Marc Voinnesson, 'otherwise it will not be noticed by consumers. Just having it displayed on (the) shelf is not sufficient.' So far, over 100 Casino-brand food products carry the index. Casino intends to maintain the index into 2013 until the government decides the direction for future environmental labelling in France, and was working on designing a unique web tool for calculating the index to be released by end of 2012 that could then be accessed by all national brands. 'There needs to be one index nationally for all products and brands, otherwise consumers will not be able to compare,' adds Voinnesson.

Commercial Impact of the Pilot

With the launch of the Carbon Index, which was expanded into a multi-criteria Environmental Index in 2011, Casino is seen as one of the pioneers of environmental labelling in France. The retailer has received recognition in the form of a number of sustainable business awards (for example, the Green Business Award 2010).

The lessons learned in conducting lifecycle analyses have contributed to efficiency gains and cost savings in the supply chain. Among consumers and civil society, Casino has gained a high level of environmental credibility for its products, and as a result significantly enhanced its reputation.

REFERENCES

Agri-Food Trade Service, Agriculture and Agri-Food Canada, *Food Labels in Europe: Changes to E.U. Labelling Regulations and New Eco-labels in France*, International Markets Bureau Market Indicator Report, September 2010, www.ats.agr.gc.ca/eur/5646-eng.htm (accessed 2 June 2013).

Blaikie, Heenan, 'Disclosing Carbon Emissions on Product Labels: Yah, Sure – When Pigs Fly, Right?', *Green Marketing & Advertising Law Update*, Issue 1, www.heenanblaikie.com/en/Publications/2010/Disclosing-Carbon-Emissions-on-Product-Labels-Yah,-Sure-When-Pigs-Fly,-Right-.html (accessed 10 June 2013).

Interview with Marc Voinnesson, Director of Sustainability Projects, Casino Group.

Ministère de l'Écologie, du Développement Durable et de l'Energie, 'Expérimentation de l'affichage environnemental' (description of the development of the Environmental Labelling Experiment), www.developpement-durable.gouv.fr/National-experimentation-for-the (accessed 2 June 2013).

Ministère de l'Écologie, du Développement Durable et de l'Energie, *National Experimentation on the Environmental Labelling of Consumer Products, National Experimentation Presentation Pack*, www.developpement-durable.gouv.fr/IMG/pdf/expaffichage-ang-b.pdf (accessed 2 June 2013).

OECD Global Forum on Trade: Trade and Climate Change, Paris, 9 and 10 June 2009, *Counting Carbon In The Marketplace: Part I – Overview Paper*, www.oecd.org/dataoecd/29/40/42886201.pdf (accessed 2 June 2013).

PCF World Forum, 8th PCF World Summit, 26–27 September 2012, Berlin, 'Renewable Resources in the Value Chain: A Viable Option for Reducing Environmental Footprints?', www.pcf-world-forum.org/tag/grenelle-2/ (accessed 2 June 2013).

Picard, Corrine, 'The Age of the Eco-label', 8 April 2009, www.packaging-gateway.com/features/feature52586 (accessed 2 June 2013).

Presentation by Marc Voinnesson, Director of Sustainability Projects Casino Group, on the Casino Environmental Index at the 6th PCF World Summit, Berlin, 26–27 October 2011.

Presentation by Sylvain Chevassus, French Ministry of Sustainable Development, at the 6th PCF World Summit, Berlin, 26–27 October 2011.

12 *The Supplier Perspective – Best Practice Cases*

Best Practice Case 5: The Tchibo and GIZ Worldwide Enhancement of Social Quality (WE) Project

IDEA AND INSPIRATION

Idea behind the WE Project

In 2005–2006, the German retailer Tchibo was targeted by the Clean Clothes Campaign due to critical working conditions in supplier factories in Bangladesh. It was the first time Tchibo had been confronted with the need to build up professional sustainability management. The privately-held company took the decision to make sustainability an integral part of its business strategy. The Corporate Responsibility(CR) department was set up to ensure the incorporation of sustainability into core business functions and processes, reporting directly to the CEO. As one of the first priorities, the Tchibo management team considered how best to tackle the issue of working conditions in the supply chain. 'We analysed existing approaches,' remembers Nanda Bergstein, who was the WE Project Manager for Tchibo, 'and at that time social auditing was the focus of most brands and retailers. Due to its top-down approach, however, this instrument is not very effective in initiating improvement. In fact, most audits are considered to be manipulated or faked and thus do not drive social change.' Therefore, the first driver for the WE Project, jointly initiated by Tchibo and German development organization GIZ,[1] was that an alternative to audits had to be found. Secondly, the Tchibo team learned that ensuring human rights in the workplace is primarily about building up relations between workers, their representatives, managers and buyers. In Asia, a lot of discrimination exists in factories, as well as a real communication gap between workers and managers. Apart from the consequences for the way workers are treated, this leads to disruptions in the production process, with a negative impact on economic sustainability. Bergstein adds:

> Based on these drivers, our idea was to work on the factory floor, to empower managers and workers to bridge the communication barriers and to achieve real improvements in working conditions, but also to be part of this process as a company. A clear challenge emerged here: we found that there was a lack of local qualified trainers familiar with the culture and local language.

---

1   Deutsche Gesellschaft für Internationale Zusammenarbeit ('German Agency for International Co-operation').

What inspired Tchibo to take a different approach to sustainable development in the supply chain was the insight that real change needed to happen, and that existing tools and approaches were not creating the necessary change because they did not take into account the complexity of the issue, which is illustrated by Figure 12.1. Bergstein says 'Tchibo has a corporate culture which is very hands-on and results-oriented. We want our initiatives to have an impact and lead to sustainable change.' To achieve this objective, Tchibo worked with GIZ to pilot a change methodology based on dialogue. An integral part of the pilot was to train local facilitators to act as multipliers of the approach.

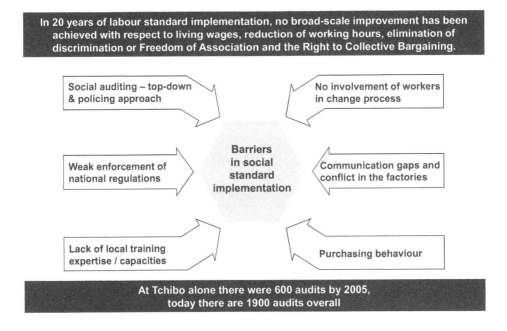

Figure 12.1 Barriers to realizing labour standards
Source: Reproduced courtesy of Tchibo GmbH.

PROPOSITION AND IMPLEMENTATION

Concept of the WE Project

The WE Project was initiated jointly by Tchibo and GIZ, the German development agency, and supported by consultancy SusA (Sustainability Agents). The key objective was to achieve significant improvements in the working conditions of suppliers in China, Bangladesh and Thailand. The project adopted an innovative approach by moving away from top-down-driven audits to a collaborative method, emphasizing the dialogue between managers and workers in factories, as well as between retailers (for example, Tchibo), importers and suppliers/producers. The focal point of the approach was to improve the relationships between workers, their representatives and managers, and to integrate all relevant actors within the improvement process. This trust-building was also meant to function as a stepping stone to realizing mature industrial relations.

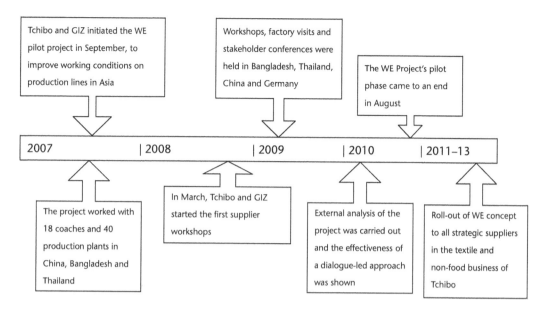

Timeline of the WE Project

Are there any campaign-specific communication principles?

Table 12.1 shows the campaign-specific communication principles of the WE Project case.

Table 12.1 Campaign-specific communication principles – WE Project

Principles	Examples
1. Transparency	To initiate change, transparency needs to highlight the actual realities and issues which are faced by workers and managers alike. Transparency is created through trusting that openness about difficulties in the factories will not result in punitive actions against the workers by managers, or the suppliers by customers. An enabling environment is necessary, in which the factory participants feel comfortable sharing their views. Good-quality solutions are based on root cause analyses, transparency of interests, and an understanding of everyone's goals.
2. Integration, putting workers and managers centre-stage	Effective change is created when all relevant stakeholders have been integrated into designing the 'good-quality solutions'. At a factory level, this means including in particular the workers, their representatives, middle managers and top managers; in the supply chain, the buyers, and in the overall local and international environment, governments, trade unions, non-governmental and international organizations.

Table 12.1 Campaign-specific communication principles – WE Project *continued*

Principles	Examples
3. Local ownership and motivation	A learning and ownership-building process among workers, middle managers and top managers is initiated that shows them that a systematic in-house dialogue is effective, as it helps to achieve better working conditions and business performance. In this context, managers are motivated to gradually move from informing workers to consulting them on specific matters (quality circles, suggestion boxes) and involving them in decision-making processes (for example, roundtables, worker representative committees).
4. Participation	Participation by buyers and other stakeholders in the workshops is important. Progressively involving buyers and relevant local stakeholders helps to address issues related to external framework conditions. Also, it is imperative to create awareness and understanding of commonalities and of differences in interests within factories, with the intention of empowering managers and workers to develop and decide on solutions in order to gain as much backing in a factory as possible. Participation also requires giving workers a platform to voice their concerns in a protected environment through building managers' trust in their abilities and their stake in the factories.
5. Process	A key to successful implementation and scaling lies in the application of the WE dialogue process: a clear sequence of tools, instruments and tasks for training participants, gradually balancing out hierarchical differences. This is methodologically done with the help of the six-step method (see Figure 12.2).
6. Action learning	A key principle as well as a key success factor of the WE approach is 'action learning'. Experience shows that lasting change results from working on actual, tangible problems, from defining concrete action points, executing those points and reflecting on the results. That reflection in turn results in adaptation and revised actions. It generates a positive momentum towards step-by-step improvement. Action learning implies that making mistakes and learning from these mistakes is part of the process, and ensures that action is not hampered by unnecessary perfectionism.

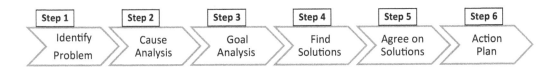

Step 1	Step 2	Step 3	Step 4	Step 5	Step 6
Identify Problem	Cause Analysis	Goal Analysis	Find Solutions	Agree on Solutions	Action Plan

Figure 12.2 The Tchibo and GIZ six-step process

Source: Reproduced courtesy of Tchibo GmbH.

Which are the key implementation parameters of the WE approach? What makes WE different and unique in the context of sustainable supply chain management?

What makes the approach unique is the focus on results and change rather than on achieving the certified application of a standard system. Demanding compliance with a standard can result in demotivation in factories, because the benchmark might seem to be very high, or even unachievable.

The GIZ adviser responsible for the WE Project, Priyani Thomas-Dirla, adds:

> From my perspective, the unique characteristic of the WE approach is its focus on long-term change of behaviour and communication processes, including (at) both the management and the workers' levels. This is key to enable the factories on a long-term basis to identify and solve challenges within the factory, which leads to self-sustaining change.

This is best illustrated by a concrete example – see Figure 12.3, which shows pictures from different workshops. Managers and workers receive training on overtime, including legal requirements as well as the different facets of the issue. They are then briefed to work through these six steps in the course over the following three hours:

1. **Brainstorming issues** – What are the issues managers and workers connect with overtime? What are the consequences for both sides? The managers complain that production quality decreases due to overtime and that they have to pay higher overtime wages. The workers indicate that they are exhausted, and have problems with their families, but also that they need to work this much to receive higher wages. The result of the discussion, therefore, is that both sides have an interest in reducing overtime.
2. **Conducting a root cause analysis** – This shows that the reasons for too much overtime are that the rejection rate is too high, product quality is deficient and working processes are inefficient (all of which reduce company profits), suppliers accepting too many orders, unprofessional production planning and late product changes by buyers.
3. **Defining goals** – Participants learn to express their goals connected to a certain workplace issue. They understand that everyone in the workplace has different goals. They are trained in how to formulate specific, measurable, achievable, relevant and time-bound goals. The individual goals are discussed, and a common goal is negotiated. Participants come to a joint agreement on their key goals with regard to a selected factory problem.
4. **Brainstorming solutions** – Together, managers and workers openly brainstorm options for solutions.
5. **Negotiating** – In a process of negotiation, managers and workers agree on a set of actions to be taken in the factories (such as setting up quality circles, changing the production and planning processes, and instigating performance-related bonuses) in order to create a win–win situation of co-operation on the factory floor.
6. **Action plan** – The results are captured in a joint action plan that is then implemented in the factory. As this plan has been developed jointly, the commitment on both sides – managers as well as workers – to execute this plan is high.

Figure 12.3 A WE training workshop in action from start to finish, illustrating the six-step problem analysis approach

Source: Reproduced courtesy of Tchibo GmbH.

A positive side-effect of this process is building trust. Managers and workers are busy with their tasks and forget with whom they are sitting at one table – which would normally seldom happen. They are entirely focused on the given task of jointly finding a solution within a clearly defined timeframe as well as the peer pressure of the other participating factories. Nanda Bergstein observes:

> *Suddenly they are communicating with each other, and with this comes the realization that they can actually relate to each other. This process is empowering, especially to the workers who show great courage when sharing their views with their owners and line managers on the issues they see in their workplaces and what they would like changed. During such a process many problems, also quite critical ones, are put on the table. The managers certainly also deserve recognition for accepting such feedback and for entering into a constructive dialogue.*

The overall programme duration is two years. The training is clearly structured, consisting of seven workshops and six factory visits. The reason for this long duration is that learning to conduct dialogue requires a paradigm shift for the parties involved and takes time. The specific programme format ensures that there is sufficient time to learn and there is positive competition through creating a platform for sharing between factories combined with individual, locally available support.

Priyani Thomas-Dirla of GIZ sums up the positive impact:

After those two years of the programme, we see that attitudes have really changed. Workers are much better able to articulate grievances openly and take responsibility for themselves. Top management have also adapted their attitudes and see a higher value in empowering and caring about their staff. This is because they have seen substantial change and progress in their factories. Thus, WE contributes to sustainable development, one of the core objectives at GIZ.

Target audiences

The pilot project targeted trainers, factory management, employees, trading companies and 40 factories in Bangladesh, China and Thailand which manufacture consumer goods such as jewellery, textiles, decorative articles and kitchenware for Tchibo. Tchibo buyers, importers, international consultants, local training providers and NGOs were involved in various project activities. To enrich the dialogue WE facilitates at the factory floor level, GIZ and Tchibo held four stakeholder conferences in Germany, Bangladesh, China and Thailand. The factories presented their results directly to the other stakeholders (including the workers), thereby creating a situation in which stakeholders and factories came together for the first time. 'This led to a very constructive atmosphere of dialogue,' Nanda Bergstein explains, 'and since everyone was present, everyone had to engage. All parties were able to speak for themselves and represent their interests directly. There was no space for dogmatism and highly theoretical discussion. The focus lay on the actual situation.'

The project is not an advertising tool to market Tchibo products to its consumers at the point of sale. Nanda Bergstein explains why:

Ensuring human rights is a basic principle of doing responsible business, not a marketing topic. Also, the methodology of WE and the dynamics behind improving labour rights are highly complex issues. They require a lot of explanation. Against this background, we have decided to have an open discussion culture with NGOs, trade unions and other interested stakeholders, but we do not use it as a communication tool at the point of sale.

Response and key benefits of the WE Project for target audiences

Despite some initial scepticism at the start of the pilot, managers and workers in all three countries demonstrated a growing openness to dialogue-oriented training. The number of participants taking part in each workshop increased as the project progressed – this applied to all hierarchical levels: top management, middle management and workers.

The most important benefits for workers and factories, the key stakeholders of the project, differ from site to site and depend on the level of ownership which the factories have taken over the project. Interestingly, it can be surmised that applying dialogue to improve social standards also has positive impacts on economic indicators.

As an example, in one production site – a kitchenware factory in the greater Shanghai region of China – the pilot resulted in the election of 18 worker representatives, creating communication channels for workers via roundtables, consultation processes, suggestion systems and worker participatory organizational health and safety (OHS) meetings.

Average wages increased by almost 50 per cent over a two-year period, and for the first time paid annual leave was given. Over the same period, the factory recorded a 30 per cent reduction in working hours. In addition to the benefits enjoyed by workers, overall factory productivity was enhanced. The production volume and the net profit of the company have increased annually by 10 per cent.

BUSINESS CASE AND RESULTS

Figure 12.4 shows the general impact of worldwide engagement in the WE Project.

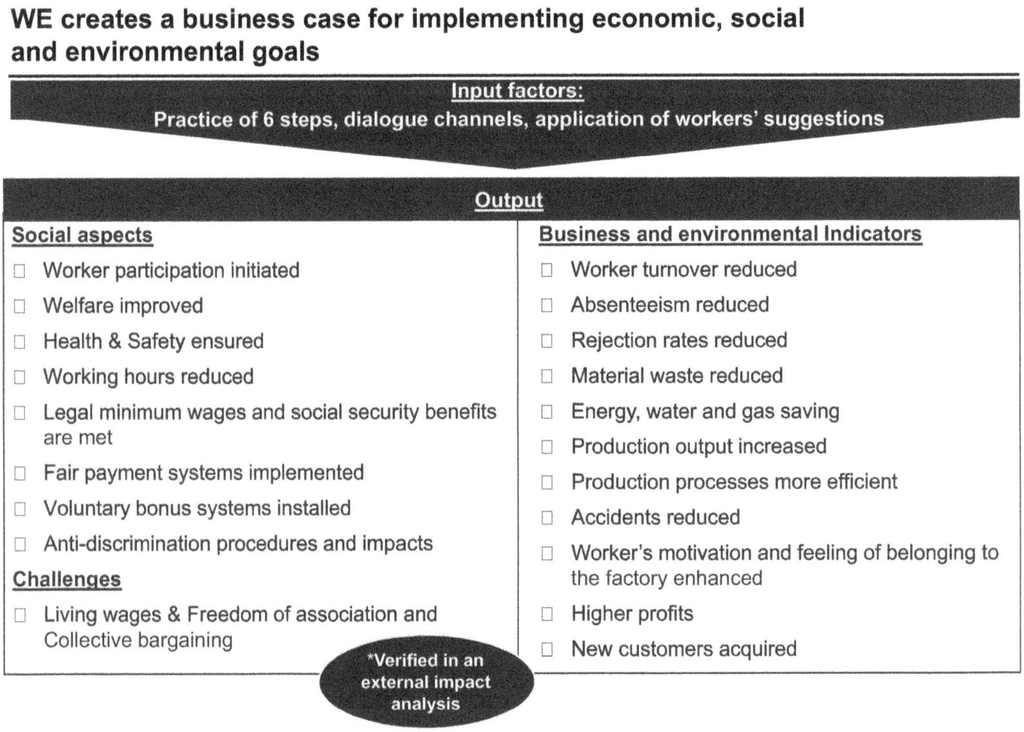

WE creates a business case for implementing economic, social and environmental goals

Input factors:
Practice of 6 steps, dialogue channels, application of workers' suggestions

Output	
Social aspects	**Business and environmental Indicators**
☐ Worker participation initiated	☐ Worker turnover reduced
☐ Welfare improved	☐ Absenteeism reduced
☐ Health & Safety ensured	☐ Rejection rates reduced
☐ Working hours reduced	☐ Material waste reduced
☐ Legal minimum wages and social security benefits are met	☐ Energy, water and gas saving
☐ Fair payment systems implemented	☐ Production output increased
☐ Voluntary bonus systems installed	☐ Production processes more efficient
☐ Anti-discrimination procedures and impacts	☐ Accidents reduced
Challenges	☐ Worker's motivation and feeling of belonging to the factory enhanced
☐ Living wages & Freedom of association and Collective bargaining	☐ Higher profits
	☐ New customers acquired

*Verified in an external impact analysis

Figure 12.4 General impact of worldwide engagement
Source: Reproduced courtesy of Tchibo GmbH.

Key societal impacts of the WE Project

For those workers involved in WE, a number of positive impacts can be noted: working hours were reduced and fair payment systems implemented, legal minimum wage levels were at least met, and social security benefits and voluntary bonus systems were instigated. Anti-discrimination procedures were put in place, health and safety standards ensured, and general welfare improved. Arguably the biggest difference was made by the introduction of worker participation, which led to motivation, empowerment, and ultimately to the development of real win–win solutions.

Challenges remain, as living wages and freedom of association and collective bargaining have not yet been achieved on a broad scale. Tchibo is working with selected factories to build model cases to generate further learning. The big solutions, however, go beyond the purview of the individual factory. This requires addressing the broader systemic issues of international competition and ensuring a strong national legislative and executive approach. This in turn requires a coalition of relevant international and national stakeholders.

Next to the improvements in social standards, the most important lesson of the pilot project was that real sustainable change is possible. Nanda Bergstein adds: 'Until WE, many of us in the field were under the impression that you cannot sustainably improve human rights at factory floor level. Now we have evidence that it is possible, but it requires a long-term commitment and process. There is no quick fix.'

Commercial impacts of the WE Project on factories

'Through the pilot, we learned that improving human rights and good business performance is not a contradiction, but highly compatible', says Nanda Bergstein:

> It deconstructs the myth that better working conditions always result in profit reduction. There is a positive business case, if the dialogue method is applied and management allows worker representation and participation! This is reflected in better product quality and higher productivity in our factories. Factories that initially may have been sceptical remained in WE because they found that the program helped them develop their organizations in a holistic manner.

On the business side, WE reduced absenteeism, worker turnover, accidents, rejection rates and material waste. On the other hand, production output increased, and the factories managed to acquire new customers. Environmentally, there were energy, gas and water savings. Overall, production processes became more efficient. Add to that increased motivation of the workers, and the net bottom-line result of WE was increased profits for the factory.

Internal impacts of the WE Project on Tchibo

The positive outcome of the pilot phase led to the company's decision to roll out WE to all strategic supplier factories by the end of 2015. Currently, 175 factories are in the process of qualification. Nanda Bergstein, formerly a member of the CR team, moved to Purchasing, and is in charge of the implementation team of nearly fifty personnel worldwide, with five Tchibo staff as direct reports, four external experts from SusA and a total of 38 local trainers on the ground across the programme countries. Tchibo covers all the related costs. The CR Department empowers the Purchasing Department by securing the programme's place in the overall corporate strategy and promoting it accordingly.

'Integrating the project into the purchasing department has made a real difference,' explains Nanda Bergstein. 'This supports a better alignment with purchasing strategy and processes.' Apart from promoting the integration of sustainability into the consumer goods supply chain, the team is now in the process of institutionalizing the dialogue between buyers and producers and building up new communication systems. This comprises new dialogue event formats and producing adequate information materials with the objective of ensuring better communication between buyers and suppliers.

Impacts on the Tchibo brand

WE helped build trust in Tchibo among external stakeholders. Nanda Bergstein states:

> *We try to keep up very open communication about what we learn, including the areas which require further work. For example, we need additional strategies to achieve living wages and freedom of association. These are systemic issues which require a coalition of governments, suppliers, brands, retailers, NGOs and trade unions to ensure broad-scale change.*

She is convinced that this openness and transparency is helping Tchibo move forward into collaboration and joint working on human rights solutions with all relevant stakeholders, moving away from singular company approaches to driving holistic, broad-scale change.

LESSONS LEARNED AND KEY SUCCESS FACTORS

Lessons learned

Nanda Bergstein explains the main lessons learned since the project's inception:

> *The main understanding gained is that change requires committed people who are willing to see things through and convince others to support it. Commitment is created through a very hands-on approach, allowing actors to learn by doing, then reflecting on the results, and then again adapting their steps based on the knowledge they have acquired.*

She adds that less is sometimes more, in the sense that in the beginning, it can be better if small decisions are taken with clear commitment and ownership. This facilitates the lesson that change is not harmful, but on the contrary, productive and helpful. With this mind shift, factories begin to set and implement more and more ambitious improvements targets.

Key success factors

'Sustainable improvement of social conditions at the supplier level cannot be forced top-down. Communication with suppliers and workers or managers at the factory level therefore cannot be one way,' says Bergstein. 'Open dialogue on expectations and barriers on all sides are required to create an understanding for the different positions, thereby opening up space for joint solutions. WE is a platform to enable dialogue between all stakeholders.'

Priyani Thomas-Dirla of GIZ adds three additional important success factors:

1. competent and culturally sensitive trainers, who are confident with social standard topics and the dialogue methodology, as well as having some knowledge of the technical production processes;
2. sincere and lasting commitment among the factory management, which is the basis for real workers' involvement as well for the implementation of joint action plans;
3. clear commitment of the buyer involved is also crucial in order to build a sustainable and strategic buyer–supplier relationship, and through this encourage suppliers to engage.

REFERENCES

GIZ, 'Success Factors: What is Special about WE', www.we-socialquality.com/WE-Specificity/First-results/Success-factors.aspx?l=2 (accessed 2 June 2012).

Interview with Nanda Bergstein, Head of Vendor Relations at Tchibo GmbH.

Interview with Priyani Thomas-Dirla, adviser at GIZ.

Tchibo, 'From Strength to Strength – with Dialogue and Participation: How Tchibo Empowers Factory Workers to Stand Up for their Rights at Work', www.tchibo-nachhaltigkeit.de/csrweb/servlet/content/649018/-/en/responsibility-supply-chains/consumer-goods/qualification-measures-for-suppliers.html (accessed 2 June 2012).

Tchibo, 'More than a Job: How Tchibo Strengthens its Corporate Culture and Promotes Employee Satisfaction', www.tchibo-nachhaltigkeit.de/csrweb/servlet/content/649084/-/en/employee-benefits/corporate-culture.html (accessed 2 June 2012).

WE Project, www.we-socialquality.com (accessed 2 June 2012).

Best Practice Case 6: ROMP – Fully Traceable Organic High Fashion

IDEA AND INSPIRATION

This case describes the rise and fall of ROMP, the first fashion brand to offer a complete couture lifestyle collection of organic products with full traceability. It is not a classic success story, for various reasons. However, the unique achievement of producing organic leather and the combination of state of the art fashion design and the 100 per cent commitment to transparency in the supply chain warrants its inclusion in this book. It has the potential to inspire, and there are important lessons to be learned. Most of the case is built on long conversations with Greg Sturmer, the mastermind behind the traceability and sustainability aspects of the venture.

The ROMP idea

Take a look at the video of 'So What' at the MTV music awards 2008. Our product is the playsuit Pink reveals after taking off her blue coat at about half time. This video sums up what ROMP was all about pretty well. The item was certified organic, traceable to source. But actually, the item was designed by Nina [Morgan-Jones] and selected by the stylist based on normal requirements, beauty, fitness, desirability, rock chick suitability and price, not sustainability. I say this video proves beyond doubt that eco-fashion can be a reality, and ROMP rocked.

This is how Greg Sturmer answered the question about the idea behind ROMP – it sums it up well. Other stars to wear ROMP were The Pussycat Dolls and The Sugababes.

ROMP was the brainchild of fashion designer Nina Morgan-Jones and Greg Sturmer, a former dealer in sheepskin and leather and a pioneer in organic leather production: 'I always felt that Nina's no-compromise attitude to fashion and my no-compromise attitude to transparency was what made the brand what it was. Squaring that particular circle is what it is all about.' It was[2] first and foremost a fashion brand, and delivered what a fashion brand needs to deliver – style. But it was a fashion brand with a key added value, and which was full transparency in the supply chain that you could experience online and in-store. Greg Sturmer explains:

The products were well-priced high fashion, but what was behind it was a bit much to comprehend, so we learned to promote it as a point-of-sale value proposition, after the initial attraction was achieved conventionally with style and comfort. The scope was quite vast, from farm to finished product in Los Angeles [where ROMP had a store], and up and down the waste streams. Each section of the supply chain was as good as it gets, and tied it all together with traceability software that allowed all supply chain partners to promote themselves both separately and as part of the project. We had both the first IFOAM-accredited[3] Certified

---

2 Nina Morgan-Jones continued to run the ROMP brand as Romp London until 2011. In 2011, she started a new label, Douek & Jones (www.douekandjones.com), which continues to carry her handwriting as a designer specializing in natural products (sheepskin, leather and suede). 'Knowing what I know about materials origin, I do the best I can, but there is no alternative to ROMP, and at present still no supplier that comes close to supplying raw materials of the calibre created by Greg,' she says, and adds: 'I still believe ROMP was a great success, in that we did what we set out to do. It's just a tragedy that we didn't get to carry on our work when it had been so flawlessly set up. As you say, to this day, there is still no other brand like ROMP.'

3 International Federation of Organic Agriculture Movement.

Organic Leather Products, GOTS certification,[4] as well as the first fully traceable (in terms of full disclosure) products for the consumer.

He continues:

ROMP being a high-end brand, certified traceable organic was out of the price point for the main market of IUV [ROMP's tannery in Slovenia]. My colleague Sonja Vavken then developed an economic leather line we called 'bali', which was a wet white, heavy metal-free, formaldehyde-free, PCP-free offering that was machine-washable to save aftercare costs and chemical use in general. The 'bali' product was offered for trial with Bernardo Fashions, an American distributor, which loved it. We furthermore successfully attracted J.C. Penney and Nordstrom in the States and had trial orders in from Marks & Spencer in the UK.

ROMP's strategy was therefore to have an own-label offering geared at securing better capacity utilization in the IUV tannery, with its own eco-credentials, including a reduced version of the traceability process, while presenting the unique, full-blown organic leather high-fashion products under the ROMP high-fashion brand. Greg Sturmer is still excited about some of the exquisite details:

The thing that tied it together was a marketing mechanism we developed for the States. Drop dead gorgeous imagery from ROMP. Rock stars wearing eco-fashion. And a hang tag we made from the tannery waste and filled with Californian poppy seeds. That said: 'Our product is different. Our waste is a rich nitrogen fertilizer which is legally safe and grows flowers better than normal soil.' This had the tracking number with the chemical data. It also quietly said: 'Ask our competitors to make you a paper tag from their waste, and just see if it's a legal fertilizer or not.' For the LA store, we were fully RFID-enabled[5] for each item, and (had) a lot more than stock control within the store; scanners and computers were hooked up to plasma screens, so customers could check the entire history and supply chain.

Concept of supply-chain traceability

The ROMP website, with partner Historic Futures, which built the traceability software for ROMP, gives a glimpse of what it was like to trace a product's supply chain online (customers were able to purchase the products online) – see Figure 12.5.

Customers could enter the traceability code and the product code, and the myString traceability software would allow them to follow the history of the product (in this case, a leather product) all the way back to the receipts for the hides that were going into the leather production.

Simon Warrick, Chief Technology Officer at Historic Futures, who collaborated with Greg Sturmer to develop the traceability system, talked about how the traceability idea developed:

---

4   Global Organic Textile Standard.

5   Radio Frequency Identification, a wireless method of transferring data.

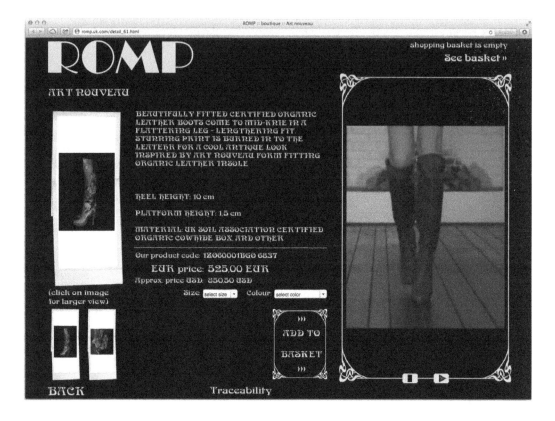

Figure 12.5 Designed by London designer Nina Morgan-Jones, ROMP leather products were pioneers of organic leather, offering full product traceability

Source: Reproduced courtesy of Janusz Krek, web design (www.kreksi.net), and Luis Monteiro, photography (www.luismonteiro.com).

> *Greg had been trading leather for some time, saw quality getting worse and worse, knew about all the toxic dyes and so on used in conventional leather production, and felt there had to be a better way of doing it. He looked at organic meat and skin, and saw he could add value to what they were doing. Our great idea was to introduce traceability into the supply chain. Greg really wanted to tell a great story rather than just solving business issues in the supply chain. We felt you needed to marry the two. Greg was a good five years ahead of the big brands back then in 2003, which have only now [2010] started to catch up.*

Together with the UK Soil Association, which certified the leather as organic, and Historic Futures, ROMP set up a fully transparent production system. For products to qualify as organic, the entire chain of production had to be licensed, which included the farmers, abattoir, tannery, design and manufacture of the finished product (see Figure 12.6). To meet the UK Soil Association standards, ROMP would obtain skins from livestock that was reared on sustainably managed land, given no chemical treatments against disease, and slaughtered at a licensed abattoir. He modified the production processes at IUV, ROMP's tannery in Slovenia, to eliminate toxic dyes, heavy metals and other chemicals typically used in leather tanning.

Figure 12.6 The labels ROMP's IUV factory produced for US retailer J.C. Penney were as 100 per cent organic as the clothes and leatherwear themselves

Source: Reproduced courtesy of Greg Sturmer, Director and co-founder of ROMP.

PROPOSITION AND EXECUTION

What are the communication principles behind ROMP?

The key target audience of the ROMP brand was female buyers of high-fashion items, including clothes, shoes and accessories. At the tannery, ROMP also produced own-label products that were slightly more high street fashion (for example, for Bernardo's USA), as mentioned above.

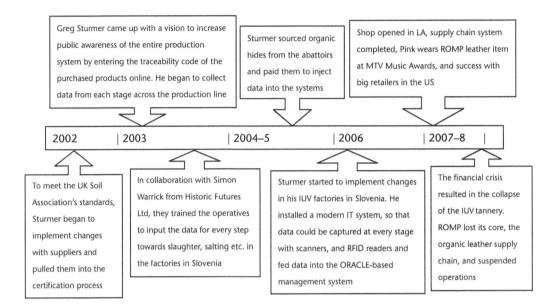

Timeline of ROMP and its fully transparent supply chain

BUSINESS CASE AND RESULTS

Environmental impacts of ROMP and its traceability system

Changing leather production to an organic process on a larger scale would have a significant positive environmental impact, as the conventional tanning process carries a heavy environmental footprint.

Commercial impacts of ROMP and its traceability system

Greg Sturmer says:

> ROMP as a brand never got the opportunity to show its full potential in its own right. But as a marketing mechanism to leverage-market the 'bali', it was extremely successful. Our customer Bernardo will still tell you he had issues about shutting the marketing side down when the supply failed. At the time, he was questioning our ability to license bali production and supply 60 million feet if the trials were successful. Bali was a genuine son-of-ROMP product, and it broke open the doors to retail sales. There was no failure in that regard.

However, following the global financial crisis that started after the Lehmann collapse in September 2008, IUV, the tannery in which ROMP had set up its organic supply chain and which Greg had been recruited to change in 2006, faltered. While ROMP was doing well playing its part in attracting interest, sales of the 'old' chromium-based products finally collapsed, exactly as Greg had predicted they would during the original discussions. That product range was dated, and the Chinese had caught up in terms of quality and surpassed IUV in reliability and proximity to the remaining global factories, also by then in China. Like General Motors, sales collapsed 50 per cent in one month, but unlike General Motors, there was no bail-out. Indeed, far worse, an election removed Slovenian Finance Minister Andrej Bajuk from office, and the new government had no interest in or understanding of just how close ROMP had come to saving the tannery. Greg was removed from his position, and three months later the tannery shut its doors for the last time. It should be noted that in May 2008, the 'bali' represented 35 per cent of all sales in the tannery in just its first trial year. ROMP lost the supply chain in which it had invested six years of hard work: 'In the end, it was wider business management, internal marketing, cultural differences and labour regulations, coupled with the crash, that eventually caused the failure of IUV, and that took ROMP with it,' says Greg Sturmer, adding with some cynicism: 'Next time round, I will check the foundations before I try to fix the hole in the roof.'

In hindsight, it was of little relevance that the order books were full, ROMP was at the height of its media success and had been a nominee for the RSPCA Good Business Awards 2008 due to its focus on animal husbandry, nor that the 'bali' product sold better than like-for-like in the trials.

LESSONS LEARNED AND KEY SUCCESS FACTORS

Lessons learned

The main lessons from the ROMP case were that:

- There is a market for sustainable fashion. The early success and the interest from major retailers proved this.
- A production process to produce organic leather exists.
- Full transparency can be achieved with up-to-date traceability systems (that have developed significantly since ROMP initiated its system) which can serve to educate consumers about sustainability in the supply chain.

Key success factors

If there had not been a financial crisis in 2008, then ROMP would most likely have enjoyed more success. The key success factors shown in Table 12.2 explain why it was successful up until the crisis hit.

Table 12.2 Key success factors – ROMP

Key success factors	Description
1. Combination of style and sustainability	The market needs brands like ROMP. Sustainability and sustainable products need to be fun, attractive and desirable – not boring, frumpy and bland. To get it right, any brand needs to be 100 per cent in delivering its core benefit before even starting to talk about its sustainability credentials.

Table 12.2   Key success factors – ROMP *continued*

Key success factors	Description
2. Lifecycle thinking	Behind the traceability system was lifecycle thinking. Where do the ingredients/materials my product is made of come from? How are they obtained? How is it manufactured? What happens in production in terms of environmental or social footprint? Greg Sturmer paid extremely close attention to each and every process step in leather production, and managed to find environmentally friendly alternatives to every one of them so that he was able to obtain organic certification.
3. Usability	Technology is one thing – making it accessible to consumers who are not geeks is another. ROMP and Historic Futures managed to build a traceability system that was intuitive and fitted into the world of the high-fashion brand. If ROMP were still around today, the system would long ago have been a smartphone app.

REFERENCES

CSRwire, 'CSR Press Release: ROMP "World's First Soil Association Certified and GOTS Certified Couture Fashion House" by London Designer Nina Morgan-Jones at New West Third St. LA Boutique Opening on Earth Day April 22', www.csrwire.com/press_releases/14455-ROMP-World-s-First-Soil-Association-Certified-and-GOTS-Certified-Couture-Fashion-House-by-London-Designer-Nina-Morgan-Jones-at-New-West-Third-St-LA-Boutique-Opening-on-Earth-Day-April-22 (accessed 2 June 2013).

International Labor Rights Fund, 'Supply Chains: Working on a Chain Gang – Brand Strategy', http://lrights.igc.org/press/sweatshops/supplychain_brandstrategy_11205.htm (accessed 2 June 2013).

Interview/email exchange with Nina Morgan-Jones, co-founder of ROMP.

Interview and conversations with Greg Sturmer, co-founder of ROMP.

Interview with Lee Holdstock, Soil Association UK.

Interview with Simon Warrick, Chief Technology Office at Historic Futures.

Montgomery, Della, 'Cradle to Grave Certified Fashion', *Feelgood Style*, 11 October 2008, http://feelgoodstyle.com/2008/10/11/cradle-to-grave-certified-fashion/ (accessed 2 June 2013).

Tyrrell, Paul, 'Now Slip into Something Organic', *The Financial Times*, 19 November 2005, www.ft.com/cms/s/0/80b7da4e-58a1-11da-90dd-0000779e2340.html (accessed 2 June 2013).

CHAPTER

13 *The Employee Perspective – Best Practice Cases*

Best Practice Case 7: SKF BeyondZero

The SKF Group is a Swedish world leader in bearings, seals, mechatronics, lubrication systems and services with 40,000 employees worldwide. This case illustrates how a sustainability strategy can be effectively communicated within a global organization and become a critical driver of business strategy.

IDEA AND INSPIRATION

Idea behind the BeyondZero initiative

'The idea is very much an ambition and a vision,' explains Sim Tee Lam of the SKF Sustainability Team. Peter Gündling, who was in SKF Training and Development at that time, remembers:

> It started at a conference hosted by Christian Azar at Chalmers Institute of Technology in Gothenburg in 2004. Our CEO at that time, Tom Johnstone, was inspired by a question Professor Azar posed to him: 'Tom, have you discussed the implications of climate change in your management team and what it means for SKF?'

At that stage, they hadn't, but after the conference, he put together a team he called the 'Tiger Team' – young leaders from different backgrounds and nationalities, only two of whom had previously been involved in environmental sustainability. Sim Tee Lam, who was one of those young leaders along with Peter Gündling, explains:

> Our task was to define 'What would SKF's response to sustainability be like?' We brainstormed for two days, developed a vision for the next five years, pictured what we would say, and produced a video. What we came up with was the idea of 'beyond zero' – namely, that we could reduce our environmental impact to zero. But with our products, we could go even further to provide a positive impact. If we take a look at external sources like the Global Compact principles, we see that both aspects are there – reducing impact and in parallel finding innovative solutions.

Needless to say, Tom Johnstone was excited about the idea, so the vision was agreed and trademarked, and the new strategy was launched within SKF in 2005.

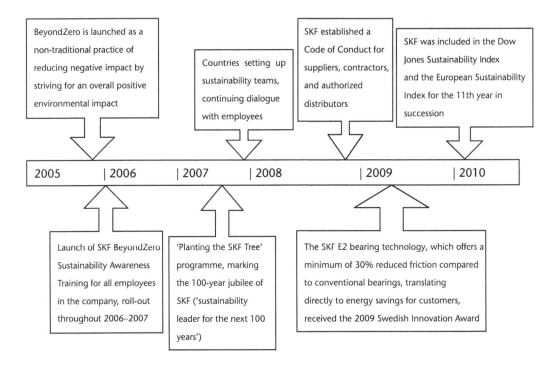

Timeline of BeyondZero

PROPOSITION AND EXECUTION

Concept of BeyondZero

BeyondZero has two aspects: reduce and innovate – reducing the negative environmental impact of the group's operations, and creating innovative products, which helps their business customers improve their environmental performance.

In order to bring this concept to life within the organization, raising awareness about sustainability within the company was key. Therefore, step one was to run a Sustainability Awareness Training Program globally. Peter Gündling proposed a train-the-trainer approach, and trained 200 trainers in 2006–2007 across all business units on all continents. Those 200 trainers subsequently inspired over 40,000 SKF staff in 50 countries. 'The key topics were climate change and social responsibility,' he explains, 'The reactions were very positive. Our colleagues were touched and felt that their work was becoming more meaningful and they were proud of being part of this company.'

The second step was a CO_2 reduction programme that ran from 2005 to 2009, which achieved a 5 per cent annual reduction in absolute terms and was flanked by programmes reducing other environmental impacts, like those of chemicals. Step three was moving into product innovation. 'In 2009, the work with the divisions on product innovation started,' says Sim Tee Lam, 'and we formed working groups to develop the positive side of BeyondZero.' This quickly bore fruit, and the E2 ('Energy Efficient') bearings that have a 30 per cent higher efficiency in terms of energy use than previous comparable products were awarded with the Swedish Innovation Award in 2009. Another example is the welding robots that are used by Daimler-Benz in automotive production.

What is special about BeyondZero is that through a holistic approach, it generates understanding of a product's environmental impact from raw material extraction through manufacturing to the product's use and disposal. It integrates the environmental lifecycle management of products into its core business processes.

Are there specific communication principles that apply to BeyondZero?

Table 13.1 shows the campaign-specific communication principles of the SKF BeyondZero initiative case.

Table 13.1 Campaign-specific communication principles – SKF's BeyondZero

Principles	Example
1. Vision	It started with a vision endorsed by the CEO which has served as a guiding light throughout the project so far and continues to provide direction. It serves to include all parts of the business in working towards sustainability
2. Inside-out	There was a strong conviction that the primary target audience were not customers, but managers and employees. They were the main drivers of communication, and needed to understand sustainability and the idea of the BeyondZero vision in order to live and breathe the 'Spirit of SKF' (as Sim Tee Lam calls it) and pass it on by word of mouth. It has become a way of working, and that translates into external communication, such as sustainability reporting.
3. Multiplication	A key principle of the internal communication programme to create sustainability (and strategy) awareness was the train-the-trainer approach. The 200 trainers became ambassadors for sustainability within SKF, acting as multipliers for the BeyondZero idea.
4. Lifecycle approach	On the innovation side, SKF took a holistic product lifecycle approach at the start, which translated into supplier guidelines and codes of conduct, among other innovations.

Target audiences

The key target audience for BeyondZero are the SKF employees. Sim Tee Lam distinguishes four sub-groups:

1. They show full SKF commitment and do not need convincing: they are the ideal multipliers.
2. They feel it is their job to create value for the company. They need to hear how highly SKF prioritizes sustainability.
3. They really need the examples and best practice cases, for instance through the intranet and SKF News.
4. They are reluctant to change.

Sim Tee Lam is convinced that 'If we are able to motivate 80 per cent of the organization, we have come a very long way.'

Suppliers and customers are the other two important audiences.

Key benefits of the BeyondZero initiative for the target audiences

As mentioned above, BeyondZero inspires employees and gives them a sense of pride. They gain a sense that their work is meaningful. Motivation, loyalty and staff retention are some of the benefits for SKF.

To customers, many of whom also have sustainability strategies and goals, the benefit is that innovative BeyondZero products by SKF help them to reduce their environmental impact. In the case of car manufacturers, which are faced with ever more stringent CO_2 per kilometre regulations, purchasing ball bearings with lower resistance like the E2 product family of innovative bearings may be a fairly straightforward business case.

BUSINESS CASE AND RESULTS

Key societal impacts of the BeyondZero initiative

The 'reduce' aspect of BeyondZero has brought significant environmental benefits. Overall, SKF's emissions reduction in 2008 was 9.1%. In the use of material, for example, SKF applies the near-net-shape concept to achieve high efficiency in material consumption. This is a process technology to form components as closely as possible to their final shape in the production of bearings. It minimizes the amount of material used for the required finished state. The use of metal as a raw material decreased by 4% to 523,000 tonnes in 2011, compared to 546,000 tonnes in 2010.

SKF also aims to minimize waste and increase recycling. In 2011, a total of 103,000 tonnes of all the scrap metal from its operations was recycled, while the recycling rate of grinding swarf[1] was 68%. As for water consumption, the group saved 0.1 million cubic metres of water in 2011 compared to 2010 through a combination of technologies, including rainwater harvesting and waste water recycling.

Sim Tee Lam comments:

We have come a long way, but as IKEA puts it, it is a 'never-ending job'. We are looking at waste, recyclability, and taking the product lifecycle perspective. We want to develop more products in the areas of environmental technology, particularly helping traditional customers to become more efficient.

Commercial impacts of the BeyondZero initiative

The initiative has not only made a positive environmental impact on the business, it has also benefited it commercially. Energy saving measures and innovative technology have reduced the group's production costs. For example, the water usage of SKF's sealing solutions factory in Salt Lake City, Utah was reduced by 50% during 2007–11, with a 20% increase in production.

---

1   Grinding swarf is industrial waste which is usually deposited into landfills.

Figure 13.1 It is estimated that using SKF bus door actuators instead of pneumatic actuators results in a 2.6 per cent improvement in city bus fuel economy

Source: Reproduced courtesy of SKF Group.

The 'innovate' aspect has strengthened SKF's position in the market, as the new CO_2-reducing products provide an important added value to many customers (see Figure 13.1). It has brought both new business and new orders. 'So on the one hand we have seen cost reduction, and on the other top-line growth. We need to make these business effects more trackable, measurable and transparent, which we are working on,' says Sim Tee Lam.

Impacts on the SKF brand

'Up until now we see BeyondZero more as the "Spirit of SKF",' says Sim Tee Lam:

This is how we want to work inside the company. It is the SKF commitment. We have not yet launched it to the outside world like GE has with ecomagination, and we are not sure we want to go down that road. If it is and remains the 'spirit', the outcome will be normal business. We are not doing it because it is a programme.

Internal impacts of the BeyondZero initiative

'BeyondZero represents our commitment and has had a strong impact on motivation. It has added to the pride in working for SKF,' says Sim Tee Lam. More recently, SKF has set up five campuses worldwide to take the sustainability awareness training approach to the next level. These academies provide training on sustainability topics for employees and aim to inspire more sustainable thinking and behaviour.

Another example of the impact of BeyondZero is Brazil SKF: the business unit. During 2009–11, Brazil SKF was elected as 'one of the best companies to work for in Brazil'. Alongside the BeyondZero commitment, the group acts as a role model for staff.

LESSONS LEARNED AND KEY SUCCESS FACTORS

Lessons learned

The main lesson from the implementation of the SKF BeyondZero initiative is that the 'inside-out' approach has proven effective and successful, explains Sim Tee Lam:

> *What we have also learned is that we need to use different tools in different cultures or areas of the business. If there are regional good practice examples, we have seen that it is very motivating if these sites are visited by those that are seeking to learn about sustainability. It really motivates the people in those locations because they receive recognition for their achievements.*

Another lesson is that creating awareness is an ongoing process. 'We need an awareness foundation *plus* regular internal communication *plus* job-specific "academics"', says Sim Tee Lam.

Key success factors

Table 13.2 shows the key success factors of the SKF BeyondZero initiative case.

Table 13.2 Key success factors – SKF's BeyondZero

Key success factors	Description
1. Top-level commitment	Without the high-level commitment, starting with the CEO, BeyondZero could not have been realized.
2. Walking the talk	'We felt from the onset that BeyondZero would only be achievable if the entire organization was fully behind it,' says Sim Tee Lam. The operations sections in particular needed to buy into the new approach, as without their full commitment the footprint reductions could not have been achieved. And only if the reduction is achieved can the positive element, the innovation part, fly.' Walking the talk also is the basis for credibility – internally as well as externally, particularly among investors.
3. Simplicity	The BeyondZero concept is very straightforward – 'reduce' and 'innovate' are terms that are easy to understand and to apply in different contexts.
4. Engagement	Continuous communication and dialogue at all levels within the organization are key. Management is regularly provided with sustainability updates and they pass those on to their teams. On the middle management level there are dedicated sustainability managers who act as multipliers and ambassadors. While very interactive communication with employees on the shop floor is difficult, there are feedback opportunities on the intranet and via email, which is used a lot.

REFERENCES

Corporate Register, *Sustainability Reporting by SKF*, www.corporateregister.com/a10723/Skf05-sus-swd.pdf (accessed 2 June 2013).

Interviews with Sim Tee Lam and Peter Gündling.

'Q&A With Bart G. Bartholomew, Vice President, SKF® Reliability Systems North America', *IMPO Magazine*, 25 January 2008, www.impomag.com/articles/2008/01/q-bart-g-bartholomew-vice-president-skf-reg-reliability-systems-north-america (accessed 2 June 2013).

Best Practice Case 8: IBM's World Community Grid – Technology Solving Problems

> *IBM's World Community Grid (WCG) [is] an unprecedented effort to deploy ordinary people's idle computers to create a free, open source lab for researchers around the globe. Massive computational research is broken down into discrete problems and distributed across a vast network.[2]*

IDEA AND INSPIRATION

Idea behind IBM's World Community Grid

'We are very proud of our CSR traditions and initiatives,' explains Robin Willner, Vice President of Global Community Initiatives at IBM Corporation:

> *It is part of the IBM DNA and core to our business strategies and the way we do business. We are proud of it because of the combination of technology, and volunteerism and its link to science. For the last fifteen years we have focused our Corporate Citizenship and CSR efforts on what we call talent technology and services, bringing IBMers and their skills and talents to the table. That is better than any cheque we can write – and (the) World Community Grid is one of our favourite projects.*

She goes on to explain how the World Community Grid came about:

> *We regularly ask when reviewing our strategy, 'Is there something here that we can translate into a community project?' For instance, if IBM is doing work on voice recognition technology, we may think how that can help children learn to read. In 2004, grid technology became a topic. One of our business partners started www.grid.org and wanted to showcase grid technology, but lacked the funds. So at first IBM did cash sponsorship and got very positive feedback. We then thought: perhaps instead of cash sponsorship, we should build a better and more robust grid with more functionality and bring the idea to a higher level, doing more research, involving more participants and on a higher technological level. We saw that this technology could be a great innovation in supporting medical research. In parallel, it coincided with the volunteering trend. So this proved a new way of doing volunteerism.*

---

2   Chuck Salter, 'How IBM's World Community Grid is Helping Cure AIDS, Cancer and World Hunger', *Fast Company*, 1 May 2010, www.fastcompany.com/1615161/how-ibms-world-community-grid-helping-cure-aids-cancer-and-world-hunger (accessed 2 June 2013).

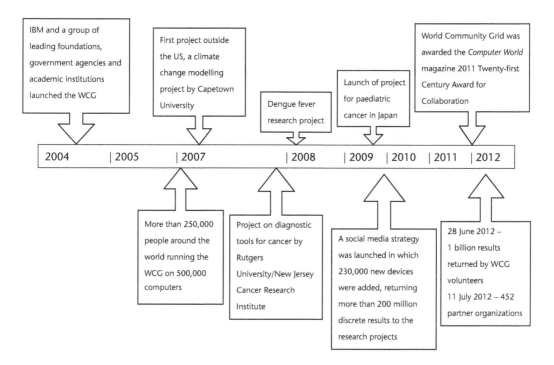

Timeline of IBM's World Community Grid

PROPOSITION AND EXECUTION

Concept of IBM's World Community Grid

The concept of IBM's World Community Grid is very simple. Whomever wants to participate and support important research projects can do so by allowing the WCG to use their idle computer power, for example from their laptop or desktop computers, while they are not working on them. By installing World Community Grid software, the users enable the processing power of hundreds and thousands of computers to work together and to be linked up to form a supercomputer. That computing power is offered to major scientific research projects, particularly in the medical field, which need this high-level computing power but lack the funds for supercomputers. A lot of disease-related research that is of little or no interest to the pharmaceutical industry falls into this category.

The World Community Grid allows research organizations to harvest the idle time of millions of individual personal and business computers in people's homes and offices around the world while their processor capacity is not actively employed (for example, while reading a website when browsing) and makes them into useful tools to help solve some of the world's most demanding health (for example, cancer, malaria, tuberculosis and AIDS) and societal problems by running the WCG client and computing the tasks distributed to it (see Figure 13.2). In addition, the WCG builds awareness about these issues and motivates people to volunteer their time as well as their computing power to some of these causes. 'Volunteering becomes very easy,' says Robin Willner, 'you download World Community Grid onto your computer, tell others about it and share it on Facebook.'

Figure 13.2 The IBM World Community Grid supports a wide spectrum of causes
Source: Reproduced courtesy of International Business Machines Corporation.

IBM's World Community Grid software acts like an agent. It is comparable to a screen saver, and shows computer users which of the projects they have signed up for the machines on which they are currently working. Each individual computer connected to the WCG requests data on a specific project from the WCG's server when idle, and informs the WCG about current tasks, requests new packages and reports back results on completed tasks. Each computation accelerates the pace of the research. Overall, more than 600,000 individuals and organizations are part of WCG, with a total of two million devices (see Figure 13.3).

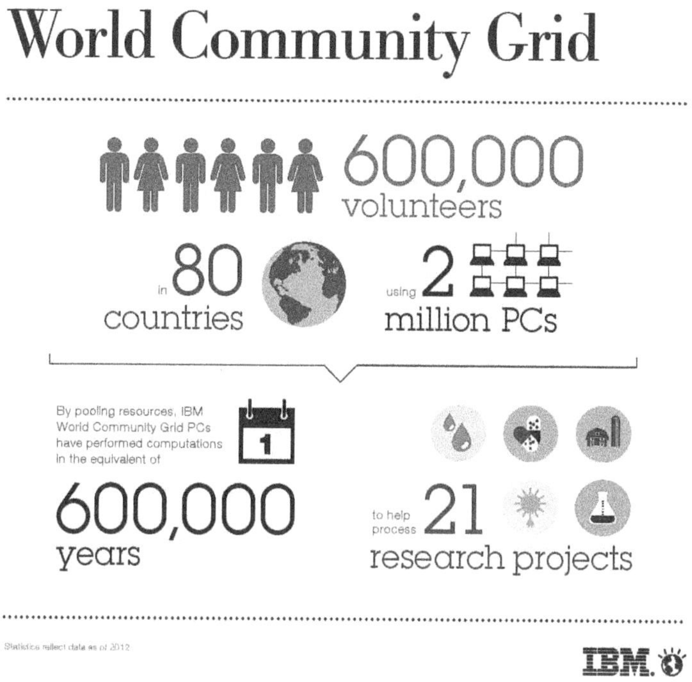

World Community Grid

Figure 13.3 IBM's World Community Grid is a truly global community
Source: Reproduced courtesy of International Business Machines Corporation.

Are there any campaign-specific communication principles?

Table 13.3 shows the campaign-specific communication principles of the IBM World Community Grid case.

Table 13.3 Campaign-specific communication principles – IBM's World Community Grid

Principle	Example
1. Word of mouth	One basic way of getting new users was through word of mouth. A colleague or customer would ask: 'What kind of interesting screen saver do you have there?' Word of mouth was and is flanked by marketing campaigns of different kinds, either web-based or through people on the ground, such as country Citizenship Managers, participating in events, giving speeches, working with press and the like. In 2008, a Facebook widget was launched through a 'Facebook garage meeting' where one of the Citizenship Managers participated and talked about WCG. The Facebook widget was the starting point for the WCG social media strategy inaugurated in December 2010, which enabled automated posting of messages and weekly contributions to the Facebook walls and Twitter feeds of volunteers who chose to participate. This gave wide exposure and visibility to the initiative on social platforms and attracted more individuals to become involved in the project.

Table 13.3 Campaign-specific communication principles – IBM's World Community Grid *continued*

Principle	Example
2. Partnerships	The WCG has many partner organizations across the globe (as of July 2012 there were 452), including corporations, non-profits, professional associations, education institutes and foundations. Examples include Sony Electronics and the Cancer Society of Finland, among many others. These partner organizations play an important role in promoting the initiative to the public in different sectors throughout the world, by putting information about WCG on their websites and encouraging their associates to get involved. More importantly, partnering with these organizations has established a high degree of credibility for the initiative.

Target audiences

Robin Willner explains the three target audiences for IBM's WCG: 'First: anyone who has a laptop or PC that is under three or four years old. This is a very large target audience!' Her German colleague, Peter Kusterer, adds: 'We call the core of that target the forward thinkers, those people that share responsibility and are open to new technology.' Robin Willner continues:

> *Second: IBMers – we encourage them to run WCG so that they see how IBM gives them the opportunity to engage very simply and volunteer. Third: Universities, research organizations and NGOs, such as the American Cancer Society. The first two groups are the ones who join and provide the computer resources as a new kind of volunteering. The third group are those people that run projects which can benefit from having the computing power WCG offers. This is obviously a much narrower target audience.*

Key benefits of IBM's World Community Grid to important stakeholders

The primary benefit to the participants in the WCG is that they can contribute effortlessly and without sacrifice to worthwhile causes (and obtain an attractive, dynamic screen saver). In addition, IBM staff have an interesting story which they can be proud to tell, for instance to customers or potential customers, also exemplifying IBM's corporate citizenship strategy to help the social cause by contributing with company strengths rather than mere chequebook philanthropy. For the researchers whose projects are supported, the main benefit is access to the virtual supercomputer power at no cost, high flexibility and high security standards. IBM benefits because it gains feedback on technology development and provides volunteering opportunities to its staff, which has a positive effect on motivation and retention. It communicates the IBM brand to broader audiences than just customers, and allows for major media stories which also support PR.

BUSINESS CASE AND RESULTS

Key societal impacts of IBM's World Community Grid

Generally speaking, the WCG benefits society globally by: (1) accelerating difficult humanitarian research that would otherwise require years of laboratory work; (2) expanding research in previously unsponsored or neglected areas; (3) focusing on global humanitarian issues, and (4) encouraging computationally rich approaches resulting in new data to help resolve long-standing problems.

Specifically, scientists engaged in research supported by IBM's WCG have gained the greatest immediate benefits. During 2004–12, more than 500,000 years of computer run-time provided at no cost have delivered over one billion research results (or computational assignments) for scientists free of charge for 35 research projects in six countries. For example, scientists identified at least two significant drug possibilities for the Fight AIDS project in six months, which would have taken five years with normal computing resources. In 2012, two million devices were running within the WCG system. Also, the WCG helped Harvard University's Clean Energy Project to discover a significant molecular compound that could lead to cheaper and more efficient solar cells which can be coated on surfaces like windows and walls.

Most significant is the time saved by the WCG: one hundred to two hundred years of research collapsed into six to twelve months on average. A lot of this is the unglamorous but necessary work that won't necessarily lead to spectacular breakthroughs, but which makes those breakthroughs possible.

Commercial impacts of IBM's World Community Grid

The WCG represents an important element of IBM's business strategy, which epitomizes the new IBM vision of a 'Smarter Planet' – changing the way the world works through intelligent systems. The initiative is also connected to 'Project Big Green', a $1 billion investment to increase the efficiency of IBM products. It adds considerable marketing value to IBM's business in grid computing solutions. These solutions, comprising software and services, are an essential component of the IT marketplace. The WCG is therefore an important reference point for IBM's business in the IT marketplace.

Impacts on the IBM brand

'The impact is indirect but plausible,' says Peter Kusterer. 'We do not measure it like we measure marketing campaigns. And nobody internally questions it because it makes so much sense intuitively.' Robin Willner agrees, and explains that it provides the brand with a story as well as with differentiating features:

> Even though I cannot name a specific client who signed a deal with us because of WCG, there are many instances when we will be talking to clients in the health care field – and in all those cases the World Community Grid is a way of entry into potential accounts and a way of distinguishing IBM from competitors. We get into conversations based on the screen saver – we tell our sales people to have it on their laptops. They may be sitting in a public place or talking

to a prospect. There is no better way into a conversation about the technology IBM offers. The same goes for recruitment of talent – no better way of getting the attention of prospects!

It is fair to say, even without market research proof, that the WCG provides significant benefits for IBM's brand and reputation, as it generates significant online and offline visibility – among others, Google has reported over 8,700 blogs posting about the WCG since 2008. It demonstrates leadership and expertise in technology, and it emphasizes IBM's strong reputation for excellence in basic science – the company invests more than $6 billion annually in R&D. From a CSR point of view, it shows IBM's commitment and supports the company's solid reputation as a responsible corporate citizen.

Internal impacts of IBM's World Community Grid

'It helps all of us in terms of motivation, atmosphere and culture,' says Peter Kusterer. 'You feel proud that your company does something like that and that builds loyalty.' The World Community Grid initiative is managed by IBM's Corporate Citizenship team with more than a hundred staff worldwide as part of their mandate to promote and execute IBM's corporate citizenship strategy and activities. IBM also provides support for the WCG in areas ranging from hosting and security to marketing and communications. The wide involvement of employees helps to further raise awareness for the project internally. In many countries, a significant proportion of employees participate in IBM's WCG initiative

LESSONS LEARNED AND KEY SUCCESS FACTORS

Lessons learned

The main lesson from IBM's World Community Grid implementation is that 'we have learned a lot of things about technology through the project,' says Robin Willner. 'From a CSR communications perspective, we learned that you have to find new ways to tell your stories every day. It is not sufficient to have a great project, with great technology. You continuously need to find new ways of engaging new audiences.' Peter Kusterer adds that a main hurdle has been, and continues to be, security issues:

We cannot guarantee 100 per cent security, so many companies refuse to allow their staff to run the World Community Grid. We understand, and encourage them to run the programme at home on their private computers instead. And we continuously work to keep the security of the World Community Grid at the highest levels.

From a more general point of view, IBM's WCG is an excellent example of how a company leverages its core business competences to further social and environmental purposes. This creates a win–win situation between the three dimensions of sustainability. Always asking the questions, 'What good could come out of the application of our technology or service offering? What social and environmental benefit could we deliver?' can produce unforeseen positive societal and business-related results.

Key success factors

Peter Kusterer identifies three key success factors of the World Community Grid (see Table 13.4).

Table 13.4   Key success factors – IBM's World Community Grid

Key success factors	Description
1. Clear link to business and brand strategy	'There needs to be a strong link to the business and brand strategy, and at the same time a convincing societal benefit. The balance is key. If in doubt, the balance should always be in favor of the societal benefit. The clear link to core business and the right balance gives us authenticity and credibility. What must never happen is that it is seen as a marketing bubble.'
2. Low hurdles to engage	'The hurdles to participate and volunteer are very low.' Installing the programme takes only a few minutes, and there is no cost attached.
3. Social media marketing	'The World Community Grid is in itself a kind of marketing, primarily via the Internet.' One could say that WCG is a kind of 'social network'. Social media activities have been very powerful in generating awareness of the WCG: an average of 200 volunteers join daily as a result.

REFERENCES

Basu, Sanjay, Bickel, Rolf and Philip, John, *Bridging Technology and Society: Social Networks: Research and Practice at IBM*, 30 April 2009, http://stoa.usp.br/schwartz/files/-1/8654/IBM+Social+Network+Research.pdf (accessed 2 June 2013).

IBM, *2010 Corporate Social Responsibility Report*, www.ibm.com/ibm/responsibility/report/2010/communities/technology-communities.html#world_community_grid (accessed 2 June 2013).

Interview with Peter Kusterer, Head of Corporate Citizenship and Corporate Affairs, IBM Germany.

Interview with Robin Willner, at the time (12 May 2010) Vice President Global Community Initiatives, IBM (until May 2012).

Salter, Chuck, 'How IBM's World Community Grid is Helping Cure AIDS, Cancer and World Hunger', *Fast Company*, 1 May 2010, www.fastcompany.com/1615161/how-ibms-world-community-grid-helping-cure-aids-cancer-and-world-hunger (accessed 2 June 2013).

World Community Grid, 'About Us', www.worldcommunitygrid.org/about_us/viewAboutUs.do (accessed 2 June 2013).

14 *The Customer Perspective – Best Practice Cases*

Best Practice Case 9: Cadbury Dairy Milk goes Fairtrade

IDEA AND INSPIRATION

Idea behind Cadbury Dairy Milk Fairtrade chocolate

Cadbury Dairy Milk is an icon – one of the biggest chocolate bar brands in the world. If such an iconic brand goes Fairtrade, it is more than a piece of news in *Marketing Week* – it is a paradigm shift, a step change. Sustainability is moving mainstream! Now all the big chocolate brands have announced that they will Fairtrade-certify their chocolate as well, but they followed Cadbury. How did that step change come about? Like all great stories, it is fairly simple.

'Cadbury had been in Ghana for over a hundred years,' says Alison Ward, Sustainability Director at Cadbury at the time of the interview:

> *We realized that the farmers that supplied our cocoa were not well off. They were ageing, and so were their plants, and their yield had dropped to 40 per cent compared to previous times, so they actually did not have a sustainable livelihood out of cocoa farming. We looked into the business case and realized that we were dependent on sourcing from Ghana, so it turned out to be an unsustainable situation for both sides.*

Cadbury started working with farmers in 2005, aiming to help them raise their productivity and get more out of their cocoa. In 2007, research commissioned by Cadbury identified major risks to future supply. It highlighted low incomes, the rural-to-urban migration of young people and poor productivity as cocoa production risks, not only to future supply, but also to Cadbury's reputation in important consumer markets. The Cocoa Partnership was founded in 2008, committed to investing £45 million into improving farmer productivity. Moving to Fairtrade was almost a logical next step, says Alison Ward: 'We chose Fairtrade because in the UK it is a very well recognized mark and well-established in Ghana, so we felt it would work both on a consumer and a producer or supply chain level.' She explains why Cadbury did not create its own standard:

> *It is important to people, to consumers, that Fairtrade is an independent mark, and they trust it. We needed endorsement and credibility, and chose an established mark because it would have taken so long to establish our own mark. You could say it was a short cut, but one we are happy about.*

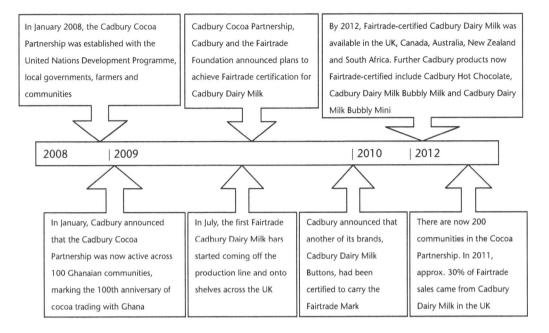

| In January 2008, the Cadbury Cocoa Partnership was established with the United Nations Development Programme, local governments, farmers and communities | Cadbury Cocoa Partnership, Cadbury and the Fairtrade Foundation announced plans to achieve Fairtrade certification for Cadbury Dairy Milk | By 2012, Fairtrade-certified Cadbury Dairy Milk was available in the UK, Canada, Australia, New Zealand and South Africa. Further Cadbury products now Fairtrade-certified include Cadbury Hot Chocolate, Cadbury Dairy Milk Bubbly Milk and Cadbury Dairy Milk Bubbly Mini |

| 2008 | 2009 | | | 2010 | 2012 |

| In January, Cadbury announced that the Cadbury Cocoa Partnership was now active across 100 Ghanaian communities, marking the 100th anniversary of cocoa trading with Ghana | In July, the first Fairtrade Cadbury Dairy Milk bars started coming off the production line and onto shelves across the UK | Cadbury announced that another of its brands, Cadbury Dairy Milk Buttons, had been certified to carry the Fairtrade Mark | There are now 200 communities in the Cocoa Partnership. In 2011, approx. 30% of Fairtrade sales came from Cadbury Dairy Milk in the UK |

Timeline of Cadbury Dairy Milk Fairtrade-certified chocolate

PROPOSITION AND EXECUTION

Concept of Cadbury Dairy Milk Fairtrade-certified chocolate

The key aim of the establishment of the Cadbury Cocoa Partnership and its Fairtrade programme is to help build a better future for many thousands of cocoa farmers, their families and their communities, while at the same time ensuring quality cocoa supply for Cadbury (now part of Kraft Foods). Through buying Fairtrade-certified products, marginalized farmers are given the opportunity for more secure and sustainable livelihoods.

Are there any campaign-specific communication principles?

Table 14.1 shows the campaign-specific communication principles of the Cadbury Dairy Milk Fairtrade chocolate case.

Table 14.1 Campaign-specific communication principles – Cadbury Dairy Milk Fairtrade chocolate

Principles	Example
1. Partnerships	The commitment to move to Fairtrade cements the long partnerships Cadbury has had with its cocoa farmers through the Cocoa Partnership. In addition to the farmer partnership, there is close collaboration with the Fairtrade Foundation, which provides Cadbury with additional reach and capability in supporting farmers to increase their productivity. Other partnerships include governments, NGOs and international organizations, as well as the UN Development Program.
2. Independent certification	Fairtrade does not just offer independent certification, which is important for credibility, it offers a strong brand in its own right.
3. Creative communication	The launch campaign used state-of-the-art creativity and imagination. Rather than just announcing 'Cadbury Dairy Milk – now with Fairtrade chocolate', the one-minute commercial celebrated Ghanaian culture and *joie de vivre*, taking Fairtrade out of a slightly moralistic context into an optimistic, life-affirming tonality.
4. Engagement with Consumers	The Cadbury Dairy Milk chocolate marketing team developed a TV, Internet and print campaign showcasing Ghanaian craftspeople, artists and dancers, with a music video available for download on iTunes. As part of Fairtrade Fortnight 2011, 20% of the profits from Cadbury Dairy Milk bars sold during the period funded solar power projects in Ghana, further strengthening the brand's reputation for assisting social and economic development in the country. The campaign's online activity included banners on supermarkets' websites and a blog carrying regular updates on progress direct from Ghana. The focus and tone of these communication activities is positive and non-threatening, direct and immediate, emotional and personal, as well as visual and imaginative.

Target audiences

The target audiences of the Fairtrade programme are on the one hand cocoa farmers and their communities in Ghana, India, Indonesia and the Caribbean. On the other hand it is the mainstream consumers, purchasers of Cadbury Dairy Milk in the UK, Canada, New Zealand, Australia and, since 2011, South Africa.

Key benefits of Cadbury Dairy Milk Fairtrade-certified chocolate for the target audiences

Going mainstream makes a big difference. Cadbury and its partners are addressing Millennium Development Goal 1 (to end poverty and hunger) and Goal 4 (to promote gender equality) by providing farmers with training and opportunities to increase their incomes through the Cadbury Cocoa Partnership. Around 10,000 farmers and their families in 100 cocoa farming communities and 55,000 members of the Kuapa Kokoo farmers' co-operative in Ghana are benefiting from efforts to more than double cocoa production. By 2012, Kraft Foods sourced 20,000 tons of Fairtrade cocoa a year, and thereby quadrupled the volume of Fairtrade cocoa from Ghana. The incomes of farming communities have obviously improved. Apart from income, the awareness of issues related to child labour and gender equality through education and empowerment programmes has increased. For example, approximately 30 per cent of partnership communities are run by women.

While UK consumers are not prepared to pay for sustainability alone, there are significant segments (40–50 per cent, some research suggests) that appreciate a Fairtrade mark as an added quality dimension, as long as the chocolate is as tasty as before. 'Enjoying with a good conscience' is an added value to a growing number of mainstream consumers.

BUSINESS CASE AND RESULTS

Key societal impacts of Cadbury Dairy Milk Fairtrade-certified chocolate

Cadbury Dairy Milk Fairtrade chocolate was launched in the UK, Canada, Australia, New Zealand and South Africa, and has transferred over £1 million to cocoa-growing communities. The Cadbury Dairy Milk Fairtrade programme has directly invested in 10,000 farmers in 100 communities. To put this in proportion, 55,000 farmers in 1,300 communities were directly invested in through Fairtrade itself, making Cadbury a significant contributor. Bonuses for farmers, additional farm equipment and training resulted in a doubling of productivity and income for some farmers. Community projects were undertaken, focusing on water, sanitation and health, including building wells and mobile health clinics, as well as funding for carbon reduction schemes. In Ghana, Cadbury has quadrupled the volume of cocoa sold under Fairtrade terms, resulting in over £6 million in Fairtrade social premiums. The local communities within the Kuapa Kokoo co-operative have used the premiums to support its 55,000 farmer members in the following key areas: (1) farmer bonuses, farm equipment and farmer training aimed at driving productivity; (2) mobile health clinics to visit 100 communities and conduct full health assessments, and (3) community projects with a focus on water and sanitation.

Commercial impacts of Cadbury's Dairy Milk Fairtrade-certified chocolate

The Cadbury Fairtrade programme generated £1.9 million of PR value in 2010 (£0.7 million advertising equivalent value). Cadbury Dairy Milk receives better positioning from key retailers during Fairtrade Fortnight (see Figure 14.1). By investing in the sustainability of the cocoa supply chain, Cadbury Dairy Milk chocolate production is reducing the risk of higher costs and the potential for an inadequate supply of cocoa in the future. And with all major chocolate manufacturers moving into sourcing certified chocolate, Cadbury retains its first-mover position, which remains a differentiating feature.

Brand impacts of Cadbury Dairy Milk Fairtrade chocolate

Cadbury Dairy Milk Fairtrade chocolate has significantly improved Cadbury's reputation. In 2008, it was ranked twenty-fifth in Britain's Most Admired Companies for the Society and Environment Award; by 2010 it was ranked fourth. Sixty-seven per cent of Cadbury Dairy Milk consumers say that Fairtrade is extremely important in their purchasing decisions.

Figure 14.1 Cadbury Dairy Milk's colourful point-of-sale promotion during launch supported Fairtrade Fortnight

Source: Reproduced courtesy of Mondelez International.

LESSONS LEARNED AND KEY SUCCESS FACTORS

Lessons learned

A key lesson learned from the Fairtrade programme is that the partnerships with governments, NGOs, farmers and the Fairtrade Foundation provide assurance that the company is doing the right thing. Working in partnership has two key benefits: (1) to help to deliver social and environmental programmes locally funded by the Fairtrade premium, and (2) to communicate the message simply and effectively to consumers. Moving to Fairtrade is a confirmation that the brand can be trusted to do business in the right way, recognizing sustainability as an important social concern.

Sustainability only works if it is part of the soul of the brand, and integral to its core values, not just an add-on. Therefore, businesses should ensure the relevance of sustainability to their brands and the commitments of the organization. Cadbury Dairy Milk chocolate is a good example in this regard, because the company sees sustainability as part of a crucial aspect of the brand. It embeds the concept of sustainability from production to marketing though the management of the supply chain.

Key success factors

Table 14.2 shows the key success factors of the Cadbury Dairy Milk Fairtrade chocolate case.

Table 14.2   Key success factors – Cadbury Dairy Milk Fairtrade chocolate

Key success factors	Description
1. Sustainability focus aligned with brand value	Moving to Fairtrade has attributed additional ethical values to Cadbury, complementing its brand values of generosity and optimism. The association with Fairtrade, supported by the Cadbury Cocoa Partnership, demonstrates a robust business action to strengthen the supply chain in Ghana and the company's relationship with farmers. The Fairtrade mark was aligned to the Cadbury brand values, key cocoa sustainability issues and business actions. This resonated with consumers. It also gave the brand a critical 'first-mover' advantage. What was important was to integrate sustainability into the brand model, creating a holistic proposition for consumers in order to influence their behaviour.
2. Engage consumers in practical and fun ways	A music video and the online blog provided effective ways to raise awareness and educate consumers about complex sustainability issues. Utilizing social media can also extend coverage to a broader range of consumers. By building a movement and giving people opportunities to participate, those tools and activities show how consumers' individual actions can lead to mass change through collective action.
3. Collaboration	External partnerships always bring new expertise and opportunities. The Cocoa Partnership relies on a network of partners, which helps to ensure the success of partnership activities.
4. Take the initiative	Being the first mainstream chocolate brand to go Fairtrade gave Cadbury an absolute competitive advantage over other chocolate brands and enhanced its reputation. The brand found new ways of sourcing and making products, which often involved working collaboratively with suppliers. Cadbury was successful in strengthening its supply chain in Ghana through sourcing Fairtrade cocoa. Therefore, the key to its success is that co-operation and innovation can help to sustain the development of raw material sources as well as increasing sales.

REFERENCES

Cadbury Australia, 'Fairtrade Certified™ Cadbury Dairy Milk Hits Australian Shelves', www.cadbury.com.au/About-Cadbury/Fairtrade.aspx (accessed 2 June 2013).

Cadbury Dairy Milk UK product page, www.cadbury.co.uk/products/dairy-milk-2360?p=2360 (accessed 2 June 2013).

Interview with Alison Ward, formerly Sustainability Director, Cadbury.

Best Practice Case 10: The innocent Big Knit Campaign

IDEA AND INSPIRATION

Idea behind the innocent Big Knit Campaign

Since 2000, over 150,000 older people have died in the UK from cold-related illnesses during the winter months; thousands more have had to choose between heating and eating. To help keep older people warm in winter, innocent launched the innocent Big Knit campaign. 'It was a crazy idea we had in 2003,' says Gurdeep Loyal of innocent's marketing team. 'We spoke to Age Concern,[1] they volunteered the knitters, and off we went!' It ran simultaneously with Age Concern's Fight the Freeze campaign highlighting the plight of older people in winter. innocent supported Age Concern's campaign, and called for generous people to knit hats for its smoothie bottles. For every behatted bottle sold in Sainsbury's and Boots stores nationwide, innocent gives 25p to Age UK to fund programmes such as winter warmth measures, including improved insulation and providing hot meals (see Figure 14.2).

Figure 14.2 Granny with hundreds of hats for innocent – 25p from each bottle sold is donated to help keep older people warm during the winter

Source: Reproduced courtesy of innocent.

---

1   Now merged with Help the Aged, and named Age UK.

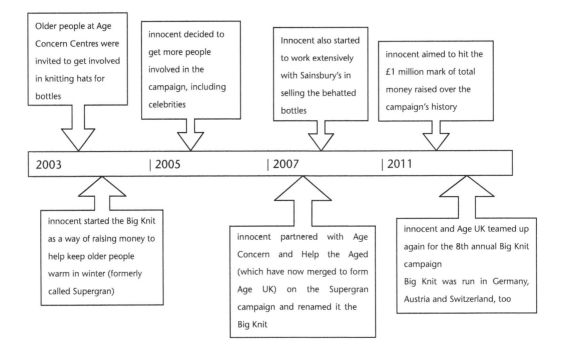

Timeline of the innocent Big Knit campaign

PROPOSITION AND EXECUTION

Concept of the innocent Big Knit Campaign

The insight of the campaign is that consumers not only want to donate money to charity, but also to make personal contributions and to find fulfilment in fun and creative ways. With a limited budget, innocent launched the simple Big Knit campaign in partnerships with retailers. The objective was to convince the public to knit hats for its smoothie bottles and to donate money raised from the smoothie purchases to Age UK.

   Gurdeep Loyal explains how it works in practice:

Months before the campaign, we start to engage with consumers through the knitting elements. Age UK volunteers lead communication through their local centres, supplying knitting patterns and knitting packs, coloured yarn – lots of things to make it exciting. They are older people who do not rely on the Internet. Then our retail partner Sainsbury's involves staff, sends them mails, encourages them to knit and organize staff competitions. We work with knitting magazines, and of course a lot of online social media. This works really well towards countdown, and it is a way of getting news to very engaged people. When the campaign is about to hit the stores, we start offline advertising – media and press adverts to communicate the mechanics. In-store, we have supporting material, displays, and of course the products with the hats.

Are there any campaign-specific communication principles?

Table 14.3 shows the campaign-specific communication principles of the innocent Big Knit campaign case.

Table 14.3   Campaign-specific communication principles – innocent Big Knit campaign

Principles	Example
1. Brand identity	CSR and responsibility are integral to the innocent brand. 'We have a responsibility for the impact our business has on the environment and society,' says Gurdeep Loyal.
2. Humour and fun	It is a serious topic, but it is portrayed and communicated in a fun and at times humorous and tongue-in-cheek way, consistent with the overall innocent tonality.
3. Online interaction	innocent created the Big Knit Hat tag on Facebook and Flickr, which encourages innocent fans to interact with the little hat and to take funny photos with it. The person who takes the best photo is awarded a big box of innocent smoothies. Also, innocent established a blog featuring 'Hats of the Week' and patterns for knitting mini-beanies. Creating a social media platform was an entertaining way for the brand to engage with online users and expand its online network. The online interaction helped to create a unique brand experience for consumers and enhance their engagement.
4. Offline marketing	innocent also introduced the behatted bottles to the public by organizing interesting outdoor promotional events, such as staging huge, behatted bottle displays and in-store knitting activities. This helped to enhance the public presence of the campaign. 'The point is to get communities involved,' says Gurdeep Loyal.
5. Media	innocent encouraged consumers to embrace the Big Knit campaign through the national broadcaster – RTE in Ireland. On-air interviews were held with both innocent and charity representatives.
6. Partnerships	innocent partnered with Age UK, Sainsbury's and Boots. The campaign leveraged the work and resources from its partners. The woolly hats were knitted by local Age Concern users and employees of Sainsbury's and innocent, as well as the general public.

Target audiences

The general public, consumers and elderly people were the major target audiences of the innocent Big Knit campaign.

Key benefits of the innocent Big Knit Campaign for consumers

'Firstly, it is just surprising and delightful for them,' says Gurdeep Loyal:

Supermarkets are not the most exciting places, and individual knitted hats make people smile. It is a serious message presented in a pleasant way. Secondly, I know that I am buying a product that someone has spent time on – and I am helping with the donation. Thirdly, they have the hats – and put them on their pets, use them as Christmas decorations – there is no wasted element at all. People love to collect them!

Another benefit is the active involvement of knitting the hats. Some older people found it enjoyable to knit with younger people (see Figure 14.3). And obviously, the campaign raises funds, helping many older people in need to stay warmer in winter. Furthermore, it raises consumer awareness regarding the importance of contributing to society and caring for older people and has brought people together in knitting groups, creating new friendships and tackling the social isolation of older people.

Figure 14.3 Innocent's delightful little hats make a good cause fun
Source: Reproduced courtesy of innocent.

BUSINESS CASE AND RESULTS

Key societal impacts of the Big Knit Campaign

In 2007, the innocent Big Knit campaign raised £115,000 for Age UK. The money raised has benefited around 55,000 older people in the charity's centres across the UK. More than 500,000 little bobble hats for innocent drinks raised over £250,000 in 2009. By end of 2011, the donation to Age UK had exceeded £1 million, with 650,000 hats knitted in that year alone. The increased funds and resources enabled centres to provide more comprehensive services for older people, including helping them to claim winter fuel allowances and funding shuttle buses to take them shopping.

Commercial impacts of the Big Knit Campaign on innocent

There was a significant increase in sales over a six-week period after the launch of the innocent Big Knit campaign. The campaign resulted in a record-breaking uplift in sales for innocent smoothies. It also led to innocent's biggest week of unit sales in Sainsbury's in 2007. In 2009, the December sales of innocent's smoothie product increased by 11% year on year. It sold 94% more Big Knit units in 2009 than in 2008. 'There is definitely an uplift,' says Gurdeep Loyal, 'about 20% above normal price promotion, and a significant impact on penetration and weights of purchase and sales per shop. We have even seen a small increase in baseline penetration.'

Impacts on the innocent brand

Gurdeep Loyal is convinced of the longer-term brand impact of the promotion: 'What the campaign really drives is brand metrics: how ethical, exciting, interesting, how much buzz, how much consumers love the brand. And that builds loyalty.' It is part of what makes the innocent brand what it is – one of the few true 'love brands'.

Internal impacts of the innocent Big Knit campaign

Gurdeep Loyal explains:

> We are a very consumer-led company, and we are very focused on consumers. So when we know that consumers want and love the Big Knit, that has an automatic impact of getting everyone at innocent excited internally about it. This is the thing that is so special about the campaign – it engages all stakeholders!

And that excitement and commitment is essential, because what looks like a fun campaign from the outside requires incredibly hard work from the organization: 'We need to fundamentally change the supply chain for the campaign, and that requires motivation and absolute commitment, particularly from suppliers on the logistics side. But we do it because the consumer loves it and it's a great, worthy cause to help older people.'

LESSONS LEARNED AND KEY SUCCESS FACTORS

Lessons learned

Gurdeep Loyal identifies the main lesson learned from the innocent Big Knit campaign:

> We have learned that no matter how big our target, we know we can make it. Every year we have thought: 'How big should we go next year?' We have been a bit scared, but ended with a higher goal than we set out. Our motto is: 'Think of the biggest number you can think of – and then up it.' This stretches the organization to give 110 per cent because we are so passionate about it.

The second lesson is that innocent realized it needed to understand the link between its three main constituents – consumers, customers and beneficiaries (which it calls its 'holy trinity') – even better. And thirdly, everyone in the company and all partners need to be fully behind the campaign – only then can it be realized successfully.

Looking at it from the outside, one lesson is to be innovative and courageous. It is possible to link creativity, fun and consumer engagement with a serious social topic. It is possible to inspire a wide range of audiences and the general public if you think outside of the box, and to achieve a 'triple-win' situation between Age UK and the old people it helps, Sainsbury's as the retail partner and innocent – plus, of course, all the happy people involved in knitting the hats.

Key success factors

Table 14.4 shows the key success factors of the innocent Big Knit campaign case.

Table 14.4   Key success factors – innocent Big Knit campaign

Key success factors	Description
1. Building on core values	Gurdeep Loyal is convinced: 'You need to base your CSR communication on your core values – otherwise why should the consumer believe that you are credible in supporting a certain cause?' innocent was certainly credible.
2. Thinking out of the box	The idea of the Big Knit campaign was innovative and original – and a little mad. Whoever thought of hand-knitting little woolly hats for a mass market product before?
3. Empowering consumers	innocent realized that consumers do not want to be patronized, but are very keen to contribute actively and participate in campaigns if they consider them worthwhile – in this case, knitting for a good cause.
4. Strong partnerships	The strong partnerships with Age UK and the retail partner (in the UK case, Sainsbury's) are vital. Without them, such a campaign will not fly.

REFERENCES

Age UK, 'innocent Drinks – Award-winning Cause-related Marketing', www.ageuk.org.uk/get-involved/corporate-partners/cause-related-marketing/innocent/ (accessed 2 June 2013).

innocent, 'So What is the Big Knit?', www.innocentdrinks.co.uk/bigknit (accessed 10 June 2013).

Interview with Gurdeep Loyal, innocent Marketing Team.

Interview with Jessica Sansom, innocent Sustainability Director.

Irish Marketing Journal, The Media Awards Winners Book 2011, http://edition.pagesuite-professional.co.uk/launch.aspx?referral=other&pnum=33&refresh=9p1WyB600qX2&EID=e29f7a0f-2b01-4c3f-9964-7a8af83189b9&skip=&p=33 (accessed 2 June 2013).

Mitchell, Alan, 'Good Work', Tasweeq Today.com, http://tasweeqtoday.com/articles/field-related/37-general-subjectstopics/54-good-work- (accessed 2 June 2013).

Best Practice Case 11: Max Burgers, Climate on (the) Menu

IDEA AND INSPIRATION

Idea behind the Climate on (the) Menu initiative

Meat production has a huge impact on the climate. The meat industry accounts for approximately 18 per cent of global greenhouse gas emissions, making it one of the largest contributors to greenhouse gases. With meat as its core business, the owners of Max Burgers[2] realized their business was part of the climate problem. 'Actually, we started sustainability with a programme in 2002 that focused on employing disabled people, through collaboration with Samhall, a partly government-owned company,' says Pär Larshans, Chief Sustainability Officer at Max Burgers:

> That initially had nothing to do with climate change. Rather, it helped us understand that disabled people do not just have problems, but they compensate and have abilities that other people do not have. Then we came across The Natural Step and found it easy to understand because their thinking was so similar to our thinking in the social area, so we could easily adapt it to the environmental area.

Prompted by discussions with The Natural Step, Max Burgers became part of the solution by analysing the climate impact of its food production from farm to table. Max Burgers was the first restaurant chain to add carbon labels to its menus so that customers could make informed decisions based on environmental information. This initiative is known as Climate on (the) Menu. Apart from targeting customers, the company has made voluntary carbon offsets throughout its supply chain to support reforestation projects in Uganda and Mozambique. It actively supports offsetting projects which strengthen local agro-forestry, entrepreneurship and ecosystem services. Pär Larshans explains:

> We choose to offset our emissions since it's not possible to be 100 per cent sustainable today. We are not able to get meat from farms that are 100 per cent carbon-neutral; today you can only try to reduce the methane through different cattle feed and reduced fossil fuel use by farmers. And when it comes to waste, most of it is burned, whereas we would prefer to recycle and reduce. Unfortunately, current legislation stands in the way.

PROPOSITION AND EXECUTION

Concept of the Climate on (the) Menu initiative

There were three major objectives for Max Burgers in putting climate on the menu. First, it aimed to inspire customers to choose climate smart alternatives on the menu. Secondly, it got customers involved in reflecting on the climate impact of food in general. And lastly, the carbon label could help Max Burgers stand out as the best fast food restaurant choice for concerned customers. In developing its sustainable business strategy, Max Burgers has adopted the fundamental interpersonal relations orientation (FIRO) theory,

---

2   'Max Hamburgare' in Swedish.

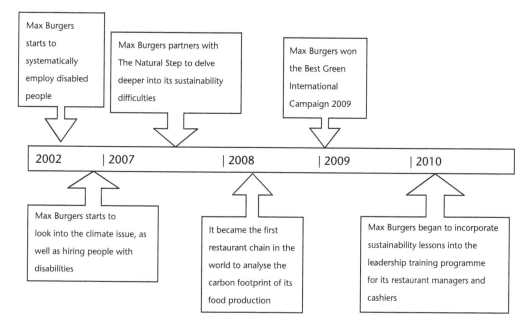

Timeline of the Climate on (the) Menu initiative

which stresses that the better the understanding of human behaviour on an individual level and during interaction, the more effective it is in improving relationships, building trust and establishing high-performing teams. This FIRO theory ('The Human Element') combined with the use of The Natural Step framework is used as the starting point of Max Burgers' climate initiative: this aims to create a culture of sustainability and make it a sustainable company from the inside out. It is essential for the company to ensure that its staff understand its climate initiative, making them ambassadors, and enabling them to communicate and spread the message.

'We conduct carbon reduction in three steps: (1) we measure the carbon impact; (2) we take concrete steps to reduce carbon emissions, and (3) we compensate,' says Larshans. 'The compensation works like an internal tax, so the more we reduce, the less we have to offset.'

Are there any campaign-specific communication principles?

Table 14.5 shows the campaign-specific communication principles of the Max Burgers' Climate on (the) Menu case.

Table 14.5 Campaign-specific communication principles – Max Burgers'
Climate on (the) Menu

Principles	Example
1. Consumer engagement	In order to raise climate awareness among consumers, Max Burgers communicates its sustainability initiative by telling customers the climate story through carbon -labelling, menu boards, posters and so on. They are therefore given a bigger picture and the opportunity to choose to reduce their climate impact.
2. Internal communication	Staff at Max Burgers play a crucial part in telling the climate story, sharing information on sustainability and responding to feedback from customers. To succeed, it is essential that employees understand the company's position on sustainability and the purpose of the initiative. As a result, the company has provided a series of courses, training events and workshops for employees to help them build trust in and recognition of the values of the climate initiative. For example, cashiers and managers take a four-hour and eight-hour sustainability course respectively.
3. External communication	Max Burgers' climate initiative has received a significant amount of Swedish and international media attention. A number of interviews have been conducted regarding the Climate on (the) Menu sustainability initiative. Speeches about its climate initiative to audiences of opinion leaders have created a word-of-mouth narrative. The company has also been mentioned in numerous books, and spreads the word using its own social media channels, such as Facebook and Twitter. All these external tools help to expand the coverage and enhance the credibility of the company's CSR initiative, as well as raising public awareness about the climate impact of food production.

Target audiences

The primary target audience was the restaurants' customers, who are assumed not to be specifically interested in environmental issues. Secondary audiences include the food industry and opinion leaders within the sustainable development field, as well as political stakeholders.

Key benefits of the Climate on (the) Menu initiative for target audiences

'When it comes to taste, numerous tests put Max as the winner when compared with competitors,' says Pär Larshans. 'However, we want Max Burgers not only to taste good, but do good, so we take responsibility, both social and environmental, which becomes a bonus to our customers.' By providing carbon labels on its food menu, Max Burgers raises consumers' climate-awareness. Customers are given the opportunity to compare the emissions of various burgers and make climate-smart choices of meals through the information given to them on sustainability.

BUSINESS CASE AND RESULTS

Key societal impacts of the Climate on (the) Menu initiative

To date, Max Burgers is responsible for the discharge of approximately 60,000 tons of CO_2 equivalents each year. In 2010, it offset its total climate impact 100 per cent by planting 66,000 trees in Africa, and to reduce the company's carbon impact resulting from energy use, all restaurants are powered by 100 per cent wind energy (see Figure 14.4).

Figure 14.4 Max Burgers works in many ways to reduce the carbon footprint of its burgers, including planting trees and supporting wind energy

Source: Reproduced courtesy of Max Hamburgerrestauranger AB.

Commercial impacts of the Climate on (the) Menu initiative

Max Burgers' sales have doubled in five years, tripled in seven years and quadrupled in nine years. In 2011, turnover reached 1,475 million kronor. Max has 88 restaurants in Sweden and three in Norway. There was a 15 per cent relative increase in sales of climate-smart alternatives from the menu. These gains are not only earned from expansion and innovation, but also by lowering the operating costs for energy and waste. 'People more actively look for Max restaurants as a choice in fast food, making establishing new restaurants in new locations a more immediate success,' according to Larshans. Brand preference has tripled in the last five years.

Impacts of the Climate on (the) Menu initiative

Max Burgers has received a number of awards for its 'Climate on the Menu' initiative. For example, Richard Bergfors, CEO of Max Burgers, was awarded the title Green Capitalist of the Year by the leading Swedish business magazine *Veckans Affärer* ('Business Week') and Climate on (the) Menu was named Best Green International Campaign in 2009. In 2011, Max Burgers received the Corporate Social Responsibility Award for Leadership, and in the same year, *Fast Company* magazine ranked Max as one of the 10 most innovative companies in the world.

A survey conducted by Mindshare found an increase in customer loyalty of 27 per cent for Max Burgers between 2007 and 2009, which concluded that much of the brand's success be attributed to the carbon labelling on the menu. In 2011, Max Burgers was ranked by Sustainable Brands as the most sustainable company in the restaurant and hotels sector in Sweden.

Apart from the awards and survey results, 131 articles have been written by journalists about Max Burgers' carbon label, equivalent to a PR value of £340,000 in 2009 alone.

Internal impacts of the Climate on (the) Menu initiative

Max Burgers has launched a leadership programme which offers managers opportunities to develop self-awareness, and a series of sustainability courses for employees. Apart from that, Max Burgers actively seeks to employ disabled workers. These programmes significantly help employees to understand the values and motives behind the climate initiative and helps build their trust in the company.

LESSONS LEARNED AND KEY SUCCESS FACTORS

Lessons learned

Pär Larshans identifies the main lessons learned from Max Burgers' Climate on (the) Menu initiative: 'You have to take an inside-out approach and do it right from the start. You can't paint the walls green, the change has to be real.' Being the pioneer also has an impact – Max Burgers was the first fast-food service chain in Sweden to put carbon labels on its menus, publishing carbon emissions data to enable its customers to make better choices. Climate on (the) Menu plays a role in influencing customers' behaviour and helps to raise their awareness about sustainability and climate issues.

However, the question is how much impact carbon labelling has on customers' understanding of sustainability, enabling them to make climate-friendly choices. Even though customers are given information enabling them to compare the carbon emissions of different burgers, they may not genuinely understand the real impact of the various levels on climate change. In this regard, there may be a need for the company, as well as the food industry in general, to further increase its interaction with customers to ensure their genuine understanding of environmental effects, instead of providing one-way information in the future.

Nonetheless, Max Burgers has taken an inside-out approach by strengthening sustainability values within the company and expanding the concept to include the community at large. It has been organizing a series of courses on sustainability and leadership training workshops to change attitudes and educate staff. Offering personal development training to employees is indeed evidence of a view to the long term. This helps to develop employees' sense of belonging as well as their trust in the company, and in return they will strengthen the company's values by communicating them to outsiders.

Key success factors

Table 14.6 shows the key success factors of the Max Burgers Climate on (the) Menu case.

Table 14.6 Key success factors – Max Burgers' Climate on (the) Menu

Key success factors	Description
1. Effective internal communication on sustainability	Max Burgers values its employees' recognition and understanding of sustainability. It took strategic steps to make the company sustainable from the inside out by adapting the FIRO theory in its management. It launched an FIRO-inspired leadership programme, including courses to help managers and cashiers build confidence and competence in, as well as commitment to, sustainability. The programme aims to communicate sustainability in a credible and clear way, so that employees can spread the message and answer enquiries from customers. The company sees the importance of engaging every employee with it corporate values. Trust and a sense of belonging are built by including and involving staff in climate initiatives. This facilitates the process of building good relations between the company and customers, and communicates the sustainability message to society.
2. Social and traditional media	Max Burgers makes effective use of both traditional and online media. It has created a Facebook fan page and spread s the message about the importance of making climate-friendly choices in food consumption through public relations. Third-party coverage of the climate initiative has broadened awareness and enhanced its credibility.
3. Multi-stakeholder considerations	Max Burgers keeps all the company's stakeholders involved when designing the climate programme, including employees, customers and the wider food industry. It partnered with The Natural Step, meaning that third-party involvement could bring a more holistic and objective approach to planning the strategy.

REFERENCES

CSRwire, 'CSR Press Release: Max Hamburgers from Sweden Revolutionize Fast Food Industry and Tour US, 19 October 2010, www.csrwire.com/press_releases/30891-Max-Hamburgers-from-Sweden-Revolutionize-Fast-Food-Industry-and-Tour-US (accessed 2 June 2013).

International Green Awards, 'Climate on the Menu – Max Hamburgerrestauranger AB: Best Green International Campaign', www.greenawards.com/winners/winners_2009/best_green_international_campaign-2 (accessed 2 June 2013).

Interview with Pär Larshans, Chief Sustainability Officer, Max Burgers.

McCallum, Neil, 'Max Hamburgers Joins Global Sustainability Conference Planet Under Pressure', Det Naturilga Steget, 7 March 2012, www.naturalstep.org/en/max-hamburgers-joins-global-sustainability-conference-planet-under-pressure (accessed 2 June 2013).

SOCAPmarkets, *The New Era of Sustainable Business, Powered by The Human Element*, 10 May 2012, www.youtube.com/watch?v=B9XL5xrysjg (accessed 2 June 2013).

The Natural Step, *A Natural Step Case Study: Max Hamburger and The Natural Step*, 2010, www.thenaturalstep.org/sites/all/files/Max-TNS-CaseStudy-FINAL.pdf (accessed 2 June 2013).

15 Sustainable Consumption and the Social Responsibility of Marketers and Advertisers – Best Practice Cases

Best Practice Case 12: Coop Switzerland Sustainability Brand Communications

IDEA AND INSPIRATION

Background and idea for the sustainability umbrella brand campaign and the sustainable competence brands

In the past, Coop Switzerland's concept of sustainability was always communicated through own-label product brands, the so-called 'competence brands'. Although this has been effective and continues to work very well, Coop Switzerland wanted sustainability-related communication which enhanced the retail or umbrella brand Coop in addition to these product-related brands. A key reason for this was that the leading Swiss retailer needed to find a way to reach younger target audiences with sustainability messages for those who would not otherwise read about them (Coop Switzerland's own weekly paper has 60 per cent coverage of Swiss households) and would not purchase competence brand products. Dr Thomas Schwetje, Head of Marketing at Coop Switzerland, recalls: 'This future generation will be at the receiving end of our unsustainable lifestyle. We felt we needed to talk to them in their own language. It was our objective to create a lightbulb experience, an "aha-reaction" regarding sustainability, using strong visuals and music.'

Without the establishment of the competence brands, the umbrella message would not have had the foundation and credibility it needed. Coop had started very early, in 1989, to systematically develop its portfolio of sustainable competence brands (see Figure 15.1), starting with oecoplan (1989 – household cleaners and so on), naturaplan (1993 – organic food), naturaline (1993 – organic cotton), Pro Montagna (2007 – food specialties from the Swiss mountain regions) and naturafarm (2007 – organic meat and eggs), thus building its reputation as a sustainability leader in the perception of the Swiss population.

Figure 15.1 Coop Switzerland offers a wide range of sustainably sourced and organic products across many food and non-food categories

Source: Reproduced courtesy of Coop Switzerland.

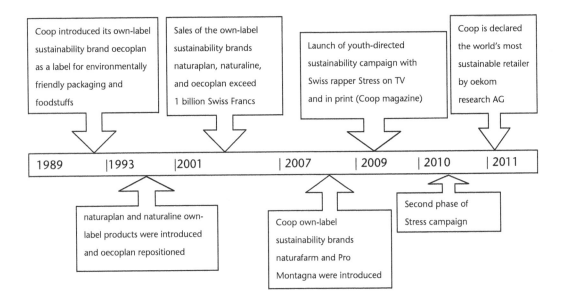

Timeline of Coop sustainability brand communications

PROPOSITION AND EXECUTION

Concept of the sustainability umbrella campaign featuring the rapper Stress

What makes this campaign different from other sustainability communications is that Coop focuses on raising consumer awareness of sustainability issues, rather than illustrating what the company is doing in the field of sustainability: 'Our aim was to talk to young people and raise their awareness about the issues and problems we saw before presenting them with a solution,' explains Thomas Schwetje. 'With the Stress campaign, we explained to them why we do what we do, what our motivation is.' Thomas Schwetje is convinced that Coop was only able to run a campaign like this due to the retailer's long history in the area of sustainability, with its pedigree of own-label sustainability brands:

What you need to bear in mind is that the umbrella campaign ran in parallel to our sustainability- related product brand campaigns that explain what we do. So the umbrella brand tells the story about why we are active in sustainability while the competence brands inform them about our concrete actions.

The media plan for the campaign was straightforward: the rapper Stress (see Figure 15.2) appeared on national TV, and raised awareness primarily among young people. It was flanked by an online campaign in which school classes could win a day with Stress to explore the subject of sustainability. 'We believe involving people is key in the context of sustainability,' adds Thomas Schwetje.

Figure 15.2 Switzerland's number one rapper Stress became Coop's spokesperson to help raise awareness of sustainability among the younger generation
Source: Reproduced courtesy of Coop Switzerland.

In parallel with the TV campaign, Coop Switzerland ran a print advertisement series in its own magazine, *Coopzeitung*, and in other print media: in the former, the adverts aimed to raise awareness about sustainability among the older target audience; in addition, *Coopzeitung* provided much deeper background information geared to heads of households.

Online communication focused on Coop's own website rather than social media, as their own site is one of the highest-traffic sites in Switzerland. It was similar to the print campaign, with the addition of making videos and the above-mentioned schools initiative.

Are there any campaign-specific communication principles?

Table 15.1 shows the campaign-specific communication principles of the Coop Switzerland sustainability brand communications case.

Table 15.1 Campaign-specific communication principles – Coop Switzerland's sustainability brand communications

Principles	Example
1. Target audience-specific	Coop was determined to find a way to reach young people with the sustainability message. Joining forces with Stress, one of Switzerland's most prominent rappers, was a clever move. The decision to create 60-second TV adverts and air them in prime time was courageous given the usual audience, and proved the company's commitment. The fact that Coop backed up the youth-directed campaign with a print campaign and PR geared to the heads of households doing their shopping at the retailer's outlets made the package complete.
2. Integration	The way Coop used a combination of media and built the campaign on the product brand campaigns was the reason for the massive impact Coop's sustainability communication has had on sustainability awareness in Switzerland and the perception of the Coop brand as a sustainable brand.
3. Values	The values Coop demonstrates as a socially responsible company and its commitment to sustainability are the basis for both the Stress campaign and the sustainability competence brands.
4. Authenticity and credibility	Authenticity and credibility come from Coop's perceived substance due to its sustainability competence brands. Pro Montagna is a good example: the entire value chain is in the mountain areas. naturaplan shows this, too – Swiss organic standards are a lot more stringent than the EU or German standards. 'We look extremely carefully at being totally credible on the product side,' affirms Thomas Schwetje.

Target audiences

The campaign's primary audience is young people. Secondarily, the print campaign targets heads of households – middle-aged consumers, with a focus on women.

Consumer response to the campaign

'The target audience received it very positively,' Thomas Schwetje recalls. There were reactions like "Finally someone's advertising in our language" and "It's cool that you're taking our music into the mainstream media."' Stress's CD sold very well, and he won the Swiss Music Award for the campaign theme song.

Heads of households and parents applauded the fact that Coop was managing to talk about sustainability with young people. In assessing the overall campaign, this target audience did not distinguish between the print communication and the TV commercials, because both were placed in the mainstream media.

Overall, there was very little negative feedback, despite the fact that rappers are usually controversial.

There was no specific communication directed at NGOs or other critical stakeholders – nor was there any negative response from that quarter.

BUSINESS CASE AND RESULTS

Key societal impacts of the campaign

It can only be assumed from the consumer response that the campaign has had a positive impact on sustainability awareness, particularly among young people. While no before/after surveys are available, according to Thomas Schwetje, the feedback from students, parents and teachers was so positive that Coop is more than convinced that there has been a significant impact.

Commercial impacts of the 'Stress' campaign

It is not possible to attribute a direct sales effect to the umbrella campaign. However, the sustainable competence brands have shown disproportionate growth, and sustainable investment rating company oekom research rated Coop Switzerland as the most sustainable retail brand in 2011, with communication as one of the criteria that made a difference.

Brand impact of the 'Stress' campaign

Due to the campaign, sympathy values have increased, particularly among the younger target audience, but also among heads of households and parents. Coop has gained further credibility, and is clearly perceived as the leader in sustainability communication by Swiss consumers, despite usually being head-to-head with rival Migros.

Internal impacts of the 'Stress' campaign

Coop's employees are seen as ambassadors, serving as the primary point of contact with customers. In 2011, Coop expanded its existing internal training courses and included sustainability-related content. One important event was a large-scale motivational training conference in 2011 in Interlaken for approximately 1,800 staff. Games and a variety of activities were used to inspire employees and increase their understanding of Coop's sustainability approach and the sustainability competence brands and quality labels.

LESSONS LEARNED AND KEY SUCCESS FACTORS

Lessons learned

Thomas Schwetje identifies the main lessons from the 'Stress' campaign:

> We walked a tightrope as we filmed the commercials with Stress at Lake Aral and in Australia. There was some criticism along the lines of 'How can that be sustainable?' despite the fact that we compensated for the CO_2 emissions. We decided to communicate our decision proactively and transparently, because we were convinced we were doing the right thing.

The lesson is that there are times when you need to make a call and pursue your course despite opposition and criticism, communicating the rationale for your decision actively and openly.

The second lesson is that it pays to speak the language of the target audience. The 'Stress' campaign proved that, as does the most recent oecoplan campaign, which has a 'twinkle in the eye' element and shows that sustainability does not have to be a dry topic, but can be fun.

The third lesson is that in sustainability communication, the involvement of consumers creates authenticity and helps build emotional proximity. The 'Stress' campaign included interactive elements, such as the schools campaign. Thomas Schwetje cites the Coop Switzerland wildflower campaign as a good example: 'You need to involve consumers as much as possible to do something themselves. In the wildflower promotion, we handed out seeds to them and encouraged them to sow them.' If consumers were able to document that they had actually planted the seeds with a photo, they qualified to take part in a competition. In return, for each participant, Coop also enriched one square metre of meadowland with wild plants.

Key success factors

Table 15.2 shows the key success factors of the Coop Switzerland sustainability brand communications case.

Table 15.2 Key success factors – Coop Switzerland's sustainability brand communications

Key success factors	Description
1. Product-related	Stay close to the product and run an umbrella brand or corporate campaign; communicate on the product side in parallel, because the audience requires proof.
2. Point-of-sale experience	Create a point-of-sale experience. Coop runs naturaplan promotional weeks every year. At the store level, consumers get the (ultimate) proof.
3. Consumer involvement	Involve consumers actively to create a deeper level of awareness and to build emotional proximity.
4. Credibility first	Start building credibility for sustainability through what you do before communicating actively. If you are not perceived as credible, your campaign will be seen as greenwashing.

REFERENCES

Coop Group Annual Report 2011, www.coop.ch/pb/site/common/get/documents/coop_main/elements/ueber/geschaeftsbericht/2012/_pdf_gbnhb_2011/COOP_GB_2011_low/COOP_GB_2011_e_low.pdf (accessed 2 June 2013).

Interview with Dr Thomas Schwetje, Head of Marketing, Coop Switzerland.

Nexum Consulting & Design, 'Coop Puts its Commitment to Sustainability on the Web', 22 June 2010, www.nexum.de/en/newsroom/news-and-media/details/article/1/Coop-bringt.html?no_cache=1&cHash=47820bbad6abebdae9371b47a13a6cc0 (accessed 2 June 2013).

Best Practice Case 13: Puma's Clever Little Bag

IDEA AND INSPIRATION

Idea behind the Clever Little Bag and how it originated

'The key question in our minds was: "How do you make a better shoebox from environmental packaging?"' says Antonio Bertone, at the time of the interview (June 2012) Chief Marketing Officer at Puma and the driving force behind the project that led to the Clever Little Bag. Shoeboxes account for millions of tons of waste. 'Our goal was to re-engineer the box. What we had in mind was a packaging that would explain itself to the consumer on the spot and would create an immediate response.' The project was started in 2008. Antonio Bertone approached designer Yves Béhar and his company FuseProject, and 90 days into the venture, the team had the first designs on the table (see Figure 15.3).

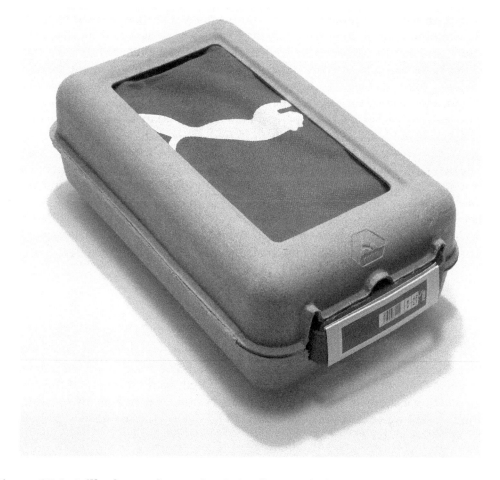

Figure 15.3 Still a box – the result of the first optimization phase did not convince the Puma development team

Source: Reproduced courtesy of Puma SE.

Antonio Bertone recalls: 'Yves shared our mindset. We wanted to do this without design for design's sake, without screwing up the supply chain. We wanted warehouse people to love it, too!' The project team conducted a comprehensive survey of what worked from a production and supply chain point of view and what did not, thus defining the design brief and the boundaries. 'This part of the process was critical in order to get it right,' Bertone remembers:

> Then at one point, we had a very nice design that did what it should do from a consumer perspective. However, when looking at it from a supply chain and product lifecycle point of view, this paper foam and bag design did not do the job. That was a pretty devastating realization almost two years into development. It was a massive education for us, but we knew we had to stick to our conviction. It was not a very popular project at that time! We sat there, and were trying to understand why we failed, looking at the lifecycle assessment [LCA] part of it, asking what would change the metrics. 'How can we make the meal, but with different ingredients?'

From the LCA,[1] they knew they had to get rid of the paper foam, because it was very energy-intensive in production. They also realized that they wanted to retain the box in a minimized form to provide stability for the new design. And they kept the bag construction: Enter the Clever Little Bag! 'And then we also managed to reach the LCA benchmarks we had set ourselves!' Getting from the setback phase to the final design was actually fairly speedy: 'We were sitting in a conference room, with scissors and cardboard, and basically making it by hand.' When it came to turning the prototype into production-ready packaging, the experts at Material ConneXion were a great help to the Puma development team, supporting them in finding the right source materials for the bag.

The new packaging was launched on the market in 2010, and by 2011 most of Puma's shoes were shipped in the Clever Little Bag. The team continued their work, and an even slimmer and further improved version was due to be launched by end of 2012. Also, further clever packaging solutions have been created, including the Clever Little Hanger and a paddleboard packaging called EcoCradle made from mushrooms. The Clever Little Bag has become part of what Puma internally now calls 'Clever Little World'.

PROPOSITION AND EXECUTION

Concept of the Clever Little Bag

The Clever Little Bag is a half-bag and half-box design which uses 65 per cent less cardboard than traditional shoeboxes (see Figure 15.4). The design firstly aims to reduce water, energy and paper consumption as well as CO_2 emissions throughout the lifecycle of the traditional shoebox. Secondly, it provides customers with a handy reusable bag, aiming to raise awareness of eco-packaging and reducing the use of plastic shopping bags.

---

1   See PE Americas/PE International, *Life Cycle Assessment of Different Shoe Packaging Design*, Puma, April 2010, www.puma.com/pdfs/lca-report.pdf (accessed 2 June 2013).

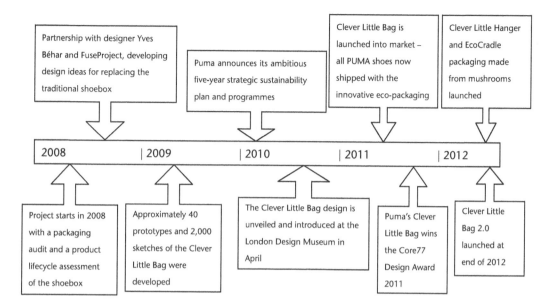

Partnership with designer Yves Béhar and FuseProject, developing design ideas for replacing the traditional shoebox

Puma announces its ambitious five-year strategic sustainability plan and programmes

Clever Little Bag is launched into market – all PUMA shoes now shipped with the innovative eco-packaging

Clever Little Hanger and EcoCradle packaging made from mushrooms launched

2008 | 2009 | 2010 | 2011 | 2012

Project starts in 2008 with a packaging audit and a product lifecycle assessment of the shoebox

Approximately 40 prototypes and 2,000 sketches of the Clever Little Bag were developed

The Clever Little Bag design is unveiled and introduced at the London Design Museum in April

Puma's Clever Little Bag wins the Core77 Design Award 2011

Clever Little Bag 2.0 launched at end of 2012

Timeline of the Clever Little Bag

Figure 15.4 The Clever Little Bag marks a new era in Puma's sustainability programme
Source: Reproduced courtesy of Puma SE.

What are the campaign-specific communication principles of the Clever Little Bag?

Table 15.3 shows the campaign-specific communication principles of the Puma Clever Little Bag case.

Table 15.3   Campaign-specific communication principles – Puma's Clever Little Bag

Principles	Example
1. Humility	'It needs to have a humble voice,' explains Antonio Bertone, 'needs to be truly clever, and it needs to hit a benchmark in terms of environmental performance as measured by an LCA.' Thus, the humility implies both transparency and having strict benchmarks and boundaries, realizing that you can always improve. Puma was to launch version 2 of the Clever Little Bag a little more than a year after the first one hit the market. The fact that Puma decided to develop this project in partnership with Yves Béhar and later Material ConneXion illustrates its collaborative approach. The mushroom packaging was developed with experts Ecovative.
2. Brand icon	The Clever Little Bag is an iconic addition to the PUMA brand. The new packaging is designed to fit within the parameters of the brand's corporate identity and enhances the brand wherever it appears.
3. Self-explanatory	It fulfils Antonio Bertone's expectation that it should speak for itself. In that way, it creates its own viral marketing and produces a lot of earned (versus paid-for) media coverage. Puma has added to that with a video circulating on the Internet that is welcome fodder within the social Web. Consumers are encouraged to upload photos showing how they use the bag on Puma's website, thus spreading the word even further and encouraging creativity and imagination.
4. Eco win–win	The key to its success with consumers is that it offers added value in terms of convenience and added functionality, as well as superior environmental performance.
5. Mass-market	'It is not a niche, it is everything. It is not a design experiment!' says Antonio Bertone. All Puma shoe packaging was switched from the traditional red shoebox to the Clever Little Bag, not just an 'eco-line' of products.

Target audiences

The key target audience is the consumer, for whom the bag is made, bearing in mind that shoes are usually taken home from the shop in plastic shopping bags and that most people like to store shoes somehow, particularly when they are travelling. In addition, it relays the message that sustainability can be cool, is compatible with attractive design, and encourages the use of reusable versus disposable bags.

The secondary target audiences are retailers which are resellers of Puma shoes and suppliers which produce Puma's shoes and packaging or supply materials. With the LCA in hand, Puma can show suppliers where environmental improvements can be made and potential cost savings can be made. Thus, Puma also contributes to raising awareness of sustainability up and down the supply chain.

The third target audiences are key opinion leaders and critical stakeholders, like the NGOs which scrutinize all of the sustainability-directed activities of big business.

The fourth target audience is Puma employees, who have to work with the new packaging, either in the supply chain or in sales.

Responses to the Clever Little Bag

'Consumers have been awesome about it,' explains Antonio Bertone. 'They really appreciate it and what it does for them. We had a lot of positive feedback at shop floor level.'

The response from retailers has been mixed: 'Some retailers still do not like it because they do not like change. Some see it as truly innovative.'

As for significant opinion leaders and stakeholders: 'They have been good, they like it. For the most part they appreciated the transparency and how we handled the LCA, the independent survey and our metrics.'

In terms of employees, as in most cases, there was a mixed reception: 'You have the cheerleaders and also the naysayers. Now everybody is collectively proud of it because of the good results, the awards, the accolades. Even the critics are charmed by it.' The salespeople may still be the most critical, as they have to deal with the retailers, their customers. 'I am not sure what they would say if I put them on a lie detector,' muses Antonio Bertone, 'perhaps they would ask, "Why did we do that?"'

BUSINESS CASE AND RESULTS

Key societal impacts of the Clever Little Bag

Puma estimates that the Clever Little Bag cuts water, energy, and fuel consumption during manufacturing alone by 60 per cent – the design saves 8,500 tons of paper, 20 million megajoules of electricity, 1 million litres of fuel and 1 million litres of water each year. Also, by not providing plastic bags to customers, 275 tons of plastic is being saved, which correspondingly saves another 500,000 litres of diesel due to lighter shipping weights.

Commercial impacts of the Clever Little Bag on Puma

The big fear within Puma was that the new packaging would add significant cost to its products. However, according to Antonio Bertone, the result is that the cost of the Clever Little Bag is almost the same as that of the traditional red shoebox, but with significant positive environmental effects. He adds: 'What really justifies it from a commercial point of view is the massive amounts of earned media it has generated. We cannot be sure whether it has directly added to sales.'

Impacts on the Puma brand

Antonio Bertone is excited about the impact the sustainable packaging innovation has had on the Puma brand:

The brand got a lot out of it! The reason is innovation – the Clever Little Bag does so much talking for itself, for such a little bag it does a lot of communication, particularly every time the bag is used for something other than its original purpose, like carrying bottles of wine. Here at Puma's newly designed Boston headquarters, we've incorporated them into a lighting fixture, creating a sculptural effect.

Internal impacts of the Clever Little Bag

As mentioned above, it has created internal awareness about sustainability in the production context. However, at times it was challenging for the sales staff, due to the opposition to innovation expressed by some major retail customers.

LESSONS LEARNED AND KEY SUCCESS FACTORS

Lessons learned

In the 13 March 2012 edition of the British magazine *Marketing Week*, Unilever's Vice President of Marketing, Marc Mathieu, cited Puma's Clever Little Bag as an example of a brand that can have a successful sustainability agenda.

For Antonio Bertone, one of the main lessons is that you have to be prepared to be internally unpopular if you are passionate about change:

You can be really committed to people who are already on board. But sometimes someone has to be the leader and run with it. If you want to change the paradigm, you have to be brave and march forward. It is so easy for a company to talk itself out of change.

He mentions that he was grateful to have the support of senior management, especially of the then CEO, Jochen Zeitz.

With the Clever Little Bag, Puma has demonstrated that sustainable and creative leadership should go hand in hand. The lifestyle brand has shown that a stock market-listed business can successfully undertake an ambitious sustainability commitment and make it accessible to consumers. The example also shows the power of sustainability to stimulate the innovation agenda – if managers are prepared think, quite literally, 'outside the box'.

Key success factors

Table 15.4 shows the key success factors of the Puma Clever Little Bag case.

Table 15.4 Key success factors – Puma's Clever Little Bag

Key success factors	Description
1. Behaviour change first	'The first and most important step is that your behaviour truly changes and the product starts behaving differently. This product behavioural change has to carry over to organizational business behaviour,' says Antonio Bertone. For him, credible product responsibility is thus the key success factor. 'Only when we feel even more comfortable with our behaviour do we earn the right to use the Clever Little Bag and sustainability in advertising.'
2. Tenacity and passion	As mentioned above, there is always resistance to change, both inside and outside organizations. Passion for sustainability and tenacity will be vital.
3. Stakeholders as gatekeepers	Part of Puma's humble approach to CSR communication in the production context is that the company annually invites stakeholders to help it fine-tune both behaviour and language, according to Bertone.

'The ultimate objective from a communication point of view would be top-of-mind awareness by consumers that Puma cares. That would be a massive success. I would love that as an unprompted response, as a sign that sustainability is part of the brand atmosphere,' says Antonio Bertone.

REFERENCES

Baker, Rosie and Snoad, Laura, 'Marketers Call for a "Rebrand" of the Industry', *Marketing Week*, 13 March 2012, www.marketingweek.co.uk/news/marketers-call-for-a-rebrand-of-the-industry/4000597.article (accessed 2 June 2013).

Core77, '2011 C77DA Packaging: Winner Professional, Designer: FuseProject – Yves Behar, Project: Clever Little Bag, Client: Puma, Question and Answer', Core77 Design Awards, www.core77designawards.com/2011/recipients/puma-clever-little-bag/ (accessed 2 June 2013).

GreenerDesign Staff, 'Puma's "Clever Little Bag" Slashes Sneaker Packaging', GreenBiz.com, www.greenbiz.com/news/2010/04/13/puma-clever-little-bag-slashes-packaging, 13 April 2010 (accessed 2 June 2013).

Interview with Antonio Bertone, Chief Marketing Officer, Puma.

PE Americas/PE International, *Life Cycle Assessment of Different Shoe Packaging Design*, Puma, April 2010, www.puma.com/pdfs/lca-report.pdf (accessed 2 June 2013).

Puma, *Group Management Report for Financial Year 2010*, http://about.puma.com/wp-content/themes/aboutPUMA_theme/media/pdf/IAS_Konzernabschluss_e2010_03022011.pdf (accessed 2 June 2013).

The Dieline, 'The Dieline Awards 2011: Best of Show – PUMA Clever Little Bag', *the dieline*, www.thedieline.com/blog/2011/6/24/the-dieline-awards-2011-best-of-show-puma-clever-little-bag.html (accessed 2 June 2013).

Welbel, Jennifer, 'Puma's "Clever Little Bag"', *Brand Packaging*, 1 April 2011, www.brandpackaging.com/Articles/Brand_New/BNP_GUID_9-5-2006_A_10000000000001025819 (accessed 2 June 2013).

16 *The Shareholder Perspective – Best Practice Case*

Best Practice Case 14: Novo Nordisk Integrated Reporting

IDEA AND INSPIRATION

Idea behind integrated reporting

'We do not want the dichotomy of business and sustainability. What we really want is to communicate in a way that shows that sustainability is how we do business' explains Susanne Stormer, Vice President Corporate Sustainability at Novo Nordisk, the Danish health care company and global leader in diabetes care:

> For us, the triple bottom line is a business principle that enables us to take decisions in a way that moves us towards sustainability. It helps us to ensure that we get the balance right between concerns for business objectives, both short-term and long-term, the implications for people and communities and for the environment. So when we speak to our shareholders, we put a lot of emphasis on that. We do not see a distinction between shareholder and stakeholder interests, as the only way we can honour shareholder interests is by honouring stakeholder interests.

So the core idea behind integrated reporting is that sustainability should not be a separate message.

Novo Nordisk published its first environmental report in 1994. The 1999 report included the social dimension (responsibility towards employees and civil society), and in 2004 the first integrated report was released, based on the triple bottom line approach.

'Changing Diabetes'

Novo Nordisk is the leader in diabetes care, and its mission is to defeat diabetes. 'Changing Diabetes' is the 'brand' that embodies that mission. 'Some people may think, "With that mission, they'll put themselves out of business,' says Susanne Stormer. 'We are convinced that as a world leader in diabetes care that builds its business on people's health, or rather illness, we have the obligation to take the lead in the fight against diabetes.' Behind this vision that puts 'meat on the bone' of the triple bottom line idea, Novo Nordisk has developed a three-step approach

1. continuously developing products to provide better care for people that have diabetes already, enabling them to lead a normal life;
2. helping people that have diabetes to have it diagnosed at an early stage, as 50 per cent who have it do not know; by driving earlier diagnosis followed by earlier treatment, there is therefore an opportunity to reduce costly and painful consequences;
3. preventing diabetes (particularly Type 2 diabetes) by advocating lifestyle changes.

Susanne Stormer explains:

> In the short term, the focus on better treatment and diagnosis is pulling people into the business, while prevention is intended to keep people away from our business. Shareholder reactions are interesting: they appreciate the approach, and understand the direct link between the business and our responsibility. They ask us to build the business case from a societal point of view, because the approach could generate huge public savings.

She mentions China as an example where Novo Nordisk has worked to help build infrastructure, educating doctors and developing an alliance with the Ministry of Health over the past fifteen years:

> We were trying to ensure that diabetes is perceived as a major health threat by building awareness. Only after this period are we now promoting our products and today we have a 69 per cent market share in the insulin market in China: a strong business case indeed, and proof that CSR is basically good business. When we look at our share price compared to peers and indexes, there is clearly a premium for Novo Nordisk. We are working on showing that some of this value can be attributed to our triple bottom line approach.

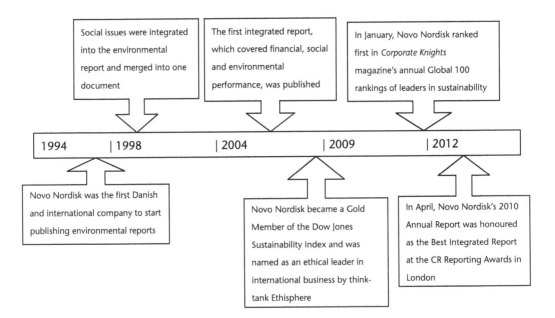

Timeline of integrated reporting

PROPOSITION AND EXECUTION

Concept of integrated reporting

The major goals of integrated reporting are to increase financial valuation and to explore the relationship between Novo Nordisk's financial and non-financial performance. These objectives have both an internal and external dimension. Internally, integrated reporting aims to enhance accountability for achieving the company's performance objectives. Externally, it aims to create more transparency and increase accountability to all stakeholders. In implementing integrated reporting, a number of activities are involved. They include an annual review of internal strategies and balanced scorecard targets; engagement with external and internal stakeholders; internal and independent reviews of the company's annual integrated report, and a review of the company's media coverage and public agenda issues. In addition, an external assurance provider is asked to review whether the non-financial performance included in the report meets the standards for stakeholder engagement: inclusivity, materiality and responsiveness.

Having said that, there is still specific sustainability and CSR communication at Novo Nordisk. Susanne Stormer explains:

> *While our aim is to streamline and to integrate CSR and sustainability into our general communication, we accept we need to cater to the needs of specific audiences in the sustainability area. That is why we have a sustainability sub-site on our website, to cater to the needs of sustainability professionals, peers, and academics as well as investors.*

What are the specific communication principles of Novo Nordisk's integrated reporting?

Table 16.1 shows the campaign-specific communication principles of the Novo Nordisk integrated reporting case.

Table 16.1 Campaign-specific communication principles – Novo Nordisk's integrated reporting

Principles	Example
1. Triple bottom line	The core principle behind the integrated reporting approach is Novo Nordisk's triple bottom line concept. For integrated reporting to work, the business needs to be aligned with this paradigm.
2. Strong vision	'Changing Diabetes' is a vision that combines the societal and the economic dimension. Business can be aligned behind that vision. The vision provides the business rationale for the triple bottom line approach.
3. Stakeholder engagement	Novo Nordisk has been actively engaged with multiple stakeholders for many years, to address key issues in its business and decision-making process. Long-standing engagement has created an open dialogue between the company and stakeholders, building solid relationships. This helps develop both sides' trust and understanding in order to find common ground for more sustainable solutions. For instance, the 'Blueprint for Change Programme' was launched in 2010 to facilitate stakeholder engagement and demonstrate how the company delivers value to both business and society through rigorous assessment.

Target audiences

Investors and shareholders are the primary target audiences for the integrated annual report, while stakeholders and the general public are secondary targets.

Key benefits of integrated reporting for the target audiences

The following key benefits were identified:

- Novo Nordisk's integrated reporting provides greater clarity about the relationship between financial and non-financial key performance indicators (see Figure 16.1). This helps shareholders make better management and business decisions, because of better measurement and information.
- The integrated report enhances the transparency of internal business operations, and therefore increases market trust, as well as facilitating improved relationships between shareholders and stakeholders.
- The report demonstrates the strong values orientation of Novo Nordisk, which helps to increase stakeholders' understanding and awareness of sustainability.

BUSINESS CASE AND RESULTS

Commercial impacts of integrated reporting

There is no direct financial impact from sustainability reporting, integrated or not integrated. However, there is potentially a business case for integrating sustainability into the business. The financial success of Novo Nordisk has accompanied its sustainability recognition. In 2012, the company announced that it enjoyed a 19 per cent increase in fourth quarter earnings over 2011. As mentioned above, the share price has developed compared to the company's peers, even though so far it has not been possible to attribute it unambiguously to the integrated triple bottom line approach. Susanne Stormer says: 'There is a clear business benefit that you can quantify and assess in terms of reputation, employee engagement and level of innovation.' The business case for integrating the 'Changing Diabetes' approach has been explained above.

Susanne Stormer adds:

> We are not looking to appeal to day traders, but to institutional investors that take a long-term approach, like Al Gore's Generation Investment Management. Novo Nordisk was one of their very first investments, and they have stayed invested because our business model is consistent with their investment strategy. They appreciate the fact that we have a vision combined with strong financial performance today and the prospect of a solid long-term performance based on that vision.

Brand impacts of integrated reporting

Novo Nordisk is renowned nationally and internationally for its integrated reporting. Since 2004, the Global Reporting Initiative has pointed to Novo Nordisk as a model for the quality of its integrated reporting. In 2012, its 2010 Annual Report was honoured as

For nearly 90 years, Novo Nordisk has combined drug discovery with technology to turn science into solutions for people with diabetes. We also provide treatments for people with haemophilia and growth hormone deficiency and for women experiencing symptoms of menopause. We leverage our expertise with protein molecules, chronic disease management and device technology to provide innovative treatments that make a difference in quality of care.

Novo Nordisk has more than 32,000 employees in 75 countries and markets products in more than 190 countries. Our B shares are listed on NASDAQ OMX Copenhagen and our ADRs are listed on the New York Stock Exchange under the symbol NVO. For more information about our company, visit novonordisk.com.

> We leverage our expertise to make a difference in quality of care.

We report on our financial, social and environmental performance in one integrated report and we report additional information online. This public filing contains references and links to information posted on the company's website; such information is not incor - porated by reference into the publ ic filing. The management review, as defined by the Danish Financial Statements Act, is com prised of pp 2–54 and 100–101.

Material and business-critical information is reported in the annual report. Information for specific stakeholder groups is reported at annualreport2011.novonordisk.com . We value feedback and welcome questions or comments about this report or our perfor-mance at annualreport@novonordisk.com .

Figure 16.1 The table of contents of the Novo Nordisk report provides a comprehensive and thorough guide to business, governance, social and environmental impact

Source: Reproduced courtesy of Novo Nordisk A/S.

the Best Integrated Report at the CR Reporting Awards in London. It is the fourth time the company has won the award in integrated reporting. Earlier in the year, it ranked number one in the Global 100 Most Sustainable Corporations in the World Index published by *Corporate Knights* magazine. The initiation of integrated reporting has clearly enhanced the profile and visibility of the Novo Nordisk brand. On top of that, the company's integrated report has provided more product and marketing information to its stakeholder network, which has fostered additional goodwill for the company's brand.

Internal impact of integrated reporting

Novo Nordisk's integrated reporting demonstrates the importance of business and sustainability links to internal stakeholders. Before publication, internal stakeholders are involved in consultations to identify key priorities, set targets and so on to establish the annual financial and non-financial objectives. After publication, the report serves as an internal communication instrument for improving understanding of the strategic importance of sustainability at both employee and management levels.

'Internally having an integrated vision like "Changing Diabetes" has made a huge difference,' says Susanne Stormer, 'and as an employer brand, it is extremely valuable that you're making a difference to other people's lives.'

LESSONS LEARNED AND KEY SUCCESS FACTORS

Lessons learned

Novo Nordisk has become an undisputed leader in conducting and communicating integrated reporting. It has successfully demonstrated and explained the relationship between financial and non-financial performance. Most importantly, it has brought the values of sustainability to the fore, from which other companies can learn. The company's value commitment has created an environment for innovative thinking along the triple bottom line – social, environmental and business performance. The idea of integrated reporting evolved to reflect both the financial and non-financial performance of the company. Coupled with executive management commitment, the integrated report has pointed the way to achieve long-term success on the triple bottom line.

However, Novo Nordisk has also encountered challenges in balancing financial, social and environmental considerations in integrated reporting, particularly in its commitment to the triple bottom line principle. It has to ensure that all areas where the company has a significant impact are covered and addressed. In addition, companies which intend to start or improve their integrated reporting should note the need to improve metrics to measure non-financial performance progress. Novo Nordisk is working on developing those metrics to underpin the business case that investors want to see.

Key success factors

Table 16.2 shows the key success factors of the Novo Nordisk integrated reporting case.

Table 16.2   Key success factors – Novo Nordisk's integrated reporting

Key success factors	Description
1. Integrated management	Integrated reporting requires integrated management – whether that is called 'triple bottom line' or 'embedding sustainability into business processes'. Businesses intending to move towards integrated reporting need to first assess how integrated their business processes are.
2. Quantitative base	Novo Nordisk found it challenging to build the quantitative business case because it lacked baseline figures. Defining appropriate indicators and generating robust data is a prerequisite to ensure that the financial and the non-financial elements of integrated reporting are on an equal footing.
3. Speak the language of the CFO	'CSR professionals need to understand that they need to speak the language of CFOs if they want to be understood,' says Susanne Stormer. There are four building blocks to include: (1) Growth – How do CSR activities stimulate growth in terms of access to new markets and customer groups, and driving innovation? (2) ROI – What is the ROI of CSR activities, which could be associated with optimizing processes, especially in environmental management? (3) Risk management – How can the sustainability-related risks be described and quantified? (4) Management quality – In what way do CSR and sustainability influence the way the company is run, and thus improve the quality of management?

REFERENCES

Interview with Susanne Stormer, Vice President Corporate Sustainability, Novo Nordisk.

Novo Nordisk, 'Novo Nordisk Supports Global Dialogue on Integrated Reporting Sustainability', www.novonordisk.com/sustainability/news/2011-09-Novo-Nordisk-supports-global-dialogue-on-integrated-reporting.asp (accessed 2 June 2013).

Novo Nordisk, *Novo Nordisk on Integrated Reporting*, April 2011, www.novonordisk.com/images/Sustainability/PDFs/NN_GRI_QnA_.pdf (accessed 2 June 2013).

Stormer, Suzanne, 'How Novo Nordisk's Corporate DNA – "To Act Responsibly" – Drives Innovation', Management Innovation Exchange, 30 April 2012, www.managementexchange.com/story/how-novo-nordisk's-corporate-dna-drives-innovation (accessed 10 June 2013).

17 *The Media Perspective – Best Practice Case*

Best Practice Case 15: SAP Community Network

IDEA AND INSPIRATION

This case about global business software leader SAP shows how social media can be used to support and even drive sustainability-related communication and facilitate stakeholder engagement.

Idea behind the SAP Community Network

'We launched the SAP Community Network (SCN) in 2003, back then called the SAP Developer Network, at the same time we launched SAP NetWeaver,'[1] explains Mark Yolton, Senior Vice President of SAP Digital, Social, and Communities:

> To run a technical integration platform you need to provide developers and IT people with a tool to share best practices and solutions with each other. Over time we saw that we needed to broaden the SAP Developer Network to include different kinds of professionals who engage with SAP, which is why we renamed it the SAP Community Network in 2007.

The objective of SCN is to 'change the world by triggering the effect of people inspiring others'. To date, it serves over two million individual members and thousands of enterprises from more than 200 countries and regions. They work across a variety of professional roles, industries, topic areas and throughout the entire lifecycle of their relationship with SAP. These communities increase the flow of information between SAP and its stakeholders, providing openness and transparency through active engagement. 'The SAP social ecosystem consists of five components,' says Mark Yolton:

> **Social networking**, which includes our public online community [the SAP Community Network], **the SAP Store** [formerly EcoHub], our online community-powered solutions marketplace connecting buyers and sellers as a kind of app store for SAP and **partner solutions**, our physical

---

1   'The SAP NetWeaver technology platform enables the composition, provisioning and management of SAP and non-SAP applications across a heterogeneous software environment. The latest release of SAP's technology platform is used by SAP customers to complement their business applications with technology components that enable faster adaptation to their business processes, better integration into other SAP and non-SAP applications, and increased operational efficiency of their SAP systems'; 'SAP NetWeaver Technology Platform – Overview', SAP Community Network, http://scn.sap.com/community/netweaver (accessed 2 June 2013).

events (for example, conferences and seminars for community members, specifically SAP TechEd), **public social media***, which includes SAP's presence on Twitter, Facebook, LinkedIn, Weibo, YouTube, and many others, and* **SAP's primary web destination, SAP.com***, which encompasses 72 country websites in 40 languages.*

The core idea is to connect partners, developers, employees and customers in an 'ecosystem' that facilitates discussion and the exchange of information between stakeholders (see Figure 17.1). According to Mark Yolton, 'Interconnectedness is very important to SAP, as our partners will often provide solutions that are important to our customers and therefore the ecosystem that the SCN provides is vital to SAP's business strategy.'

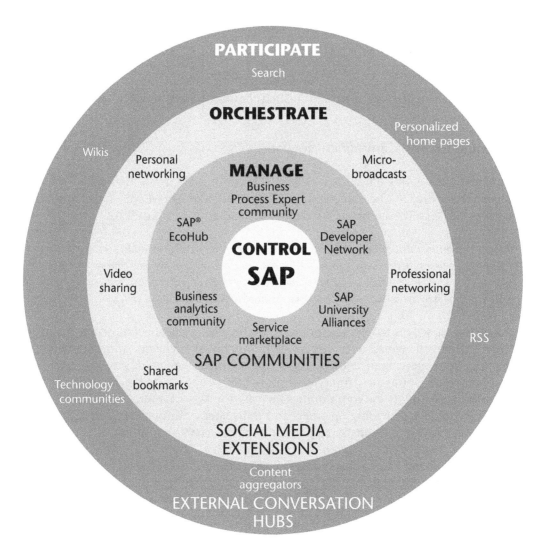

Figure 17.1 Increasing circles of influence – how the SAP Community Network functions

Source: Reproduced courtesy of SAP AG.

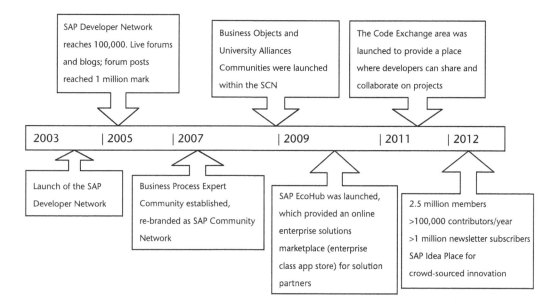

Timeline of the SAP Community Network

PROPOSITION AND EXECUTION

Concept of the SAP Community Network

The SCN involves the implementation of the best practices of social media and Web 2.0. It engages experts with real-world experience across a variety of industries and job functions, to share knowledge and collaborate on a global level. There are four main elements of the SCN:

1. **Social intelligence** – enabling customer success through sharing knowledge, solutions and best practice;
2. **Social innovation** – using collective wisdom to drive higher-quality solutions and innovation;
3. **Social commerce** – leveraging the reach of online channels and the tools of the platform to drive leads and revenues through targeted campaigns, and customer recommendations to influence prospect purchase consideration;
4. **Social insight** – extracting intelligence from customer discussions to derive insights in or about different topic areas, to give SAP and its ecosystem partners a competitive edge.

Within the SCN, there is an active CSR and sustainability area used by employees, customers and partners. They share the best CSR and sustainability practices and ideas, as well as helping to create the solutions to the problems arising from CSR. 'What we are encouraging are discussions of topics, solutions and obstacles in the CSR and sustainability arena relating to SAP software and business processes,' says Mark Yolton. The role the SCN plays is to encourage CSR customers to be active participants in the community, sharing their difficulties, approaches and solutions.

Marilyn Pratt, Social Media Advocate and SAP Community Evangelist, adds:

As community evangelists, we do not want to make sustainability into a religion. However, even in the geek community we found that some of us had a community-driven interest in social activities. The 'Change the World' initiative on the network was started by a number of bloggers, among them Tom Raftery, a top blogger on smart grids and sustainability. This then coincided with a corporate initiative by SAP and products being developed by SAP around sustainability, reporting, dashboards, performance analysis tools. As a result, we created the sustainability area within the SCN, and we have a large group of people on it.

Are there any campaign-specific communication principles? Table 17.1 shows the campaign-specific communication principles of the SAP Community Network case.

Table 17.1   Campaign-specific communication principles – SAP Community Network

Principles	Example
1. Efficiency	The SCN is a time- and cost-saving tool to share best practice and facilitate process improvements and insights. It also increases competitiveness and access to experts that would otherwise be unavailable to customer and partner developers. They can focus and build on best practice instead of starting from scratch.
2. Interconnectedness	Through the SCN, people are connected. They become more educated by engaging, asking questions and contributing to discussions about solutions and best practice on the platform. The pool of members also helps add value to their companies from the collaboration in the network through the collective wisdom of diverse perspectives.
3. Speed	The community network accelerates execution through access to technologies, learning models and a pool of expertise so that customers can be more successful and faster – gaining them competitive advantage on the path to being 'best-run' companies

Target audiences

Primary audiences mainly include developers and IT professionals. Business process and business intelligence professionals, customers and partners are also targeted.

Secondary audiences include analysts, thought-leaders, bloggers, people who are watching SAP or markets and university students. From SAP's point of view, it is important to grow the market of SAP-skilled individuals. The network can help to attract young talent.

Key benefits of the SAP Community Network for target audiences

The following key benefits were identified:

- Participating in the community helps professionals discover optimum configurations for specific industries and best practices for change management. They can get quick, high-quality answers from other customers, partners and SAP experts.
- Community members can connect with thought-leaders and thousands of others to learn about new trends, market shifts, shared difficulties and best practice in different industries. Insights can help them achieve greater business success, and to build their skills to meet market needs.
- Reputations can be built by sharing knowledge, growing skillsets and developing expertise in a particular area.

BUSINESS CASE AND RESULTS

Societal impacts of the SAP Community Network

SCN has significantly changed the world of SAP by facilitating the ability of people to inspire others. 'There is a trigger effect of people inspiring other people on SCN,' observes Mark Yolton. It provides best practice examples of CSR and sustainability initiatives for customers to take notice of, learn about and discuss. Firstly, the network acts as a monitoring system, and encourages companies to keep track of their sustainability behaviour. Companies are seeing increased demand for enhanced sustainability performance from different stakeholders. Through sharing the best practice of sustainability management and reporting in the network, there are more companies responding to the need for operational transparency. For example, SAP is working with all of the top 10 companies on the Dow Jones Sustainability World Index, which has raised the standard for other companies to learn from and measure themselves against their peers. Mark Yolton adds: 'Another physical manifestation coming from the SCN is the Sustainability Advisory Council, where SAP meets with its customers to share leading practice and engage in dialogue about emerging needs and trends.'

Secondly, there was a huge increase in the numbers of customers telling their own stories about how SAP is helping them to achieve their sustainability goals. As Mark Yolton puts it: 'One should not forget peer pressure in this context – as companies see what their peers or other SAP customers are doing, they seek to emulate those that are best.'

Commercial impacts of the SAP Community Network

While SAP does not publicly share figures that directly show the commercial impact of the SAP Community Network, the enormous reach of the SCN and its ability to bring people together is a tremendous asset to SAP as a company. It is a marketing, sales, innovation and sustainable development enabler. Some numbers illustrate the clout the SAP Community Network has gained over the past nine years (see Figure 17.2).

SAP Community Network: >2 million total members
• Growing at ~20,000 new members per month
• >200 countries and territories worldwide (including the United States, Germany, United Kingdom, and Japan)
• Includes SAP Developer Network (SDN) community, SAP Business Process Expert (BPX) community, and the business analytics community
• Over 100 SAP mentors, more than 700 storefronts on SAP EcoHub, and thousands of career center job openings

~1.5 million unique individual visitors each month
• >2 million visits per month (100,000–120,000 total visits per day)
• Average page views per day: 500,000
• >230 million page views last year
• ~20 million page views per month
• ~4–5 million pages viewed per week

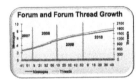

~3,000 posts per day in 350+ discussion forums
• >1.6 million topic threads
• ~7 million total messages
• Median reply time: 23 minutes
• Less than 100 of the top community contributors are designated SAP mentors
  – <100 worldwide among >2 million members
• ~5,000 bloggers
  – >60% are not SAP employees but are customers, partners, and other thought leaders
  – >250 blogs published per month (~9–12 per day)

Figure 17.2 SAP Community Network by the numbers

Source: Reproduced courtesy of SAP AG.

As of 2012, the SCN had more than 2 million members from more than 200 countries and territories, with an estimated average of 20,000 new members joining every month. The network has a monthly average of 1.5 million unique individual visitors, with over 4–5 million page views per week and 20 million page views per month. There were 3,000 posts per day in approximately 350 forums, while 1.6 million topic threads were created. Within the community network, more than 750 SAP solutions, and thousands of demos and trials were completed. With the business solutions provided by the collective input of 50,000 SAP employees and more than 100,000 customers and partners, it can be easily argued that SCN helped SAP to save and reinvest millions of dollars in efficiencies, served as a foundation for customer success and loyalty, and influenced a considerable portion of SAP's $15 billion annual revenue in 2011.

KEY SUCCESS FACTORS

Table 17.2 shows the key success factors of the SAP Community Network case.

Table 17.2 Key success factors – SAP Community Network

Key success factors	Description
1. Delivering value online and offline	One key success factor is the combination of online and offline modules. SCN events such as SAP TechEd play an important role. Online works well – if you have met in person, it often works much better, as weak ties become stronger connections.
2. Active community management	SAP employs a whole team responsible for managing and promoting the SCN. There is a substantial team of Community Evangelists, like Marilyn Pratt, and Content Strategists whose job it is to win new members and stimulate the activity and exchange on the platform.
3. High technical quality	Technical quality is not noticed if it is present. As soon as users experience hitches, capacity problems or connection errors, they usually go off the experience. Needless to say, technical quality is an important consideration for a software company, so SAP makes sure it is and remains state-of-the-art.

REFERENCES

Joint interview with Mark Yolton, Senior Vice President of SAP Digital, Social, and Communities, Marilyn Pratt, Social Media Advocate and SAP Community Evangelist, and Gail Moody-Byrd, Senior Director SAP Marketing, SAP Community Network.

SAP, *Media Kit 2012: Ecosystem Engagements for Purchase Decisions – Community-accelerated Programs*, www.erpkonnect.com/uploads/SAP_Community_Network_MediaKit.pdf (accessed 2 June 2013).

SAP, 'SAP Community Network History', Version 4, http://scn.sap.com/docs/DOC-18861 (accessed 2 June 2013).

SAP, 'SAP Integrated Report 2012: Financial and Non-financial Performance', www.sapintegrated report.com/2012/en/ (accessed 2 June 2013).

Silicon Valley Innovation Institute, 'The SAP Community Network – Driving the Social Business Future', http://svii.net/the-sap-community-network-driving-the-social-business-future-0202011/ (accessed 2 June 2013).

18 *The Academic and Expert Perspective – Best Practice Cases*

Best Practice Case 16: Research by Professor C.B. Bhattacharya on the Effectiveness of CSR Communication

RESEARCH SUMMARY

Professor C.B. Bhattacharya is an eminent academic expert on the effectiveness of CSR communication. Over the past fifteen years he has conducted quantitative research and published a number of papers on the subject. His recent paper (with Shuili Du and Sankar Sen), entitled 'Maximising Business Returns to Corporate Social Responsibility (CSR): The Role of CSR Communication',[1] is the focus of this slightly different 'case study'.[2]

Another seminal paper by Bhattacharya and Sen which contains some key research findings about the consumer response to CSR is 'Doing Better at Doing Good – When, Why and How Consumers respond to Corporate Social Initiatives'.[3]

'Maximising Business Returns to Corporate Social Responsibility: The Role of CSR Communication' presents a conceptual framework for CSR communication in light of the obstacles for companies in communicating their CSR activities to stakeholders. The authors analyse different aspects of CSR messages to stakeholders and company-specific factors that influence the effectiveness of CSR communication.

Firstly, the paper identifies stakeholders' low awareness of and unfavourable attitudes towards companies' CSR initiatives as crucial factors impeding companies from maximizing business benefits through their activities in CSR. This implies a need for companies to communicate CSR more effectively to their stakeholders, including consumers, employees, opinion leaders and investors. Put simply: if they do not know about a company's CSR activities, it cannot influence their perception. Hence, a key test in developing an effective CSR communication strategy is to create awareness in a way that reduces stakeholder scepticism and conveys the company's positive intentions.

---

1   Shuili Du, C.B. Bhattacharya and Sankar Sen, 'Maximising Business Returns to Corporate Social Responsibility (CSR): The Role of CSR Communication', *International Journal of Management Reviews*, vol. 12, no. 1 (2010), pp. 8–19.

2   Further reading and practical examples and tools on the topics covered in this case can be found in C.B. Bhattacharya, Sankar Sen and Daniel Korschun, *Leveraging Corporate Responsibility: The Stakeholder Route to Maximizing Business and Social Value* (Cambridge: Cambridge University Press, 2011).

3   C.B. Bhattacharya and Sankar Sen, 'Doing Better at Doing Good: When, Why and How Consumers Respond to Corporate Social Initiatives', *California Management Review*, vol. 47, no. 1 (2004), pp. 9–24.

In increasing the effectiveness of companies' CSR communication, company-specific factors, corporate reputation and companies' CSR positions play an essential role. An important finding of the research shows that companies with a good overall reputation tend to have higher credibility in their CSR communications. Stakeholders are accordingly less likely to be sceptical about the CSR activities of those companies. Conversely, companies with a lower overall reputation are less credible in their CSR communication and are viewed more sceptically by their stakeholders.

Lastly, the research demonstrates that the characteristics of stakeholders heavily influence the effectiveness of CSR communication. The recipients of CSR communication range from legislators, policy makers and non-governmental organizations to local communities, employees and consumers. Audiences from different backgrounds have different expectations of business, as well as different channels through which they receive company information, and therefore they respond differently to CSR communications. For instance, the general public does not actively seek CSR information about a company, but may become aware of CSR activities through the media. In contrast, opinion leaders are more active in searching for CSR information by reading companies' CSR reports. With their knowledge and expertise, they expect more from a business's CSR performance.

CSR COMMUNICATION PRINCIPLES

The research suggests a number of preconditions and communication principles leading to effective CSR communication. We illustrate them with examples in Table 18.1.

Table 18.1 CSR communication principles

Principles	Description and business example
1. Intrinsic CSR motives	A company's intrinsic CSR motive is a precondition of successful CSR communication, which will enhance the credibility of its communications and reduce stakeholders' scepticism. Companies should emphasize their intrinsic motivation for CSR and ensure the public becomes aware of this.
	For example, Carrefour explains the rationale of its environmental initiative by stating 'safeguarding the environment is a criterion we will increasingly consider' on its website.
2. CSR fit: congruence between a social issue and the company's business	Stakeholders expect companies to respond to business-related social and/or environmental issues. The more logical the association, the higher the credibility and effectiveness of the CSR communication. A sufficient connection between CSR activities and a company's business will lead to more positive reactions to its CSR performance.
	Take DenTek Oral Care as a negative example. It includes the information that diabetes can lead to tooth decay on its CSR communication. Since not many people know about the connection between diabetes and dental problems, the communication appears to be a bad fit. The company is therefore unable to demonstrate a perceived CSR fit to the stakeholders without additional education and information.

3. Corporate reputation	Corporate reputation and public trust are prerequisites for effective CSR communication. As an example, Bhattacharya and colleagues mention that Walmart had received negative coverage in the media, leading to a perception that there was insufficient support for employee welfare. Even though it announced a $500 million investment in energy efficiency to become a 'good steward for the environment', stakeholders were sceptical about the initiative.
4. Communication channels	There are a variety of opportunities for CSR activities to be disseminated to different target audiences. A company can communicate its CSR activities through a mix of communication channels, including official documents (for example, a CSR report), TV commercials, magazines, product packaging, Facebook, Twitter and YouTube. Take Diet Coke as an illustration: the brand has been running TV commercials on its CSR initiatives to raise women's awareness about heart disease. The brand has also set up a website to get customers involved in its initiatives.
5. CSR positioning	CSR positioning refers to the extent a company positions itself as responsible in the minds of consumers. Stakeholders tend to pay more attention to the CSR message of companies that position themselves clearly and distinctly in the CSR arena. For instance, Whole Foods Market in the US positions itself as socially responsible, and champions 'caring about communities and the environment' as one of its core values. This core value influences every aspect of Whole Foods' business, from sustainable sourcing to environmentally sensitive retailing. According to Bhattacharya and colleagues, this has contributed to at least an additional 5% of its annual profits.

MAIN LESSONS LEARNED

Table 18.2 shows the main lessons learned from the CSR communication principles case.

Table 18.2 Main lessons learned – CSR communication principles

Lessons learned	Description
1. Tailor CSR communication to different audiences	Since people's expectations of businesses differ depending on the perspectives of a variety of audiences, it is imperative for companies to identify the target audience for their CSR activities and to tailor their CSR communication strategies to the needs of multiple stakeholder groups.
2. Create stakeholder awareness of and support for CSR activities	Stakeholders' awareness and knowledge of social and environmental issues influences their level of support for companies on these issues. Therefore, companies need to explain and communicate their main CSR activities to their major stakeholders, to create awareness about what they are doing. Before launching CSR initiatives, companies should research stakeholder expectations, and prioritize accordingly. However, they need to bear in mind the second criterion: issue fit to core business.

Table 18.2 Main lessons learned – CSR communication principles *continued*

3. Unbiased sources of communication	CSR reporting has gone mainstream. To enhance the credibility of companies' CSR activities, companies should loosen their control of CSR message content. The research shows that the less control by the communicator, the more credibility the content has. Therefore, companies should seek positive media coverage from independent and unbiased sources in communicating their CSR messages.[4]

SPOTLIGHT: CSR COMMUNICATION AND PURCHASE DECISION

One of the core research results of Bhattacharya and Sen's 2004 article 'Doing Better at Doing Good' is that the CSR activities and communication by companies tend to influence attitudes towards the company and the brand, but only in certain cases does it influence the purchase decision:

> There is a positive link between CSR and purchase behavior only when a variety of contingent conditions are satisfied: when the consumer supports the issue central to the company's CSR efforts, when there is a high company to issue/cause fit, when the product itself is of high quality, and when the consumer is not asked to pay a premium for social responsibility. For the most part, our respondents say that if CSR plays a role at all in purchase, it matters at the margin and they are unwilling, even if they view the CSR initiatives positively, to trade-off CSR for product quality and/or price.

This touches on a key finding that is particularly relevant in the context of mainstreaming sustainable consumption: consumers are not willing to compromise on price and quality or to substitute deficits in the core benefit delivery of a product or service with CSR or sustainability attributes. In the same article, Bhattacharya and Sen explain why:

> This reluctance to compromise on core attributes such as price and quality is one of the main reasons why CSR initiatives tend to result in positive company attitudes that do not, in turn, translate into greater purchase behavior. In fact, our experimental research shows that some consumers may even penalize companies if they perceive that CSR initiatives are typically realized at the expense of investments in product and/or service quality. Such adverse effects are particularly likely to hurt sales when these consumers do not feel that the company's CSR efforts somehow improve the product (e.g., Nike's better treatment of its overseas employees leads to a better shoe), in some cases even detracting from its ability to provide or maintain a high-quality product.

To conclude, from a CSR communication point of view, another observation in Bhattacharya and Sen's article is worth noting:

---

4   Compare the interview with Professor Peter Kruse of nextpractice in Chapter 8 on the paradigm shift due to social media from one-to-many to many-to-many communication, which by default implies a loss of control over CSR communication.

Consumers are more sensitive to 'irresponsible' than to 'responsible' corporate behavior. In other words, there is an asymmetric effect and 'doing bad' hurts more than 'doing good' helps. As one of our focus group participants put it: 'I'm more likely to avoid a company that truly annoys me, like Exxon, than I am to go out of my way to buy from a company that is doing public good.' This finding was also validated by our experimental research, in which the 'irresponsible' CSR behavior was one of omission (i.e., a company not doing anything in the CSR realm) rather than commission (i.e., a company actually doing bad things).

REFERENCES

Bhattacharya, C.B. and Sen, S., 'Doing Better at Doing Good: When, Why and How Consumers Respond to Corporate Social Initiatives', *California Management Review*, vol. 47, no. 1 (2004), pp. 9–24.

Bhattacharya, C.B., Sen, S. and Korschun, D., *Leveraging Corporate Responsibility: The Stakeholder Route to Maximizing Business and Social Value* (Cambridge: Cambridge University Press, 2011).

Du, S., Bhattacharya, C.B. and Sen S., 'Maximising Business Returns to Corporate Social Responsibility (CSR): The Role of CSR Communication', *International Journal of Management Reviews*, vol. 12, no. 1 (2010), pp. 8–19.

Best Practice Case 17: The Natural Step Framework

IDEA AND INSPIRATION

Imagine the following: The scientists of an entire nation come to consensus on the roots of our environmental problems and the most critical avenues for action. The nation's head of state then gives his endorsement to their consensus report. An educational packet based on that report is prepared and sent to every household and school, so that citizens and students can learn the basics of sustainability. Then a roster of famous artists and celebrities goes on television to promote and celebrate the birth of this remarkable national project – a project that, in the long run, promises to completely reorganize the nation's way of life to bring it into alignment with the laws of nature. While this scenario may read like a fairy tale, it is already an historical fact. The name of this project is The Natural Step, the country is Sweden – and the catalyst behind this remarkable effort is Karl-Henrik Robèrt. Karl-Henrik Robèrt, M.D., Ph.D., is one of Sweden's leading cancer researchers (as well as a former national karate champion). It was his desire to dig beneath the details of the debate on the state of the environment – and to take action based on agreed-upon facts – that started a snowball that has grown to such impressively hopeful proportions.[5]

What started in Sweden has now become a global movement. The Natural Step's methods are today used across many countries and in a vast number of different contexts.

Dr Karl-Henrik Robèrt and the idea behind the Natural Step Framework

When Dr Karl-Henrik Robèrt started to reflect on sustainability from a scientific standpoint after the publication of the Brundtland Report in 1987, and discussed this with a friend who was a theoretical physicist, he realized that there was no commonly agreed upon and scientifically underpinned definition of the concept. Dr Robèrt's perspective is unusual: the former national karate champion was a medical doctor and a cancer scientist at Stockholm's famous Karolinska Institutet, which awards the Nobel Prize for Medicine. Looking at cells through a microscope, he realized that they were the 'unifying unit of all living things'. As a cancer researcher and expert on leukaemia, he studied the effect the increase in pollutants and toxins had on cells and subsequently cancer rates. He realized the link between human health and unsustainable human behaviour. From a systems perspective, he calls the process humanity started with the Industrial Revolution 'reverse evolution':

We have lost control, and are moving backwards in evolution. The extinction of species, deforestation, the greenhouse effect, acid rain, and all the other assaults on nature are but different aspects of the same mistake – increased reliance on linear processes. As we busy ourselves with tearing down more than we rebuild, we are racing toward world-wide poverty in a monstrous, poisonous garbage dump.[6]

---

5   Introduction to Karl-Henrik Robèrt, 'Educating a Nation: The Natural Step', in *Making It Happen: Effective Strategies for Changing the World* (Langley, WA: Context Institute, 1996; first published 1991), www.context.org/iclib/ic28/robert/ Spring (accessed 2 June 2013).

6   Ibid.

In his discussions with his physicist friend and other scientists, he first defined what constituted unsustainability. Based on the laws of thermodynamics, he drafted the four system conditions for sustainability. He wrote a paper on it in 1989, and sent it to 50 scientists for a peer review. He received feedback, and sent it out again. After 21 revisions, he had what he called a consensus document:

> *I managed to raise money to distribute this report to every Swedish household and every school – 4.3 million copies. The package comes with an endorsement from the King, and it employs a very simple pedagogical method: an audio cassette talks along with the pictures and explains what is wrong – the systemic errors that make up the trunk and the branches of the pollution tree – and finishes by explaining what we must do if we want both to survive and to keep our wealth, which really amounts to the same thing.*

This was the birth of The Natural Step – an organization that is committed to the acceleration of sustainable development through equipping decision makers at all levels of society with a framework that will help them make smarter, better and more strategic decisions that will lead us all as quickly as possible towards sustainability and a more genuinely prosperous society. Tens of thousands of people throughout the world have been introduced to the Framework for Strategic Sustainable Development (FSSD) through training, seminars, conferences, workshops and consensus processes. Hundreds of municipalities around the world have used the FSSD to support their regional planning and development, including cities like Madison, Wisconsin and Portland, Oregon in the US, Vancouver, Canada and Dublin. Hundreds of businesses, including more than 40 of the largest resource-users on the planet, have used the FSSD to analyse their business plans and operations and create strategies for moving towards sustainability.

Dr Robèrt switched from treating cancer patients to dedicating himself fully to advising on The Natural Step, both to municipalities and to companies, in Sweden and all over the world, and conducting research to create the scientific foundations for the four system conditions and FSSD. He now is a professor at the Blekinge Institute of Technology (BTH), which has a focus on sustainable development across all academic fields. Dr Robèrt has received widespread recognition for his groundbreaking work with The Natural Step: in 1999 he won the Green Cross Award for International Leadership, and in 2000 the Blue Planet Prize, often referred to as the 'Nobel Prize for Ecological Sustainability'. Further accolades include the Social Responsibility Laureate Medal awarded by the Global Center for Leadership and Business Ethics (2005) and inclusion in the publication *Visionaries: The 20th Century's 100 Most Important Inspirational Leaders* in 2007.[7]

---

7   Satish Kumar and Freddie Whitefield, *Visionaries: The 20th Century's 100 Most Important Inspirational Leaders* (White River Junction, VT: Chelsea Green Publishing Company, 2007).

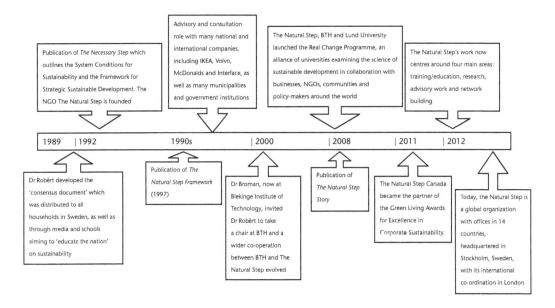

Timeline of The Natural Step

PROPOSITION AND EXECUTION

Concept of the Natural Step Framework for Strategic Sustainable Development

The FSSD aims to help corporations, communities, educational facilities and governments to develop blueprints for moving towards sustainability. Its ultimate objective is to shift an organization's thinking away from the piecemeal management of immediate problems to the creation of a long-term and strategic plan for sustainability. The FSSD is a comprehensive approach or model for planning in complex systems (see Figure 18.1).

It works with organizations to pioneer sustainable solutions, and helps them to integrate sustainability principles into companies' core strategies, decisions, operations and bottom line. It defines four sustainability system conditions (see Figure 18.2) that are reworded as the Four Principles of Sustainability Development, which organizations can use to build strategies towards sustainability (see Table 18.3).

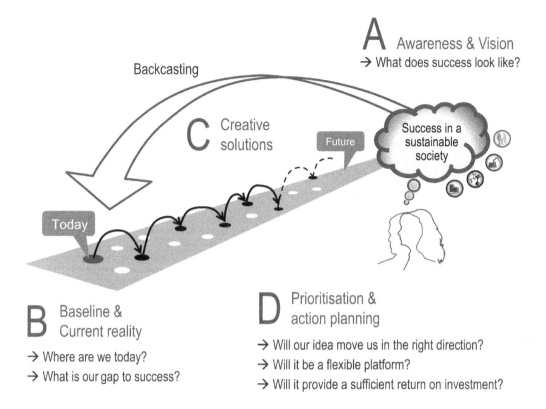

Figure 18.1 How to get from A to D – mapping The Natural Step method
Source: Reproduced courtesy of The Natural Step.

Figure 18.2 The four system conditions of The Natural Step visualized
Source: Reproduced courtesy of The Natural Step.

Table 18.3 The Four Principles of Sustainability

The four system conditions	... Reworded as the Four Principles of Sustainability
In a sustainable society, nature is not subject to systematically increasing:	To become a sustainable society we must ...
1. Concentrations of substances extracted from the earth's crust	1. Eliminate our contribution to the progressive buildup of substances extracted from the earth's crust (for example, heavy metals and fossil fuels)
2. Concentrations of substances produced by society	2. Eliminate our contribution to the progressive buildup of chemicals and compounds produced by society (for example, dioxins, PCBs and DDT)
3. Degradation by physical means	3. Eliminate our contribution to the progressive physical degradation and destruction of nature and natural processes (for example, over- harvesting forests and paving over critical wildlife habitats); and
4. And, in that society, people are not subject to conditions that systematically undermine their capacity to meet their needs	4. Eliminate our contribution to conditions that undermine people's capacity to meet their basic human needs (for example, unsafe working conditions and not enough pay to live on).

Source: www.thenaturalstep.org/en/the-system-conditions (accessed 2 June 2013).

Applying the Four Principles helps companies to understand how the current state of the world is influencing business systems, and how business systems affect the world. The FSSD provides organizations with the tools to make the most of limited resources and to envisage and move towards sustainable futures. It also focuses on education and raising awareness of sustainability by organizing workshops for organizations. The Natural Step has developed a number of tools that help companies and other organizations like municipalities to apply the FSSD, such as:

- **Backcasting from Principles** – a planning approach that starts with a vision of a desired future and asks the questions: 'What do I need to do in order to achieve that desired future? What actions will bridge the gap between reality today and the desired future state?'
- **The Funnel** – 'We use the funnel as a metaphor to help visualize the economic, social and environmental pressures that are growing in society as natural resources and ecosystem services diminish and the population's numbers and consumption grows.'
- **The three Strategic Prioritization Questions** – (1) Is this action moving you towards or away from the sustainability vision? (2) Is this action a flexible platform towards your sustainability vision? (3) Will this action offer an adequate return on investment?

What are the specific communication principles behind The Natural Step? Table 18.4 shows the specific communication principles behind The Natural Step.

Table 18.4   Specific communication principles – The Natural Step

Principles	Example
1. Scientific rigour	The FSSD is based on the scientific consensus process Dr Robèrt undertook in the late 1980s and the thorough research by many academic institutions since then to underpin the principles. Having said that, this process of scientific scrutiny remains ongoing.
2. Simplicity and applicability	The Four Principles of Sustainability/System Conditions defined by The Natural Step are simple and holistic, and are easy to communicate and understand. They clearly define the basic tenets that a sustainable business can operate within. This helps organizations to structure their business systems to achieve sustainability. Its simplicity helps experts to contribute to efforts in making smarter, better and faster decisions that lead towards sustainability.
3. Flexibility	The FSSD is flexible in its applications. It can be applied in any setting: households, products, organizations, town planning and so on. Flexibility is emphasized as an important element in developing strategy. The FSSD is flexible enough to respond to different circumstances in the future.

Target audiences

The target audiences of the FSSD include leaders of corporations, communities, educational facilities and governments. With the distribution of the first consensus document to all Swedish households, the whole population was targeted, but since then The Natural Step has expanded its activities to span large parts of the globe.

Key benefits of the Natural Step Framework for Strategic Sustainable Development for the target audiences

The following key benefits were identified:

- Having a commonly agreed definition of sustainability and how to move towards sustainability fosters much-needed clarity about the sustainability objective.
- The sustainability principles and strategies inject revolutionary and innovative thinking into new products and services, which help organizations open up new markets, increase numbers of customers and reduce risks.
- The FSSD is easy to communicate in organizations, and has the potential to more closely align them strategically towards environmental and social sustainability in an economically sound way.

BUSINESS CASE AND RESULTS

Social impacts of the Natural Step Framework for Strategic Sustainable Development

It can be argued that the national distribution of the 'consensus document', the predecessor of the FSSD, to all Swedish households and schools has had a profound effect on the awareness of sustainability in Swedish society and business. Many major Swedish companies have integrated sustainability into their core business strategies on the basis of The Natural Step system's thinking.

The FSSD significantly assists organizations in moving towards their environmental and social goals. For example, Electrolux adopted the FSSD after the loss of a multi-million-dollar deal attributed to their inability to offer a refrigeration system without chlorofluorocarbons (CFCs). The company used the FSSD principles to phase out CFCs and won back that customer. It has introduced washing machines that use less water – 12 gallons instead of 45. It has also substituted canola oil for petroleum-based oil in its chainsaws. The company's total energy consumption and hazardous waste have been greatly reduced.

Commercial impacts of the Natural Step Framework for Strategic Sustainable Development

Many companies that have applied the FSSD have experienced a significant increase in financial returns as a result of applying the Four Principles. For instance, Interface, the global market leader in carpet tiles, applied the FSSD early on in designing its sustainability approach. Its Mission Zero stipulates that Interface will be a sustainable company according to The Natural Step definition by 2020. To achieve its mission, innovative ideas including leasing carpets and powering the manufacturing factories with solar energy were developed. Design and manufacturing improvements have saved the company approximately $430 million, whereas sales have grown by $200 million, without increasing consumption of the Earth's resources.[8] Another great example is Swedish chain Max Burgers – see Best Case Study 11 in Chapter 14.

Brand impacts of the Natural Step Framework for Strategic Sustainable Development

The FSSD helps organizations to build a positive brand image through differentiating products and services. For example, the adoption and implementation of the FSSD stimulated the future development of the City of La Crosse, Wisconsin and the La Crosse County area. It helped brand the La Crosse area as a green community, thereby increasing its visibility and attracting businesses, residents and visitors to the area. Another similarly impressive example is the city of Whistler, in British Columbia in Canada. More generally, the FSSD helps organizations to clarify their sustainability vision, their sustainability gap and what they need to do in order to bridge that gap. This makes it possible for organizations to be more transparent in terms of their communication about sustainability. It is a question of building trust and credibility around your sustainability efforts – something which helps to strengthen a brand while reducing the risk of greenwashing.

---

8   See Best Practice Case 18: Interface in Chapter 19, p. 287.

LESSONS LEARNED AND KEY SUCCESS FACTORS

Lessons learned

These are the main lessons learned from the implementation of the Natural Step Framework for Strategic Sustainable Development:

1. There is the need for a framework and definition of what sustainability actually means. The Natural Step offers such a definition, which is easy to understand, easy to apply and easy to communicate while being scientifically robust and systematic. Many organizations – businesses as well as political or not-for-profit organizations – have successfully applied the FSSD.
2. Even though The Natural Step offers such a framework, it still has not been adopted as the general model. There is still a long way to go to attain consensus. How can the Swedish experiment conducted in 1989 be replicated in other countries?
3. After more than twenty years, a growing number of organizations have applied The Natural Step approach over the long term; many case studies already exist. The more these cases are rigorously prepared to underpin the business case behind The Natural Step as solidly as its scientific foundation, and the more widely they are disseminated, the more The Natural Step will be adopted by other organizations.

REFERENCES

Interview with Dr Karl-Henrik Robèrt, founder of The Natural Step.

Environmental Mainstreaming Initiative, *Profiles of Tools and Tactics for Environmental Mainstreaming, No. 6: The Natural Step*, London: International Institute for Environment and Development, 6 October 2009, www.environmental-mainstreaming.org/documents/EM%20Profile%20No%20 6%20-%20Natural%20Step%20(6%20Oct%2009).pdf (accessed 2 June 2013).

The Natural Step Canada, 'The Natural Step Canada's FREE Sustainability Toolkits', www. thenaturalstep.org/en/canada/toolkits (accessed 2 June 2013).

The Natural Step USA, 'The Natural Step US Case Study Index', www.naturalstepusa.org/case-study-index/ (accessed 2 June 2013).

19 Best Practice – Two Benchmark Cases for Communicating Corporate Sustainability

Best Practice Case 18: Marks & Spencer's Plan A

IDEA AND INSPIRATION

Idea behind Plan A and the Plan A story

Even in recession, you need to push Plan A harder.

Sir Stuart Rose

'In 2004, Stuart Rose saved the business from a hostile takeover bid,' recalls Mike Barry, Head of Sustainable Business at Marks & Spencer. 'Stuart felt passionately about the brand and the core of that brand which was trust. In order to restore some of that trust we worked hard behind the scenes on the CSR side, and in 2006 we launched 'Look behind the label'. The initiative was intended to increase and showcase business transparency and regain public trust in the brand. It was a phenomenal success, one of the most effective business-building campaigns in the history of the iconic British retailer. Mike Barry continues:

> But in the autumn of 2006, Stuart Rose came into the office and said, 'Good about CSR – need to do more!' The reason for that was twofold: (1) consumers were getting a little cynical and suspicious about greenwash, they didn't want a few nice stories, they wanted to know that everything we were doing was good; (2) the CSR space had become highly competitive in the retail sector (Co-op and Waitrose, but also Tesco), there was an opportunity to differentiate ourselves, so the CEO gave us a three months' challenge to develop a concept for moving beyond 'Look behind the label'.

The result was presented in January 2007, when Stuart Rose called a press conference and announced the launch of Plan A, 'because there is no Plan B for the one planet we've got', and promised to invest up to £200 million in a detailed 100-point action plan over the next five years geared to making Marks & Spencer into a much more sustainable business.

How did Plan A differ from CSR? Mike Barry explains that:

1. It was tackling all issues – social, environmental and welfare, not 'cherrypicking' a few, as CSR had done in the past.
2. It expressed a willingness to tackle those issues right across the value chain (suppliers, operations and customer use/disposal of products).
3. It was a change programme that sought to engage the whole business, unlike the world of CSR, which had relied on a few good people to check that 'bad things' weren't happening. While 'Look behind the label' was very much a marketing and communication initiative, Plan A was a change management and business re-engineering tool, and only parts were actually communicated. In 2009, a new communication vehicle was launched, which Marks & Spencer calls 'Doing the right thing' (see Figure 19.1), primarily targeted at customers.
4. Unlike CSR, Plan A had a clear business case, and investing in social and environmental improvements created real business benefits.

Figure 19.1 With this witty advert, Marks & Spencer communicated that it had signed the WWF's Seafood Charter

Source: Reproduced courtesy of Marks & Spencer plc.

Plan A had such an impact when it was presented because of its sheer size and ambition, and because of its very clear quantitative nature. Mike Barry says:

> It is vitally important that you back up ambition with hard targets, but you need both. Two thirds of Plan A was about tackling what we knew, and those were the hard targets. The remaining third was visionary, where we did not have exact answers yet. Those were the 'scary targets' that would stretch the business. The first two thirds were hard work, delivering today's solutions across thousands of stores, factories, farms and products, and that is very necessary. But there will be no innovation and motivation to become truly sustainable without the 'scary third'.

In the summer of 2009, Stuart Rose asked the team to review Plan A within two weeks. He had five questions (see Table 19.1).

Table 19.1 Stuart Rose's five questions

Questions	Answers the Sustainability team came back with
1. Is there more or less evidence today for growing social and environmental harm to the planet?	More – Reference: Prof. John Beddington, *The Perfect Storm* – we need 50% more energy, 50% more food and 30% more water in the next 50 years.
2. Is M&S able to make a meaningful difference, 2.5 years into Plan A?	Yes. There is evidence. For example, energy is down 10%, carrier bag usage down 20% etc. – it is working for the planet and the people.
3. Is M&S making money from protecting the planet and people?	Yes. Our plan had been to invest £40 million per year because we believed consumers would not be prepared to pay more. 2.5 years into the plan, the £40 million cost had switched to a £50 million surplus.
4. Do consumers still care for the environment and social issues during the worst recession in 50 years?	Yes, but ... concerns for the environment remain high, but shifting emphasis. 'We expect you as a business to do more, because I as a consumer can do less.'
5. Are other big businesses also involved in sustainability?	Yes. A lot of the big businesses that matter to us, like Walmart, P&G and Coca-Cola, were still very much involved and working hard in this area.

Mike Barry explains:

> When we reported back the answers, his response was: 'You have my support to accelerate Plan A even though we've not completed the first five years yet, and even though we're in a recession.' So we extended the plan from 2012 to 2015, with an additional emphasis on customers and the commitment that all the 2.9 billion items we are selling would have at least one strong sustainability story behind them.

The goal was to become the world's most sustainable retailer by 2015, and 80 points were added to the original 100-point plan.

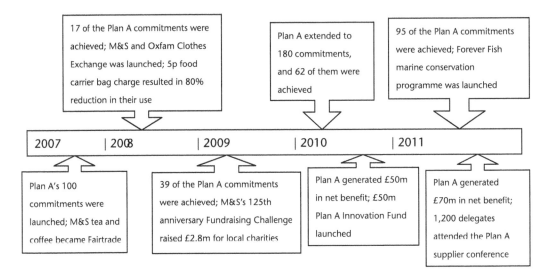

Timeline of Plan A

PROPOSITION AND EXECUTION

Concept of Plan A

Plan A is about systematically making every aspect of M&S's business, its supply chain and customers' use and disposal of its products more sustainable. It started as a five-year plan with 100 commitments in 2007, with five pillars of sustainability: climate change, waste, natural resources, fair partnership and health and well-being. These commitments affect every part of the business, from farm to factory, transport, stores and customers' homes. In 2010, M&S added 80 new commitments to the original 100, and extended a number of the existing commitments.

Are there any campaign-specific communication principles?

Table 19.2 shows the campaign-specific communication principles of the M&S Plan A case.

Table 19.2 Campaign-specific communication principles – M&S's Plan A

Principles	Example
1. Clear and measurable objectives	Plan A was so well received because 'it raised the bar for everyone' (Jonathon Porritt, Forum for the Future) and because it was clearer than any other programme before it in terms of targets across the entire business and along the whole value chain.
2. Public and transparent commitment	To step out and announce a £200 million plan and commit a big company to five years of investment and 100 action points is a bold and courageous move that requires vision and leadership. But exactly because of this boldness, even critical stakeholders like Greenpeace and Friends of the Earth applauded.

3. Reporting regularly on progress	M&S regularly reported on the progress it made on the 100 commitments, further building trust and credibility with stakeholders.
4. Stretching the envelope	Having mundane as well as 'scary' stretching goals, and balancing those two kinds of targets was key for the internal communication and the change management effect Plan A had

Target audiences

The key target audiences of Plan A include customers, the supply chain and employees, but also critical stakeholders and the financial community.

Key benefits of Plan A for the target audiences

The following key benefits were identified:

- The revised Plan A has involved more customer engagement. Within the 100 commitments in the original Plan A, 90 of them were related to supply chain and business operations behind the scenes that customers did not have a chance to be involved in. As for the new commitments, more emphasis was placed on involving M&S customers in Plan A. This helps them to make informed purchase decisions (as with the first 'Look behind the label' campaign), to make a difference to the social and environmental causes that matter to them and to develop a more sustainable lifestyle.
- Plan A has lived up to customers' expectations about contributing to society and the environment, while not requiring them to pay more for the ethically-made products (see Figure 19.2). They can purchase products with a good conscience, knowing that M&S does everything to ensure sustainable quality.
- Plan A has fostered a culture of sustainability within the company. It inspires employees and encourages ideas for innovation. Moreover, the success of Plan A has contributed to a sense of pride among employees.
- As for the suppliers who implement Plan A, the programme helps them to improve product quality and contain price inflation, despite increases in raw material, energy and labour costs.

BUSINESS CASE AND RESULTS

Environmental and social impacts of Plan A

Plan A has continued to make a positive difference to the environment and to society (see Figure 19.3) – some examples from the *How We Do Business Report 2012* illustrate that:

- M&S is the first major carbon-neutral retailer.
- 100% of its waste is recycled, none goes to landfill, and food waste was reduced by 40% over the same period.

**Figure 19.2 Marks & Spencer is actively creating win–wins for customers who
want to lead more sustainable lifestyles**

Source: Reproduced courtesy of Marks & Spencer plc.

- 31% of all products now have a Plan A attribute, driving more sustainable consumption. This adds up to almost a billion individual items sold every year at a retail value of £3 billion.
- 147 million clothes hangers have been reused or recycled, with 50p in every £1 saved to fund UNICEF activities to alleviate poverty for children and their families in Bangladesh.
- Sales of Fairtrade food by increased by 88% during 2006–2007, and M&S launched a range of Fairtrade tea and coffee, packed at source by smallholders in Kenya.

Commercial impacts of Plan A

In 2010, Plan A generated £50 million in net benefits. In 2011, £70 million in net benefits were delivered as a result of Plan A – an increase of £20 million. As of March 2012, M&S had gained £105 million net benefits per annum as a result of Plan A, with a 50% increase compared to the year before. It has saved 28% of energy across its operations with an estimated saving of £21.8m. This has delivered further benefits including the reduction of cost exposure to the Government's Carbon Reduction Commitment Energy Efficiency Scheme. As for the group revenue, the company's turnover was £9.9 billion – a 2% increase.

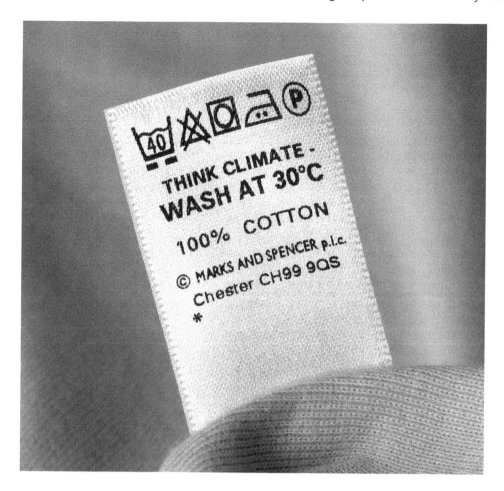

Figure 19.3 Decreasing climate change impact by urging consumers to wash clothes at 30°C

Source: Reproduced courtesy of Marks & Spencer plc.

Brand impacts of Plan A

Coming back to the original concern expressed by the then-CEO Stuart Rose, Plan A has helped the M&S brand to regain trust, and it is now considered a modern and trustworthy brand. It has received a variety of sustainable development awards, including the Business in the Community (BitC) Award for Excellence in 2012, the Queen's Award for Enterprise in Sustainable Development in 2011, and an award for Sustained Excellence in the RSPCA Good Business Awards 2011.

Lessons learned and key success factors

Mike Barry lists five main lessons learned, which can be termed the key success factors of the M&S Plan A case (see Table 19.3).

Table 19.3 Key success factors – M&S's Plan A

Key success factor	Description
1. Do the heavy lifting	The consumer wants us as a business to do the 'heavy lifting' when it comes to sustainability – it is probably 90% us and 10% them.
2. Bold vision plus specific targets	There is a mix of bold vision coupled with some very clear and specific targets ('not just pie in the sky').
3. Excellence in Project Management	It is about project management – large, complex numbers, 180 environmental and social project workstreams.
4. Internal branding and marketing	The power of the Plan A brand is internal. It makes all the disparate activity come together as a change management tool, and every M&S director has a Plan A target as part of their bonus scheme.
5. Stakeholder engagement and partnerships	Stakeholder engagement is important– listening and learning, gaining new perspectives and new ideas, making them feel understood, and partnering with them.

REFERENCES

Interview with Mike Barry, Head of Sustainable Business, Marks & Spencer.

Marks & Spencer, 'About Plan A', http://plana.marksandspencer.com/about/.

Marks & Spencer, *Your M&S: How We Do Business Report 2012*, http://plana.marksandspencer.com/media/pdf/ms_hdwb_2012.pdf (accessed 2 June 2013).

Best Practice Case 19: Interface Sustainability Communication 'Let's be Clear'

IDEA AND INSPIRATION

How sustainability communication began at Interface

In 1994, Ray Anderson initiated the sustainability programme at Interface, the world leader in carpet tiles which he founded in 1973. Why and how he realized the importance of sustainability is a captivating story, which he tells in his first book, *Mid-course Correction*.[1] The short version can be found on the Interface website:

> In 1994 Interface Chairman Ray Anderson recognised that the way industry worked was fundamentally unsustainable. Ray could see how much of the Earth's valuable natural resources industry used up and threw away, with too little regard for the future. He saw that waste from industrial processes polluted the environment and emissions from energy use were causing global warming. His conclusion: this culture cannot continue without serious environmental and social repercussions. Ray's epiphany revolutionised Interface's business strategy from that day forward, and has characterized the company's development ever since.[2]

Interface started working with some of the thought-leaders of the emerging sustainability movement, among them Amory and Hunter Lovins, Paul Hawken, Jonathon Porritt and The Natural Step founder Karl-Henrik Robèrt. Later, Janine Benyus, the originator of the concept of biomimicry and author of the seminal book *Biomimicry*,[3] joined this exclusive circle of experts which Anderson turned to in his desire to learn how his company could move from unsustainability to sustainability.

Interface's sustainability communication began when those thought-leaders started talking about what Interface was starting to do as a result of their dialogue. As always, it tends to create a lot more credibility when other people talk about you then when you do all the talking yourself. But, as Ramon Arratia, Interface Europe's Sustainability Director, says: 'This communication did not come as a stroke of luck – we simply worked with the right people.' And, it can be added, Interface acted on those experts' advice and diligently put it into practice, starting to climb 'the sustainability mountain', as Ray Anderson put it.

The idea behind 'Let's be Clear' – how and why lifecycle assessments and environmental product declarations moved centre-stage

In 1999, Interface launched Entropy, the first product developed applying the principles of biomimicry. With the launch of this product, the company started communicating what it was doing in terms of sustainability to its customers, and not just to critical stakeholders. It was Interface's first product-related sustainability communication initiative. The company followed this up with the 2003 launch of CoolCarpet, the world's

---

1   Ray C. Anderson, *Mid-course Correction: Toward a Sustainable Enterprise – the Interface Model* (Mishawaka, IN: Peregrinzilla Press, 1999).

2   'Sustainability: Mission Zero', www.interfaceflor.co.uk/web/sustainability/mission_zero (accessed 2 June 2013).

3   Janine M. Benyus, *Biomimicry: Innovation Inspired by Nature* (New York: Perennial, 2002).

first carbon-neutral carpet, which was developed applying product lifecycle assessment (LCA) for the first time.

On 12 June 2006 came the next big step for the carpet tile manufacturer's sustainability communication, with the launch of Mission Zero: 'Mission Zero is our promise to eliminate any negative impact our company may have on the environment by the year 2020.'[4]

In 2007, Interface started implementing its first recycling processes, and around that time, most competitors in the carpet market started talking about sustainability. They had visions and stories not dissimilar to Interface's Mission Zero. As Ramon Arratia puts it: 'We realized that we needed to do something more radical. That is when we started to talk about the whole lifecycle and to become more product-oriented rather than just communicating the corporate approach to sustainability. After all, people buy products, they don't buy companies.'

The starting point of the new campaign was 'Let's be Clear' in 2009. Interface had introduced environmental product declarations (EPDs), for all its products, thus creating full transparency. 'We then started a campaign to educate customers, that they really needed to look at the whole lifecycle,' remembers Ramon Arratia. Interface used the Internet, brochures, videos, and of course the EPDs themselves to communicate the new approach. They conducted training for architects and other clients in how to choose sustainable products.

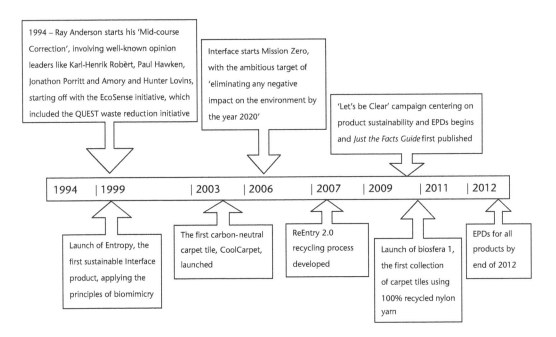

Timeline of interface sustainability communication

4   '"Mission Zero" Gives a New Voice to the Company's Sustainability Heritage', www.interfaceflor.com/UserControls/ UserModules/AboutInterface/NewsEvents/SubModules/Press/June1220061.doc (accessed 2 June 2013).

PROPOSITION AND EXECUTION

Interface sustainability communication principles

Interface's internal sustainability communication principles best sum up the thinking behind the carpet maker's differentiated approach. Even having a set of such specific and clear principles seems rather unique. Ramon Arratia explains:

> We've worked hard to build up a strong reputation for sustainability, and want to maintain that. We won't do that by shouting louder, but by continuing to communicate in a responsible way. To help us do this, we've drawn up 12 principles that we should keep in mind whenever we're working on a piece of communication.

Tell the Complete Truth

1. **Make it complete** – *Partial truths are not enough for us. We conduct an LCA assessment and consider the whole lifecycle of a product when we're making a claim. It's not right to report something that's technically correct but misleading when considered as part of the bigger picture.*
2. **Use evidence** – *We base our communications on master documents that ensure our claims are correct. These documents have been reviewed by our technical people. If it's not possible to find proof for a particular communication, ask your sustainability contact.*
3. **Consider unwritten messages** – *It's important to consider what's not being said. Sometimes it's what's left out that makes a company sound greener than it is. Always double-check to make sure we're not guilty of this.*
4. **Respect scientific evidence** – *There is so much research that it is almost always possible to find support for a specific marketing angle. However, we should consider all the scientific evidence and be guided by the overall consensus. We should refuse to twist scientific results for our own benefit.*

Sustainability is Bigger than That

5. **Be honest, sustainability is actually bigger than that** – *Conventional marketing is about strong, simple claims like 'cheapest, fastest, biggest'. Sustainability is too complex to be summarized like this, so we don't even try to. Instead, we open new angles and explore new territories. Our conversations with our customers, employees and investors are sophisticated, and where we have the expertise to be so, educational.*
6. **Face the challenges** – *Real conversations do not avoid difficult or negative points. We think it's better to be open about the challenges we face in achieving Mission Zero, particularly as we can benefit from suggestions people make.*
7. **Make it relevant** – *You can see how it happens. Many companies plan their communications by thinking 'What are our best stories?' rather than considering what's relevant to their audiences. We take care to respond to what our customers need to know.*
8. **Have one message** – *Sustainability and commercial success go hand in hand. We don't have separate sustainability and commercial messages; we embed sustainability in all our conversations, whether they're with customers, employees or investors.*

9. **Keep the right company** – *Sponsoring or partnering a brand that doesn't share our values is a shortcut to undermining our reputation. We choose our friends carefully and make sure they will help us achieve Mission Zero. We're careful using their names and logos, and make sure the partnership enables long-term change, not short-lived brand associations.*

Resist Gimmicks

10. **Reject quick-fix promotion** – *From products that grow flowers to furniture made of recycled cans, there's no shortage of green gimmicks. Our sustainability stories are based on core products, not quick fixes or attention-seeking promotions.*
11. **Use real images** – *The imagery we use for sustainability stories shouldn't be clichéd shots of polar bears and the globe. We prefer to focus on real stories. Our factories with minimum waste, our internal heroes and our sustainable products and services can speak louder than unreal imagery.*
12. **Be careful with carbon** – *We believe a company should reduce its emissions before offsetting. We also think product claims should take the whole lifecycle into account. It's not sensible to rush to claim neutrality at all costs. We do not make corporate neutrality claims.*

Executional parameters

The key, according to Ramon Arratia, is to have EPDs based on a full LCA. All Interface sustainability communication centres around that. The EPD is at the core of the company's product-oriented sustainability communication approach: 'Once you have the EPD, you need to work with R&D and your suppliers to improve products continuously from a sustainability point of view,' he explains.

Design is the second key executional parameter: 'Whatever you do in sustainability has to look beautiful. For us, design is key!' EPDs by themselves tend to be boring, technical documents. The story they tell has to be brought to life creatively and aesthetically (see Figure 19.4).

Point of difference of the Interface approach

'We are one of the few companies that makes a full commitment to transparency,' claims Arratia. 'This is a big decision, because many companies are scared to be transparent.' The second factor that makes Interface different is that 'We believe we can make a superficially boring and technical subject very sexy.' The first edition of the *Let's Be Clear* brochure is a great example of that,[5] as is 'Cut the Fluff', Interface's sustainability blog[6] and the *Just the Facts Guide* (see Figure 19.5).[7]

---

5   Interface, *Let's Be Clear*, www.interfaceflor.co.uk/webapp/wcs/stores/media/Lets%20Be%20Clear%20UK.pdf (accessed 2 June 2013).

6   Interface, Cut the Fluff blog, www.interfaceflorcutthefluff.com/ (accessed 2 June 2013).

7   Interface, *Just the Facts Guide*, 2012, www.interfaceflor.co.uk/webapp/wcs/stores/media/Just_the_facts_FINAL_24April2012mb.pdf (accessed 2 June 2013).

Figure 19.4 Interface uses sustainability as a catalyst for product innovation – its carpet tile made from 100 per cent recycled nylon is one of many examples

Source: Reproduced courtesy of Interface Inc.

Figure 19.5 The Interface *Just the Facts Guide*, which explains Interface's environmental product declaration (EPD) approach

Source: Reproduced courtesy of Interface Inc.

'We like to make jokes about the technical aspects of EPDs and LCAs,' Ramon Arratia adds, 'to make them more interesting.' He certainly takes them seriously: 'Cut the fluff and send me your EPD!'

Response to the Interface sustainability communications approach

In Arratia's view, critical stakeholders applaud the approach because of the unusual level of transparency. They believe in LCAs and have an understanding of the process. Internally, most like the course Interface is taking. There are times when the sales managers or directors in particular might prefer a more direct and aggressive approach, as customers sometimes find EPDs and LCAs a little too technical. They would occasionally favour something that is easier, but as Arratia puts it: 'Sustainability is not easy. Customers just want to tick a box rather than looking into an analysis. Once you explain it, though, they tend to get it.'

BUSINESS CASE AND RESULTS

What are the business results of 'Let's be Clear'?

It is hard to relate business success to the approach. However, as Arratia says, 'People now understand better the impact of carpet tiles and how to make decisions.' Also, the approach is unique, at least in the market for floor coverings, and that helps the Interface brand to stand out (se Figure 19.6). Even without hard, quantitative market research statistics, it seems fair to assume that this differentiation has supported Interface in consolidating its market position since the slump following the financial crisis of 2009 (it experienced 20.1 per cent growth in net sales during 2009–11), gaining a greater market share in a challenging environment.[8] Furthermore, Interface is recognized as a global sustainability leader, according to The Sustainability Survey 2011 by GlobeScan and SustainAbility (in second place, behind Unilever).[9]

What social and environmental impacts are there?

Interface is on course to achieve its Mission Zero objective of becoming the first company to be fully sustainable with zero negative impact. Because it has conducted LCAs for all its products, the entire company is aware of the key drivers of its environmental impact (primarily relating to the yarn). This helps to focus resources and to align the organization in finding ways to further reduce Interface's footprint. The 'Go beyond' initiative states that the clear objective for all carpet tile products is a closed-loop product system.

---

8   *Interface Annual Report 2011*, http://phx.corporate-ir.net/External.File?item=UGFyZW50SUQ9MTQyODA4fENoaW9aW xkSUQ9LTF8VHlwZT0z&t=1 (accessed 2 June 2013).

9   *Interface Investor Presentation 2012*, http://phx.corporate-ir.net/External.File?item=UGFyZW50SUQ9MTI5MzcwfEN oaWxkSUQ9LTF8VHlwZT0z&t=1 (accessed 2 June 2013).

Figure 19.6 Interface's TacTiles allow glue-free carpet tile installation – a groundbreaking innovation, and not just from a sustainability perspective

Source: Reproduced courtesy of Interface Inc.

Some environmental achievements include:

- an 82% reduction in waste sent to landfill since 1996 per unit of production;
- water intake in manufacturing is down 82% since 1996 per unit of production;
- total energy use is down 43% since 1996 per unit of production;
- 40% of total raw materials are recycled or bio-based materials;
- cumulative avoided waste costs have totalled $438 million since 1995.

'We are starting to look at the social impact,' admits Ramon Arratia. 'We are good at safety, but the rest of the social impact has not been in focus. That is changing now, fair trade, labour conditions and so on are being looked into.' Perhaps Arratia is a little too modest in this respect, as in 2008 Interface had already launched FairWorks, a product category based on both sustainable materials and social innovation, focusing on 'local materials and handicraft skills from across the globe to create products that address the social aspect of sustainability'.[10]

---

10   Interface, press release, 'Interface Launches FairWorks', 2 May 2008, www.interfaceflor.co.uk/web/about_us/media_centre_landing_page/press_releases/press-Interface-Launches-FairWorks (accessed 2 June 2013).

Impact on the Interface organization and on the Interface brand

Due to the EPD approach, the organization knows its environmental impacts, and is thus fully aligned behind 'that which matters, the impact of the carpet across the whole lifecycle – everybody, the production, R&D and salespeople all know what to do. Therefore, the impact has been huge,' stresses Arratia. And trust in the brand has grown as a result of the radical product transparency and the fact-based approach Interface is taking.

LESSONS LEARNED AND KEY SUCCESS FACTORS

Lessons learned

These are the main lessons learned over the last two to three years of Interface's 'Let's be Clear' initiative:

1. **Lifecycle assessments are key** – With LCAs of its products, a company learns which levers to focus on. They can therefore serve as a vital input into the strategy of any company.
2. **Environmental product declarations help to align communication** – 'We can now tell the same story to both suppliers and to customers,' explains Arratia. 'We can use the same metrics. Using different metrics for different target groups seems wrong to us.'
3. **Sustainability needs to be embedded in the product** – If that happens, sustainability automatically gets embedded into the organization, and thus the culture.
4. **You need to making sustainability attractive** – If the brand is about design, the sustainability campaign needs to be well-designed, helping to make 'boring, technical sustainability facts 'sexy'.

Key success factors

Ramon Arratia names four key success factors of effective sustainability communications:

1. Stick to the product.
2. Stick to the facts.
3. Do the job first before you communicate.
4. Realize your competitive advantage by communicating what you have done.

REFERENCES

Interface, Cut the Fluff blog, www.interfaceflorcutthefluff.com/ (accessed 2 June 2013).

Interface, *Interface Annual Report 2011*, http://phx.corporate-ir.net/External.File?item=UGFyZW50S UQ9MTQyODA4fENoaWxkSUQ9LTF8VHlwZT0z&t=1 (accessed 2 June 2013).

Interface, *Interface Investor Presentation 2012*, http://phx.corporate-ir.net/External.File?item=UGFyZ W50SUQ9MTI5MzcwfENoaWxkSUQ9LTF8VHlwZT0z&t=1 (accessed 2 June 2013).

Interface, *Just the Facts Guide*, 2012, www.interfaceflor.co.uk/webapp/wcs/stores/media/Just_the_facts_FINAL_24April2012mb.pdf (accessed 2 June 2013).

Interface, *Let's be Clear*, www.interfaceflor.co.uk/webapp/wcs/stores/media/Lets%20Be%20Clear%20UK.pdf (accessed 2 June 2013).

Interface, press release, 'Interface Launches FairWorks', 2 May 2008, www.interfaceflor.co.uk/web/about_us/media_centre_landing_page/press_releases/press-Interface-Launches-FairWorks (accessed 2 June 2013).

Interface, 'Sustainability', www.interfaceflor.co.uk/sustainability (accessed 2 June 2013).

Interview with Ramon Arratia, Sustainability Director, Interface Europe.

Summary and Outlook

CSR and sustainability communication are fascinating and dynamic subjects. They are evolving and developing, and all involved are continuously learning, not least as sustainability as a subject matter is gaining relevance due to the increasing impact of climate change and the glaring consequences of resource constraints. Talking to nearly 100 stakeholders from eight different stakeholder perspectives has shown the diversity in expectations and paradigms that all communicators in this field need to take into account. The different stakeholder groups see themselves in quite distinctly varying roles, which clearly has an effect on how companies ought to relate to and communicate with them if they want to build their brands, reputations and profits communicating what they are doing in sustainability (see Figure III.1).

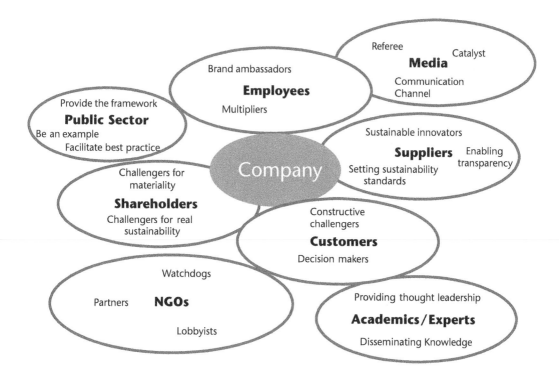

Figure III.1 Roles in the context of CSR communications

While the roles differ, they are also linked. For instance, creating transparency in the supply chain by using traceability mechanics provides suppliers with feedback on their performance. At the same time, it builds consumers' knowledge of how a product is made and what constitutes quality, and it links the two stakeholder groups together. NGOs and shareholders are sometimes portrayed as if they were natural antagonists, but when it comes to CSR communications, their roles are related. They challenge the substance of what companies do in terms of sustainability, and uncover greenwashing and cover-ups. Similarly, the media define their role as referees, but also as catalysts and (obviously) as communication channels. In many instances, employees are also communication channels - powerful multipliers and ambassadors for the CSR endeavours of corporations. Academics want to learn from companies as well as advising them and developing new ideas. They like to apply their thought-leadership to provide input to the public sector, which is responsible for defining the rules and establishing the playing field.

Figure III.2 Key success factors of CSR communication

Analysing the expectations, challenges and key success factors (Figure III.2 , Key success factors of CSR communication), 10 fundamental points stand out.

The 10 Commandments of Effective and Credible CSR Communication

1. Balance substance and perception – if in doubt, substance first.
2. Integrate sustainability into your core business and determine your direction before starting to communicate.
3. Set measurable targets, and control them rigorously.
4. Communicate honestly and with transparency – be open about threats and shortcomings.
5. Communicate from the inside out by making your employees into ambassadors for what you do in the field of sustainability.
6. Be yourself, to come across as authentic – communicate only those things you do in terms of sustainability that have a good fit with your company or your brand.
7. Shift the focus from corporate to product-related communication, for example based on lifecycle assessments or traceability, to ensure business and customer relevance.
8. Avoid one-way communication, and seek to engage actively with key stakeholders – this includes embracing social media.
9. Talk confidently about your achievements, and do not be destructively silent.
10. Invest as much creativity, craftmanship and commitment into CSR and sustainability communication as into any other advertising or corporate communication.

---

1. Balance substance and perception – if in doubt, substance first

A key to unlocking the potential of CSR and sustainability communication is to ensure that substance and perception are in balance. If the scales tip more towards perception – if there is more perception than substance – then the company runs a high risk of being found out. If, however, substance is greater than perception – the company does more than it communicates – then there is an opportunity to communicate more and create a positive impact on the company's reputation. Ideally, the two sides of the scale will be in balance.

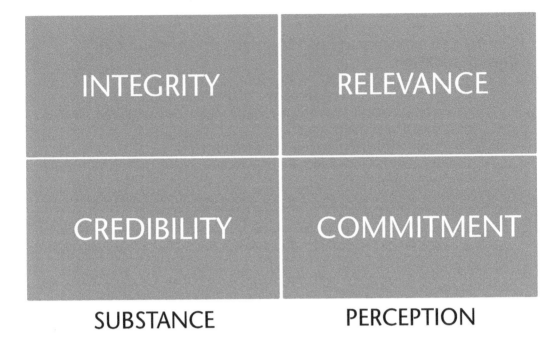

INTEGRITY	RELEVANCE
CREDIBILITY	COMMITMENT

SUBSTANCE   PERCEPTION

Figure III.3 Balancing substance and perception – the four quadrants

INTEGRITY		RELEVANCE	
IDENTITY	DIRECTION	TARGET	MESSAGE
WHO we are	WHERE we are headed	WHOM we talk to	WHAT we say
WHAT we do	HOW we do it	HOW we interact	HOW we communicate
ACTION	QUALITY	ENGAGEMENT	STYLE
CREDIBILITY		COMMITMENT	

SUBSTANCE   PERCEPTION

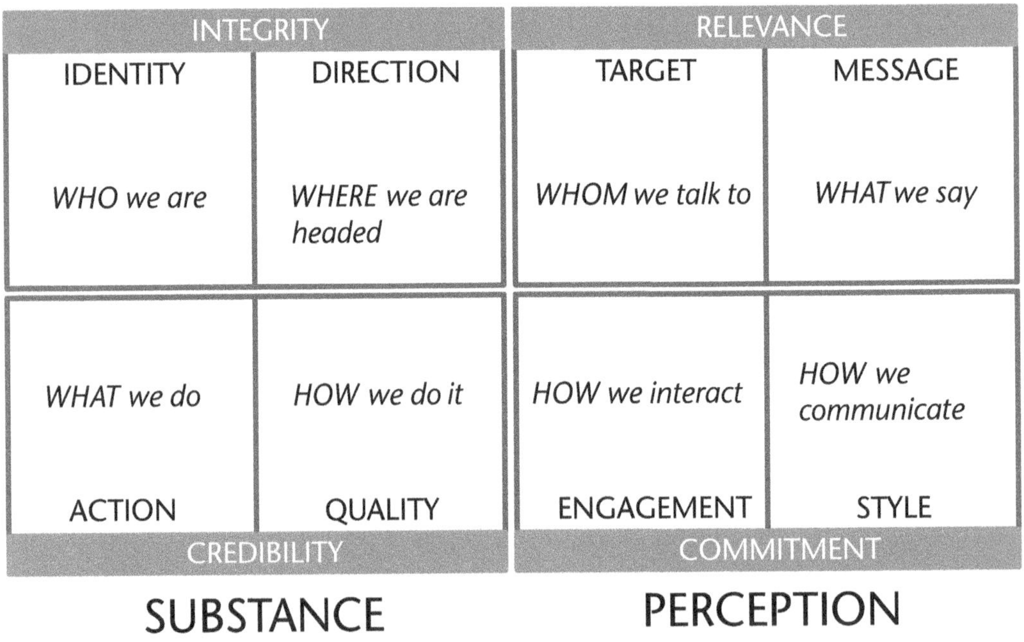

Figure III.4 Balancing substance and perception – the four quadrants in detail

When substance and perception are at a high level and in balance, CSR and sustainability communication build both brands and reputations. And because it builds trust and emotional proximity, strengthening relationships with key stakeholders, in particular customers and consumers, it will build profits as well.

Substance stems from integrity and credibility, while perception is built by relevance and commitment. Integrity consists of identity ('Who are we, as a company, what is our identity, our core?') and direction ('Where do we go? What is our vision?'), while credibility is defined as action plus quality. On the other side, target ('Who do we talk to?') and message ('What do we say?') make up relevance and engagement plus style ('How do we interact/communicate?').

2. Integrate sustainability into your core business and determine your direction before starting to communicate

Integrity is about integration. Sustainability must not be an add-on, but an integral part of the business, linked to its 'engine room'. Each company needs to ask the questions: 'What is our role in society? How do sustainability issues relate to our identity? How are environmental challenges and social issues linked to our business model? How do they affect the way we do business and how can our business have an impact on them?' General Electric's ecomagination is a response to these questions. Sustainability challenges have become the source for substantial product innovations and created new business segments for GE. Any company ought to challenge the 'business of business is business' paradigm of shareholder value as the only target as it becomes increasingly less acceptable and less realistic in the face of global sustainability obstacles, environmental, social and economic. Not having attempted to find company-specific answers to those questions, the CSR communication of some companies lacks at the very least credibility, and can develop into a significant reputational risk. Step two is to determine the direction of the sustainability efforts. If there is no direction, any path may seem the right one. Developing a sustainability vision and sustainability strategy implies deciding on what is important for the business in the context of CSR and sustainability, and what is not. Only once the questions 'Who are we?' and 'Where are we headed?' have been resolved can there be any credible sustainability communication.

3. Set measurable targets, and control them rigorously

Part of a developed CSR or sustainability strategy is to define measurable targets that are monitored openly and transparently. Marks & Spencer broke new ground in terms of rigour and dimension when it launched Plan A in January 2007, with its 100-point plan and clear five-year targets which were openly tracked. Puma set up an innovative sustainability accounting system, the Environmental Profit and Loss Account, in order to come to grips with linking sustainability and financial performance, and published its first results in May 2011:

With the announcement of initial results from the developing Environmental Profit & Loss Account (E P&L), the Sportlifestyle company Puma and the PPR Group's sustainability initiative, PPR HOME, have disclosed that raw material production accounts for the highest relative impacts of Greenhouse Gas Emissions (GHG) and Water Consumption within Puma's operations and supply chain. As the first company to provide such details, Puma has published an economic valuation of the environmental impacts caused by GHG emissions and water consumption along its value chain. Ultimately, Puma's undertaking will see the inclusion of further environmental key performance indicators in Stage 1, followed by social and economic impacts in later stages of development.[1]

4. Communicate honestly and with transparency – be open about threats and shortcomings

Across all stakeholder groups, the most dominant expectation is clearly that companies are honest and transparent in their CSR communication. Yet being particularly open about threats and shortcomings can be extremely powerful, and immunizes against potentially negative media or NGO campaigns: telling the story as it is, even if it is not positive. Nothing builds credibility faster than talking about the obstacles that a company is facing, rather than covering up the difficulties. Honesty means being accurate, well-documented and not conveniently omitting difficult truths. It implies getting by without spin. While transparency literally means being 'see-through', that is not necessarily the key point. What is important is that companies figure out what is really important to them in sustainability – for instance, via a materiality analysis – and are then fully transparent and clear, without a hidden agenda in those areas.

Figure III.5 Issues and challenges concerning CSR communication

1   'PUMA and PPR HOME Announce First Results of Unprecedented Environmental Profit & Loss Account', http://about.puma.com/puma-and-ppr-home-announce-first-results-of-unprecedented-environmental-profit-loss-account/, 16 May 2011 (accessed 2 June 2013).

5. Communicate from the inside out by making your employees into ambassadors for what you do in the field of sustainability

Employees make up the backbone of an organization and are usually a key part of the value chain – even if large parts are outsourced and there is a low level of vertical integration. As insiders, they often know more about what 'really goes on'; they can have a good feeling for whether a company's CSR and sustainability efforts are honest and sincere. A dialogue with those major stakeholders is often a first step for management to gain a better understanding of both issues and opportunities in this field. Creating awareness of sustainability and the company's sustainability strategy is a key first step to leveraging those opportunities. SKF's BeyondZero (see Best Case Example 7, Chapter 13) is a good example of how high organizational awareness becomes a value driver. And employees that collectively 'walk the talk' are a sign of high integrity.

When it comes to communicating to other stakeholder groups, employees are often the direct facilitators or communicators, particularly in the supply chain. For service or retail companies with a large number of staff, employees can act as ambassadors to customers and consumers and have a high impact, because they come across as authentic and credible. Thus, 'inside out' communication contributes to both integrity and credibility.

6. Be yourself, to come across as authentic – communicate only those things you do in terms of sustainability that have a good fit with your company or your brand

Stakeholder expectations sometimes seem very diverse and difficult to align. However, if we take a look at the expectations voiced by the different interviewees in this book, there seems to be some convergence.

Openness and transparency, honesty and truthfulness stand out, as well as dialogue and engagement and basing communication on action. Authenticity is implied in being honest and straightforward. And companies which try to be something they are not will be found out and not seen as credible, even if their intentions were good. When BP announced its 'new' logo and positioning 'Beyond Petroleum' in 1998, it seemed bold. However, as former Shell Manager Björn Edlund pointed out, insiders in the oil industry knew that moving beyond oil into other forms of energy would take decades rather than years, and the new BP positioning was therefore inconsistent with 'being yourself': 'In energy, it takes a new source 30 years to become 1 per cent of the energy mix. They were talking about what people wanted to hear rather than what was true.'

Furthermore, there are sustainability topics companies work with but prefer not (yet) to talk about or to actively communicate because they do not fit the current brand perception or might be misunderstood, due perhaps to the multi-faceted nature of the subject. For instance, consumers claim that they want transparency in the supply chain, but whether it is possible to relate to them the complexities implied, such as when it comes to improving working conditions in Asian textile factories, a company has to decide on a case-by-case basis.

What does build authenticity is humility. 'We have started to work on these sustainability subjects, but we know we have a long way to go and we are eager to learn' is an excellent approach if it is coupled with a clear direction and rigorous accountability. Humility may mean learning from others, from best practice examples like the top examples mentioned in this book (see Table III.1).

Table III.1   Top best practice examples

Brand, company, programme	No. of mentions
Marks & Spencer ('Look behind the label' and Plan A)	14
Unilever (corporate, Lipton et al.)	10
Novo Nordisk	5
Tchibo (WE Project, general)	4
Nestlé (Nespresso, Creating Shared Value)	3
Cadbury (Dairy Milk Fairtrade)	3

However, be careful not to simply copy. While adaptation may be great and generate speed, it may not fit you as well as another company.

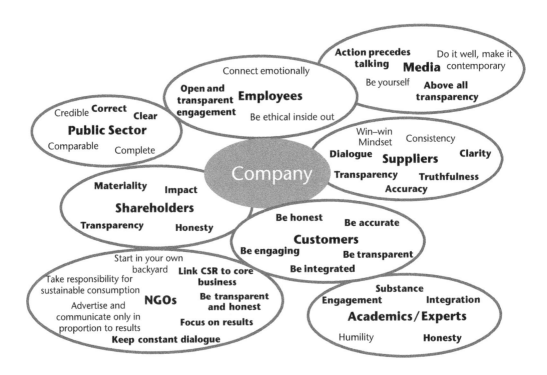

Figure III.6   Expectations towards CSR communication

7. Shift the focus from corporate to product-related communication, for example based on lifecycle assessments or traceability, to ensure business and customer relevance

From the cases in this book, we observe a trend that has developed over the past few years: the trend towards product-related sustainability. Organizational sustainability or corporate (social) responsibility is losing relevance, particularly with consumers and customers. What they are interested in are products or brands, because, as Ramon Arratia, Sustainability Director at Interface, remarks, customers want to buy products, not companies. However, shareholders and the big pension fund investors also want to invest in companies, so the corporate brand is still important! More and more companies are taking a systematic look at the environmental and to some extent also the social impact of their products by running product lifecycle assessments.[2] The result is transparency about the environmental (and sometimes also social) performance of a product. Over the next few years, one of the crucial tests for CSR or sustainability communicators will be to translate these findings for the relevant target audience. In the building supply sector, the use of environmental product declarations is becoming relatively common, not least because more and more buildings are environmentally certified and building suppliers need to provide the environmental data. The French Environmental Labelling Experiment is an important step in this direction, and will provide a lot of insights that will not just benefit the French market when it comes to creating more transparency about product-related sustainability performance.

8. Avoid one-way communication, and seek to engage actively with key stakeholders – this includes embracing social media

The words 'dialogue' and 'engagement' are mentioned almost too often in this book. Yet that frequency points to the importance of moving away from the old paradigm of one-to-many communication to at least two-way communication. This holds true generally, but particularly in the area of CSR communication. An essential part of engagement is listening and seeking to understand stakeholders. For companies which are used to controlling communication and manipulating the perception stakeholders may have of them, this is a major change. However, without listening and an open and honest exchange, the relative complexity of sustainability-related topics will lead to ineffective communication. Tchibo and GIZ's WE Project, featured in Best Practice Case 5 in Chapter 12, illustrates what genuine dialogue means: talking and discussing *with* factory managers and workers rather than talking *about* them, and seeking to change behaviour rather than manipulating it for short-term gain. Many companies which embrace sustainability create stakeholder dialogue platforms and organize stakeholder events with the explicit objective of receiving input, to learn from stakeholders and to try to understand their perspective. German retailer REWE-Group is battling with the question of how to move sustainable products from niche to mass market, and organizes dialogue forums to learn how to better educate consumers and achieve a step-change towards sustainable consumption.[3]

Social media plays a growing role in facilitating this dialogue. Companies can engage with a much larger number of stakeholders via social media than they can physically, face-to-face. At the same time, social media epitomizes the loss of control of the channels of communication. Every Facebook or Twitter user and every blogger is a media owner today, which can have a massive impact on the reputation of a large corporation.[4]

---

2   Chemical company BASF has developed a methodology called SEEBALANCE that allows it to systematically analyse not just the environmental but also the social impacts along the value chain.

3   One example is the REWE-Group Dialogue Forum 2012, 'Raus aus der Nische – wie Nachhaltigkeit für Verbraucher attraktiv wird' ('Getting Out of the Niche – How Sustainability becomes Attractive for Consumers').

4   An often-cited example is the YouTube video that showed how to open a Kryptonite lock with a BIC pen back in 2004.

9. Talk confidently about your achievements, and do not be destructively silent

There is not just an issue with talking where there is no substance – or greenwashing – there is a potentially difficult issue of underestimating silence when there is something to talk about in terms of CSR and sustainability. You could call it false humility. Joachim Schöpfer of the German advertising and media agency group Serviceplan calls it 'destructive silence'. Many companies have something to say, have answered the question of what sustainability means for them, have a clear vision of how to embed sustainability into their business model, are taking action and allow themselves to be held accountable rigorously – yet they are not willing to invest in communicating that to key stakeholder groups, especially consumers. As Best Practice Case 1: Lifebuoy in Chapter 10 showed, Unilever's creation of its much-heralded Sustainable Living Plan has involved conducting brand social imprints for its brands, yet consumers of its biggest food brands like Knorr have little awareness of the many years the brand giant has invested in sustainable agriculture and how this may benefit quality. That is a lost opportunity for Unilever, and a lost opportunity for building sustainable consumption.

In the German survey on the social responsibility of advertisers and communicators featured in Chapter 6, communicators agreed that sustainability is highly relevant for communication and will become increasingly important, yet admitted that they could be doing a better job. There is still little commitment when it comes to spending media money on communicating CSR.

Swiss retailer Coop shows how it can be done (see the Coop Switzerland Case Study in Chapter 6). By successively building sustainable competence brands in textiles, detergents and food, the retailer is growing its business based on substantial sustainability achievements. Its corporate campaign with a nationally known rapper has created broad awareness, particularly amongst teenagers.

10. Invest as much creativity, craftsmanship and commitment in CSR and sustainability communication as in any other advertising or corporate communication

Companies need to move towards supplying more and more sustainable products. And, as Marks & Spencer's Mark Barry points out, they have to do the 'heavy lifting' and not expect the consumer to actively support sustainability or even pay a price premium. But the heavy lifting in offering the products and increasing supply is only one part of the job. Another test faces the marketers and communicators: they need to take on the challenge of making sustainability fun, attractive and sexy. It is their job to create a 'want' in the consumer. It is time for the industry that (co-)created the consumer and waste society – the marketing and advertising industry – to take on its share of the responsibility, put its most creative people on the job and to drive demand for sustainable products, in the process creating awareness about sustainability issues. There are examples of this happening, some of which are mentioned in this book. The most inspiring perhaps is Coop Switzerland. Currently, the globally leading sustainable retailer is advertising sustainability with unparalleled boldness. It was able to stretch the envelope because it had so much substance to build on. Coop was able to run an awareness-building TV commercial with a famous Swiss rapper because it had built sustainability competence brands over the past ten years.

But it is not just companies which face this test. The German Bio-label was based on a highly creative campaign with unprecedented investment financed by the German government. In Sweden, a brochure and tape explaining what sustainability is was distributed to every household and every school as long ago as 1989, endorsed and supported by the King of Sweden. Arguably, this has significantly contributed to the comparatively high general level of sustainability awareness in Sweden, among business people as well as ordinary citizens.

NGOs and civil society need to create awareness, but also to develop processes and systems that facilitate sustainable consumption. Fairtrade is a good example, featured as a Case Study in Chapter 1, of a production system and quality mark that managed to move mainstream. The Rainforest Alliance has made big steps forward over the past five years, and the brand is beginning to be recognized by consumers in an increasing number of markets. In addition, agreements with global players in the coffee and cocoa areas will make that label mainstream over the next few years.

In the immediate future, CSR or sustainability communication will develop rapidly and will move into the mainstream. The pioneers will explore innovative approaches, while there is a large group of companies that are just starting to find their bearings when it comes to the whole subject of sustainability. They will make their first tentative steps in communicating their efforts once they feel confident about the substance they have created. If more and more business leaders realize the opportunities that professional, well-thought through CSR communication offers in building reputations, brands and profits and less and less of them choose to be 'destructively silent', there is a good chance that communicating sustainability will contribute to making corporate sustainability itself more mainstream by driving demand.

List of Contributors

In the context of the research for *The New Brand Spirit*, we have spoken to nearly one hundred people, most of them in the form of a structured, formalized interview. We want to express our deep appreciation and heartfelt gratitude to our interviewees for taking the time to speak with us and sharing their extremely valuable thoughts and invaluable experience as practitioners and experts in the field of sustainability and CSR communications. More than for most books, we can state with conviction that without our contributors, this book would not have come to pass.

First name	Surname	Organization
Gloria	Abramoff	Tonic Media & Productions
Simon	Anholt	Nation and City Branding
Mallen	Baker	Daisywheel Interactive and Respect
Mike	Barry	Marks & Spencer (M&S)
Nancy	Baxter	Profitable Philanthropy LLC (formerly Wells Fargo)
Sarah	Belmont	PriceWaterhouseCoopers Germany
Nanda	Bergstein	Tchibo GmbH
C.B.	Bhattacharya	European School of Management and Technology (ESMT)
Volker	Bormann	Gruner und Jahr (formerly Financial Times Germany)
Rolf	Bösinger (Dr.)	German Federal Ministry for Labour and Social Affairs (BMAS)
Dr Ingo	Braune	German Federal Ministry of Food, Agriculture and Consumer Protection (BMELV)
Paul	Brown	The Prince's Trust
Hugh	Burkitt	The Marketing Society
Tim	Callington	Edelman
Katie	Carroll	FHI 360 (formerly AED)
Göran	Carstedt	The Natural Step
Rita	Clifton	Portfolio Chairman and Director (formerly Interbrand)
Blaine	Collison	US EPA–Green Power Partnership
Gavin	Coopey	More Strategic, Australia (formerly Comic Relief)
Joanna	Daniels	Business in the Community (BitC)
Stan	Dupré	Utopies
Neil	Eccles	Institute for Corporate Citizenship, University of South Africa
Björn	Edlund	Edelman

First name	Surname	Organization
Elliot	Frankal	ESG Communications (formerly UNPRI)
Ed	Gillespie	Futerra
Gary	Glaister	NEXUS ON-DEMAND (formerly Cisco Systems)
Santiago	Gowland	Nike (formerly Unilever)
Peter	Gündling	Global Teambuilders (formerly SKF)
Michael	Hastings (Baron Hastings of Scarisbrick)	KPMG
Jeff	Hoffman	Jeff Hoffman & Associates (formerly Disney)
Lee	Holdstock	Soil Association Certification Ltd
Stephen	Howard	Business in the Community (BitC)
Erica	Jones	Walmart Inc.
Maria	Kalligeros	Kalligeros Communications (formerly Patrice Tanaka & Co)
Jeremy	Kent	RCM UK/Allianz Global Investors
Anthony	Kleanthous	Here Tomorrow (formerly WWF-UK)
Uwe	Kleinert	Coca-Cola Germany
Thomas	Krick	PriceWaterhouseCoopers (PwC)
Prof. Peter	Kruse	nextpractice GmbH
Michael	Kuhndt	Collaborating Centre on Sustainable Consumption and Production (CSCP)
Peter	Kusterer	IBM Germany
Sim Tee	Lam	SKF
Harriet	Lamb	Fairtrade International
Werner	Lampert	Werner Lampert Beratungsges. mbH
Pär	Larshans	Max Burgers
Willi	Lemke	United Nations Secretary-General's Special Adviser on Sport for Development and Peace
Céline	Louche	Vlerick Management School
Dax	Lovegrove	WWF-UK
Gurdeep	Loyal	innocent drinks
Brendan	May	The Robertsbridge Group
Barbara	McCutchen	Virginia Tech Center for Leadership in Global Sustainability and Packaging & Technology Integrated Solutions (PTIS)
Alec	McGivan	Head of BBC Outreach
Gavin	Neath	Historic Futures Ltd
Eloy	Parra	Private Public Partnership Handwashing Initiative (World Bank Group)
David	Paterson	National Association of Pension Funds (NAPF)

First name	Surname	Organization
Fabian	Pattberg	PB Consulting GmbH
Hamish	Pringle	23red
Kristi	Ragan	USAID/DAI
Jean-Philippe	Renaut	Dessau (formerly SustainAbility)
Mike	Richmond	HAVI Global Solutions and Packaging & Technology Integrated Solutions (PTIS)
Dawn	Rittenhouse	DuPont
Dr Karl-Henrik	Robèrt	The Natural Step
Nicholas	Robinson	Contact Energy Ltd, New Zealand (formerly BP)
Robert	Rubinstein	TBLI Conference BV
Tim	Samuels	Tonic Media & Productions
Kristina	Sandberg	Swedish Standards Institute (SIS)
Jessica	Sansom	innocent drinks
Veronica	Scheubel	Veronica Scheubel Organisation Development (formerly Nokia)
Greg	Schneider	3BL Media
Dr Thomas	Schwetje	Coop Switzerland
Dr Myriam	Sidibe	Unilever
Sebastian	Siegele	Sustainability Agents (SusA)
Anneke	Sipkens	Deloitte, Netherlands (formerly People4Earth)
Linda	Spevacek	The Launch Companies
Nigel	Stanley	Trades Union Congress (TUC)
Matthias	Stausberg	Virgin Unite (formerly United Nations Global Compact)
Susanne	Stormer	Novo Nordisk
Greg	Sturmer	organimark (formerly ROMP)
Ying	Sun	Sustainability Agents (SusA) (formerly TAOS Network)
Toni	Symonds	California State Legislature
Robert	Talbut	Royal London Asset Management
Jane	Tewson	Igniting Change (formerly Pilotlight, Comic Relief)
Priyani	Thomas-Dirla	German Agency for International Co-operation (GIZ)
Lesa	Ukman	IEG
Sally	Uren	Forum for the Future
Brian	Wagner	HAVI Global Solutions and Packaging & Technology Integrated Solutions (PTIS)
Claudia	Wais	Zürcher Kantonalbank (formerly SAM Indexes GmbH)
Alison	Ward	Sustainability and Communications Consultant (formerly Cadbury)
Simon	Warrick	Historic Futures
Chris	Wille	Rainforest Alliance

First name	Surname	Organization
Robin	Willner	Growth Philanthropy Network (formerly IBM)
Janine	Wood	Armadillo PR
Mark	Yolton	SAP AG

Index

Page numbers in **bold** refer to figures and tables.